Real Talk 2

Authentic English in Context

Lida Baker
Judith Tanka

PEARSON
Longman

Real Talk 2

Pearson Education, 10 Bank Street, White Plains, NY 10606

Staff credits: The people who made up the **Real Talk 2** team, representing editorial, production, design, and manufacturing, are Danielle Belfiore, Elizabeth Carlson, Dave Dickey, Christine Edmonds, Nancy Flaggman, Gosia Jaros-White, Amy McCormick, Barbara Sabella, Keyana Shaw, and Paula Van Ells.

Text composition: Laserwords
Text font: 11.5/Minion Regular
Text art: eMC Design Ltd.
Illustrations: Pat Byrnes and Steve Schulman
Map: Burmar Technical Corp.

Audio Credits: Page 16, Interview with Susan Shaffer and Linda Gordon, "Moving Back Home with Mom," 5/18/06, © 2005, Southern California Public Radio. All rights reserved. Reproduced with permission of Southern California Public Radio. **Page 43,** "Language Pet Peeves," Weekend All Things Considered, 4/21/02, © National Public Radio Incorporated. Used with permission. **Page 73,** Interview with Michelle Singletary, "Day to Day," 3/23/04, © National Public Radio Incorporated. Used with permission. **Page 125,** "Americans Agree that Being Attractive is a Plus in American Society," 1/11/03, © National Public Radio Incorporated. Used with permission. **Page 134,** lecture based on article "Male Body Image in Taiwan Versus the West: *Yanggang Zhiqi* meets the Adonis Complex," by Chi-Fu Jeffrey Yang et al. © 2005 American Psychiatric Association. Used by permission. **Page 154,** "Discovered Treasure," Motley Fool, 9/19/06, © National Public Radio Incorporated. Used with permission. **Page 181,** "Atlanta Poised to Get Tough on Panhandling," 7/18/05, © National Public Radio Incorporated. Used with permission. **Page 207,** "Pirates of the Caribbean," 7/11/05, © 2003 Southern California Public Radio. All rights reserved. Reproduced with permission of Southern California Public Radio.

Photo Credits: Page 1, © Royalty-Free/Corbis; **Page 5,** © GIPhoto-Stock/Alamy; **Page 8,** (left) © Royalty-Free/Corbis, (right) © Pankaj and Insy Shah/Gulfimages/Getty Images; **Page 16,** © Age/Fotosearch; **Page 30,** (top) © Mark Scott/Getty Images, (bottom) © Royalty-Free/Corbis; **Page 31,** (left) © Royalty-Free/Corbis, (right) © Royalty-Free/Corbis; **Page 42,** © Michael Newman/ PhotoEdit; **Page 59,** (top) Dorothy Alexander/Alamy, (bottom) © Tim Boyle/Getty Images; **Page 65,** (left) © Photodisc/Getty Images, (right) © Royalty-Free/Corbis; **Page 72,** © Fotolia.com; **Page 90,** © Royalty-Free/Corbis; **Page 94,** © Paul Carrie/Getty Images; **Page 100,** © Mel Levine/New Horizons/http://www.newhorizons.org; **Page 113,** © Photosindia/Getty Images; **Page 118,** © Chuck Savage/CORBIS; **Page 124,** © BananaStock/Alamy; **Page 130,** (left) © Stockbyte/Getty Images, (right) © Asia Images/Fotosearch; **Page 139,** © Royalty-Free/Punchstock; **Page 144,** © Royalty-Free/Corbis; **Page 153,** (left) © Judith Miller/Dorling Kindersley/Sylvie Spectrum, (right) © Neal and Molly Jansen/Alamy; **Page 159,** © Topham/The Image Works; **Page 167,** © JupiterImages/Comstock; **Page 174,** © Bob Daemmrich/The Image Works; **Page 180,** © Robert Harbison/Z.Legacy. Corporate Digital Archive; **Page 186,** © Joe Sohm/The Image Works; **Page 193,** © Everett Collection; **Page 200,** © Louis K. Meisel Gallery Inc./CORBIS; **Page 205,** © Walt Disney Pictures/The Kobal Collection; **Page 212,** Michael Newman/PhotoEdit

Library of Congress Cataloging-in-Publication Data

Baker, Lida R.
    Real Talk 2 : authentic English in context / Lida Baker, Judith Tanka.
—1st ed.
        p. cm.
    ISBN 0-13-194096-1 (student bk. : alk. paper)— ISBN 0-13-194094-5 (audio cd)—ISBN 0-13-194097-X (answer key : alk. paper)
    1. English language—Textbooks for foreign speakers. 2. English language—Spoken English—Problems, exercises, etc. 3. Listening—Problems, exercises, etc. 4. Life skills—Problems, exercises, etc. I. Tanka, Judith, 1950- II. Title. III. Title: Real talk two.
    PE1128.B2733 2007
    428.2'4—dc22

                                                            2006035253

ISBN-10: 0-13-194096-1
ISBN-13: 978-0-13-194096-3

Printed in the United States of America

CONTENTS

DEDICATION

To Paul, my eesh chayil
And to Galya, my angel-face girl

ACKNOWLEDGMENTS

My warmest thanks to the following professionals, colleagues, friends, and neighbors who consented to be recorded for this book.

Ellen Ackerman
Judy Aranoff
Mel Aranoff
Yael Aranoff
Robert Baldwin
Joyce Baker
Larry Braman
Shannon Calderone
Donna Chazanov
Matt Chazanov
Bonnie Cheeseman
Peter Converse
Jean Cox
Jonathan Epstein

Bene Ferrao
Stefan Frazier
Andrew Freund
Fran Grossman
David Johnson
Carol Eun Joo Kim
Thomas Klassen
Spencer Krull
Nira Kvart
Cindy Levey
Mark Mabray
Connie MacMillin
Rachel Miller

Karen Muldoon-Hules
Howard Nemetz
Susan Nemetz
Tara Neuwirth
Rachel Parker
Lisa Patriquin
Adam Rado
Barry Snyder
Scott Spalding
Judy Tanka
Alan Tobin
Aron Wolf
Alia Yunis

L. B.

SCOPE AND SEQUENCE

	Speaking Skills	
	Conversation Tools (Vocabulary and Functions)	**Focus on Sound** (Pronunciation)
CHAPTER 1 TURNING POINTS	• Talking about decisions • Discussing good news and bad news	• Three pronunciations of the *-ed* ending • Stress, unstress, and reductions • Linking and blending
CHAPTER 2 LEARNING A NEW LANGUAGE	• Signaling main points • Restating or asking for clarification	• Intonation of statements • Thought groups • More about stress
CHAPTER 3 IN THE MONEY	• Talking about money and banking • Learning phrasal verbs related to money	• Intonation of questions • Stress in noun compounds vs. adjective + noun phrases • Stress and linking in phrasal verbs
CHAPTER 4 MEMORIES	• Apologizing, reconciling, forgiving • Learning metaphors	• Contrastive stress • Expression of emotions
CHAPTER 5 BODY TRENDS	• Expressing support and understanding • Signaling a generalization	• Intonation of items in a series
CHAPTER 6 DISCOVERIES	• Expressing skepticism • Digressing and returning to the topic	• Modals of possibility; past unreal conditions • Reduced consonant clusters; syllable deletion • Change of *-ing* to *-in'*; more reductions
CHAPTER 7 LAW AND ORDER	• Expressing sympathy • Stating first impressions and second thoughts	• Southern American English • Linking vowels • Stress in words with suffixes
CHAPTER 8 LIGHTS, CAMERA, ACTION!	• Talking about chance, luck, and opportunity • Criticizing a work of art	• Voiced and voiceless *th*

Listening Skills	Note-Taking Skills	TOEFL® Speaking Practice
• Understanding main ideas, details, and inferences • Recognizing the past tense • Using the context to guess the meaning of idioms • Hearing the intonation of good and bad news • Recognizing signposting in a lecture	• Using signposting to organize your notes • Writing clear and useful notes	• Compare culture shock and reverse culture shock
• Understanding techniques for creating lecture cohesion • Using the context to guess the meaning of idioms • Understanding main ideas, details, and inferences	• Creating graphic lecture notes	• Explain the process of word blending
• Using the context to guess the meaning of vocabulary • Understanding expressions meaning "increase" and "decrease" • Understanding main ideas, details, and inferences	• Noting numbers and statistics	• Discuss the advantages and disadvantages of credit cards
• Recognizing contrastive stress • Understanding main ideas, details, and inferences	• Describing a process or technique • Understanding hypothetical situations	• Demonstrate the use of the keyword method to learn vocabulary
• Recognizing a variety of affirmative answers • Recognizing expressions of contrast • Understanding main ideas, details, and inferences	• Noting the organization of research reports	• Predict future research results based on current findings about body image
• Understanding reduced speech • Recognizing digressions • Understanding main ideas, details, and inferences	• Outlining assertions and points of proof	• Assess the positive or negative impact of Christopher Columbus's voyages
• Recognizing expressions of cause and effect • Understanding main ideas, details, and inferences	• Using cause and effect organization	• Explain how rising crime in China is related to theoretical causes of crime
• Listening for adjectives that describe movies • Recognizing terms for logical division	• Defining technical terms	• Define sound effects and explain the differences between these processes

TO THE TEACHER

Real Talk 2 is an innovative text that employs authentic listening segments in a variety of genuine contexts as the basis for listening and speaking skills development. The book is designed for advanced students of English in both second- and foreign-language environments. A companion text, *Real Talk 1*, built on similar principals, is aimed at the intermediate to high intermediate level.

The *Real Talk* books differ from most other listening and speaking texts in two important ways. First, the listening material consists of recordings of "real" people (not actors) speaking in authentic contexts. Natural irregularities characteristic of spoken language—false starts, fillers, hesitations, repetitions, and even errors—have not been edited out of the recorded material. Through repeated exposure to natural language and carefully designed and sequenced comprehension exercises, users of *Real Talk* learn how to identify the essential information in the imperfect and disorganized stream of sound they encounter in real English-speaking contexts.

The *Real Talk* books are also unique in their chapter organization and content. Each book consists of eight theme-based chapters. Each chapter is in turn divided into four parts named after the four contexts in which students normally hear and use English; that is, **In Person**, **On the Phone**, **On the Air**, and **In Class**. Each of these parts has a listening passage as its centerpiece. The language and skills taught in the chapter part are derived from the content of the recording. For example, Chapter 3, *In the Money*, is about finance. This theme is developed in the following four ways:

- *In Person* features a retired woman talking with a young friend about strategies for saving money. Students learn the intonation of seven types of questions and idiomatic expressions for talking about money.

- *On the Phone* presents a phone conversation between a bank employee and a visiting scholar seeking information about different kinds of bank accounts. Students learn banking terms. They also learn about stress in compound nouns such as *credit card* and adjective + noun phrases such as *monthly fee*.

- *On the Air* consists of a segment from the radio program *The Color of Money*, in which a financial advisor talks about lending money to one's relatives. Students learn about stress and linking in phrasal verbs, and they learn phrasal verbs related to money such as *do without* and *pay back*.

- *In Class* presents a lecture on the problem of credit card debt among young adults. Students practice taking notes on numbers and statistics, and they learn expressions meaning "increase" and "decrease" (*rise, skyrocket, plunge, crash*, and more).

Each of the four parts described above is divided into prelistening, listening, and post-listening sections:

Prelistening. This section includes a vocabulary preview exercise and a speaking activity in which students share their knowledge and explore their attitudes about the theme of the listening.

Listening. This section consists of listening comprehension exercises under the headings Main Ideas, Details and Inferences, and Listening for Language, respectively. The first two types of exercises are self-explanatory. The third, Listening for Language, includes skill-building activities under the headings *Focus on Sound*, which deals with phonological features of English, and *Conversation Tools*, which presents functions and idioms related to the chapter theme. As an example, in Chapter 1, *Turning Points,* a woman tells a close friend that she has accepted a job in a distant city and will be moving away. The woman begins the conversation by saying, "I've got good news and bad news." Thus the function taught in this section is "Delivering good news and bad news."

Post-listening. The section called *Real Talk: Use What You've Learned*, includes a vocabulary review and one or more communicative speaking activities that incorporate the skills and language presented in the previous two sections.

Part four of every chapter, **In Class**, differs from the other three in that it does not have *Focus on Sound* or *Conversation Tools* sections. Instead, this chapter part includes activities designed to teach students how to understand lectures and take notes. These activities appear under the headings *Lecture Form, Lecture Language,* and *Lecture Organization.*

An additional unique feature in Part 4 of **Real Talk 2** is the inclusion of a TOEFL® practice activity. This activity, called *TOEFL Practice: Synthesizing Listening, Reading, and Speaking,* mirrors the demands of the new TOEFL iBT in that it requires students to synthesize information from their listening notes and a short reading passage and prepare a one-minute oral presentation on a question related to the chapter theme. For instance, the lecture in Chapter 1, *Turning Points,* is about culture shock. The reading following the lecture is about *reverse* culture shock. In their one-minute speech students are asked to compare and contrast these two processes.

It is advisable to teach the chapters of **Real Talk 2** in order. However, it is not essential to teach every chapter of the book, nor is it necessary to cover all four parts of every chapter. The parts are sufficiently self-contained that you may choose among them according to the needs and interests of your students. Because most of the activities involve students working in pairs or groups, the book is best suited to classroom use. However, it is certainly possible for students to work independently using this textbook and the CDs. Scripts are included for convenience in the back of the book. Teachers who prefer can have students remove the scripts from the book.

This student book is accompanied by a set of three CDs and a Teacher's Manual containing answers to exercises, teaching suggestions, and chapter tests.

I sincerely hope that you and your students will enjoy using **Real Talk 2**.

Lida Baker

TO THE STUDENT

About Real Talk 2

As an advanced student of English you are probably able to understand much if not most of the English you hear. Most likely you are also able to use English to ask questions, offer opinions, and participate in conversations on a wide variety of topics. You may feel, though, that your listening and speaking skills are not as sharp as you would like them to be. Perhaps one skill is easier for you than the other; perhaps you feel there are "gaps" in your listening comprehension or your speaking fluency.

Real Talk 2 has been designed to help you overcome the gaps in your English competence and enable you to move closer to your goal of fluency in English. This innovative book uses authentic recordings as the basis for listening and speaking practice in the four natural contexts where you are most likely to hear and use English: in person, on the phone, on the air, and in class.

Chapter Organization

Real Talk 2 consists of eight chapters dealing with the following general topics: turning points, language, finance, memory, trends in body fashion, discoveries, the law, and movies. Chapters are divided into four parts, called **In Person**, **On the Phone**, **On the Air**, and **In Class**. Each of these parts has its own authentic listening passage and a variety of activities. These include:

- vocabulary and speaking activities to prepare you for listening;
- listening activities designed to help you comprehend main ideas, details, inferences, pronunciation, and language functions;
- exercises to help you learn and practice note-taking and improve your academic vocabulary;
- vocabulary review and communicative speaking activities which enable you to practice the vocabulary and language skills presented in that chapter part;
- a TOEFL practice section that calls on you to synthesize information from your lecture notes and a short reading passage and then prepare a one-minute oral presentation on a question related to the chapter theme.

The Recordings for this Book

The recordings for this book were not produced with actors in a studio. For *In Person* and *On the Phone*, the author recorded "real" people—friends, family members, colleagues, and even strangers in the street—talking about high-interest, contemporary topics. *On the Air* uses authentic radio segments, also selected for their appeal to the interests and needs of adult learners of English. Finally, *In Class* features mini-lectures delivered and recorded in front of an audience of students at the American Language Center, part of UCLA Extension in Los Angeles, California.

Speaking Activities

Every part of **Real Talk 2** includes opportunities for you to practice speaking. Most activities involve your working with a partner or in small groups. One of the unique features of the book, called *Conversation Tools*, presents lists of expressions you can use for specific purposes, such as digressing, asking for clarification, and many more. In this way the book helps you to develop your speaking as well as listening skills. Another feature, *Focus on Sound,* helps you identify tricky pronunciation features and then try to apply this information to improve your English pronunciation.

How to Use this Book

It is best to use this book in a classroom so that you can enjoy interacting with your teacher and classmates and practice your new speaking skills with them. It is best to study the chapters in order, but this is not crucial. Nor is it necessary for you to complete all four parts of every chapter. If your time is limited, focus on the type of listening that is most important for you, for example listening on the phone, listening in class, etc.

Whatever your purpose is for learning English—academic, personal or professional—we sincerely hope **Real Talk 2** will help you improve your ability to comprehend and communicate with speakers of North American English.

CHAPTER 1
Turning Points

Part One: In Person

A. Prelistening

DISCUSSION

You will hear two people talking about turning points in their education. Before you listen, discuss the questions with a partner or in a small group.

- What is a *turning point*? Give examples from your experience.

- Describe your education since high school. What is (or was) your major? How did you choose it? Do you think you made the right choice?

- In North America, people can change their college majors or their careers if they are not satisfied. Do you know of countries or cultures where this is <u>not</u> true? Explain.

VOCABULARY PREVIEW

The words and expressions are from the conversation. Check (✓) the ones you already know. Check (✓) the others as you work through the activities in Part One.

_____ (be) on the wrong track   _____ compromise   _____ start out

_____ change directions   _____ go in a different direction   _____ supportive

_____ change (one's) mind   _____ in retrospect   _____ switch gears

_____ come about   _____ regret

B. Listening

MAIN IDEAS

🎧 ① Listen to the conversation and fill in the chart. Then work with a partner and compare answers.

	Woman (Carol)	Man (Scott)
Major before switch		
Major after switch		
Future career		
Reason for switch		

DETAILS AND INFERENCES

🎧 ② Listen again and complete the tasks. Then work with a partner and compare answers.

1. Write *C* if a statement is true about Carol, *S* if it is true about Scott, and *B* if it is true about both of them.

_____ a. is good at math

_____ b. wants to have a family

_____ c. thought about becoming a doctor

_____ d. is Asian

_____ e. is religious

_____ f. wants to work with people

2. Which pair of adjectives describes the reaction of Carol's family when she first changed her major and their reaction now?

    a. surprised at first, disappointed later

    b. disappointed at first, surprised later

    c. disappointed at first, supportive later

    d. supportive at first, angry later

3. What is Carol's reaction to Scott's current major?

    a. disapproval

    b. amusement

    c. surprise

    d. admiration

How do you know? _____

4. What can Scott do if he decides later that he is dissatisfied with his career choice?

    a. become a doctor

    b. go back to school

    c. stop working

    d. any of the above

5. Draw conclusions:

    a. What does Carol imply about the expectations of some Asian families?

    _____

    b. What does Scott imply about the difference between being a doctor and being a nurse?

    _____

6. The idioms on the left are from the conversation. Match them with their meanings on the right. If necessary, listen again to hear the idioms in context.

    _____ 1. start out   a. make a mistake

    _____ 2. be on the wrong track   b. begin

    _____ 3. in retrospect   c. looking back in time

    _____ 4. come about   d. happen over time

LISTENING FOR LANGUAGE

3 Read about the three pronunciations of the *-ed* ending.

FOCUS ON SOUND
Pronouncing the *-ed* Ending

There are three ways to pronounce the *-ed* ending, depending on the sound that comes immediately before it:

- /d/ after all voiced consonants except /d/ and after all vowel sounds
  Example: changed /tʃeɪndɛd/

- /t/ after all voiceless consonants except /t/
  Example: passed /pæst/

- as a separate syllable /əd/ after /d/ and /t/
  Example: wanted /wɑntəd/

4 Listen and repeat the three groups of past-tense verbs. Focus on pronouncing the endings correctly.

Group 1: /d/	Group 2: /t/	Group 3: /əd/
changed	passed	decided
considered	stopped	interested
happened	switched	needed
planned		started
realized		wanted

5 Work with a partner. Student A says the base form of one of the verbs in Exercise 4. Student B says the past form. Take turns.

Example:

Student A: pass

Student B: passed / pæst/

6 Study the idiomatic expressions for making and changing decisions.

Making a Decision	**Changing a Decision or Course of Action**
Carol **made[1] (reached) a decision** to change her major.	At the last minute, Pierre **changed his mind** about getting married.
Scott **made up his mind** to become a nurse.	We've been working very hard. It's time to **switch gears** and relax.
	After getting a bachelor's degree in art, Hannah **changed directions (went in a different direction)** and enrolled in law school.

7 Work with a partner. Take turns making sentences about Carol and Scott. Use the answers from Exercises 1 and 2, verbs from Exercise 4, and expressions from Exercise 6. Pay attention to the pronunciation of -*ed* endings.

Example:
Carol *changed directions* in her third year of college.

---

[1]American English: make a decision; British English: take a decision

C. Real Talk: Use What You've Learned

Vocabulary Review

1 The new vocabulary from Part One is listed below. Review the list with a partner.

STEPS FOR REVIEWING VOCABULARY

- Say each item and state the part of speech—noun, verb, adjective, etc. Indicate whether an item is an idiom or slang expression.
- Define it by describing, explaining, using a synonym, or using it in a sentence.
- If you still do not know the meaning, look at the audioscript on page 235. Find the item and try to use the context to figure out its meaning.
- If necessary, use a dictionary or ask your teacher.

(be) on the wrong track	go in a different direction	start out
change directions	in retrospect	supportive
change (one's) mind	make (reach) a decision	switch gears
come about	make up (one's) mind	turning point
compromise	regret	

2 Use the vocabulary to complete the short dialogues. Then work with a partner and compare answers. Practice reading the conversations together. (*Note:* Some items have more than one correct answer.)

CONVERSATION 1

A: Hey Adam. How's school?

B: It's all right . . .

A: Are you sure? You don't sound very enthusiastic.

B: Well, the truth is, I'm pretty unhappy with my major. I feel like

I'm _____, but I'm worried that it may be too late to
                    1

_____. I'm already in my third year.
            2

A: Come on. It's never too late. If you don't _____ now, you
                                                              3

may _____ it for the rest of your life.
            4

CONVERSATION 2

A: How did you become a pilot, Sharon?

B: Well, I _____ as a geology major in college, (5)

but I _____ after I took a course in astrophysics. (6)

I became really fascinated with space and flight. That's when I

_____ to become a pilot. (7)

A: It sounds like taking that course was a real _____ in your life. (8)

CONVERSATION 3

A: It looks like we're going to be moving to Cleveland.

B: Really? How did that _____? (9)

A: The company offered me a management position there. And a big salary increase, of course.

B: How does your wife feel about the move?

A: She's pretty _____. Her family lives in Chicago, so we'll (10)

be closer to them.

CONVERSATION 4

A: How did you become a graphic artist?

B: Well, I had planned to become a painter, so this is something of a

_____. But I make a good salary, and I still paint on (11)

weekends.

A: Do you think you made the right choice, _____? (12)

B: Yeah, I really do.

DISCUSSION

Work in small groups and discuss the questions. Focus on pronouncing *-ed* endings correctly.

1. What is the hardest or most important decision you have made so far in your life? In retrospect, did you make the right decision, or do you regret it?
2. Have you ever changed your mind about something important, such as your education, a relationship, or your career? What caused you to change your mind? Was your family supportive?
3. What will happen if, five or ten years from now, you are unhappy with your career? Will you go in a different direction?

INTERVIEW

Interview an English speaker about a turning point in his or her life.

1. Write three questions for the interview on a separate piece of paper. Use new vocabulary from page 6.

   Example: What is the most important turning point in your life so far?

2. Interview the person and take notes on his or her answers.
3. In class, tell a classmate about the person you interviewed. Focus on pronouncing *-ed* forms correctly.

Part Two: On the Phone

A. Prelistening

DISCUSSION

You will hear two women talking about some important news. Before you listen, discuss the questions with a partner or in a small group.

- Where are the women in the photos on page 8?
- How do you usually tell someone important news: by phone, in person, in an e-mail, or in another way? Give examples.

VOCABULARY PREVIEW

The words and expressions are from the conversation. Check (✓) the ones you already know. Check (✓) the others as you work through the activities in Part Two.

_____ downside   _____ put (something) in a different perspective

_____ give notice (at work)   _____ stunned

_____ out of the blue

B. Listening

> **Culture Note**
>
> "VP" stands for "vice president." A VP is a high-level executive in a company, but a company may have more than one VP. Some large companies have many VPs, each with a different area of responsibility (marketing, design, public relations, etc.).

MAIN IDEAS

1 Listen to the conversation and fill in the chart. Then work with a partner and compare answers.

Tara's good news	Shannon's reaction

Tara's bad news	Shannon's reaction

DETAILS AND INFERENCES

2 Listen again and answer the questions or complete the task. Then work with a partner and compare answers.

1. Where is Shannon?

    a. at home

    b. in Atlanta

    c. in her car

    d. at work

    How do you know? _____

2. Who went to Atlanta?

    a. Tara, David, and their kids

    b. Tara and David

    c. Tara and Shannon

    d. Shannon and Tara's kids

3. What position was Tara offered?

    a. regional vice president

    b. sales manager

    c. marketing executive

    d. president of the company

4. Besides the new job, which of the following facts influenced Tara's decision?

    a. She is unhappy in the place where she lives now.

    b. Her husband was offered a good job in Atlanta too.

    c. She wants the experience of living in a different place.

    d. She wants to live in a warmer climate.

5. Which of the following things will *not* be different in Atlanta?

    a. the weather

    b. the language

    c. the food

    d. Tara's job

6. The idioms on the left are from the conversation. Match them with their meanings on the right. If necessary, listen again to hear the idioms in context.

_____ 1. out of the blue

_____ 2. downside

_____ 3. put (something) in a different perspective

_____ 4. give notice at work

a. suddenly, unexpectedly

b. tell your employer you are going to resign

c. disadvantage or negative aspect

d. make (something) appear less (or more) attractive than it did at first

LISTENING FOR LANGUAGE

③ Study the expressions for telling good or bad news.

CONVERSATION TOOLS
Good News, Bad News

Some expressions can be used to introduce either good or bad news, but the tone of voice will be different. For good news, there will be more "energy" in the voice and more movement from low to high pitch. For bad news, the voice will sound more "flat," with less movement.

	Giving News	Responding to News
Good News	Guess what!	I'm (so) thrilled / happy / delighted / glad for you.
	Surprise!	Congratulations.
		(That's) fabulous / great / fantastic / awesome / super.
Bad News	The bad news is . . .	I'm sorry to hear that.
	The downside is . . .	How awful / terrible / sad.
	There's a (real) downside.	That's too bad.
	I don't know how to tell you this, but . . .	(What a) bummer. (*informal*)
Either Good or Bad News	I've got good / bad news (for you).	I'm surprised / shocked / stunned.
	Are you sitting down?	That's amazing / interesting / shocking.
	You won't believe this, but . . .	

🎧 **4** Listen to the conversation again. Look at the Conversation Tools on page 11. Circle the expressions you hear.

5 Read about stress and reductions.

FOCUS ON SOUND

Stress, Unstress, and Reductions

In English, words that convey important information, such as nouns, verbs, negatives, and *Wh-* words, are normally *stressed*. This means they are pronounced more clearly and with a higher pitch and volume than other words in a phrase or sentence. In contrast, function words such as prepositions and articles are usually *unstressed*. They are lower than stressed words in pitch and volume. Furthermore, some unstressed words and phrases are *reduced*, meaning that sounds are dropped or combined. The result of these variations is that spoken English sounds different from the way it is written. In the following example, stressed words are written with capital letters, unstressed words with lowercase letters, and reductions with italics.

A: *Whaddaya* DOING tonight?

B: My MOM said SOMETHING about TAKING me SHOPPING. WHY? *Didja wanna* get TOGETHER '*n*' STUDY?

🎧 **6** Read the sentences from the conversation. Stressed words are written with capital letters, unstressed words with lowercase letters, and reductions with italics. Then listen and repeat the sentences exactly as you hear them.

1. I've been BUSY with WORK '*n*' the KIDS '*n*' EVERYTHING . . .

2. . . . I got this CALL *outta* the BLUE from the PRESIDENT and he OFFERED me the JOB.

3. . . . you've WORKED so HARD for all these YEARS '*n*' *yer* SO TALENTED . . .

4. . . . the THING is, we *HAFta* MOVE to ATLANTA.

5. WELL, you're NOT *gonna* TAKE it, ARE YOU?

🎧 **7** Listen to more sentences from the conversation. Circle the stressed words. Underline the reduced words and phrases.

1. Well, you know David and I have been talking about it . . .

2. Well it's not just a job, Shannon. It's my dream job.

3. I think I am going to have to take it.

4. It's so different, it's so far, I mean the food, the climate . . .

5. And I'd like to just, you know, try it for a couple of years because we can always move back.

8 Work with a partner and compare answers. Practice saying the sentences in Exercise 7 with natural stress and reductions.

C. Real Talk: Use What You've Learned

VOCABULARY REVIEW

1 The new vocabulary from Part Two is listed below. Review the list with a partner. (See Steps for Reviewing Vocabulary on page 6.)

bummer	out of the blue
downside	put (something) in a different perspective
give notice (at work)	stunned

2 Work in small groups and discuss the following questions. Use the vocabulary. Remember to stress important words.

1. What is your opinion of Tara's decision to move to Atlanta?
   a. What are the advantages of the move? What is the downside?
   b. What would you do if you were in Tara's place?
   c. How would your friends and family react if you took a job far away from them?
2. Tell about a time when you received good or bad news out of the blue.
3. Have you ever quit a job? How much notice did you give before you left?
4. Have you ever moved to a new place? Were you unhappy at first? Did anything happen later to put things in a different perspective?

ROLE PLAY

1 Work with a partner. Read the good news / bad news scenarios. Choose one and prepare a three- to five-minute role play using vocabulary from Exercise 1 and from Conversation Tools on page 11.

Scenario	Student A	Student B
1	You are getting married and moving to the city where your future husband / wife lives.	You are Student A's best friend. You are happy that he/she is getting married but very sad that your friend will be moving.
2	You have been offered a one-year job on a cruise ship that sails all over the world. If you take the job, you will have to drop out of college.	You are Student A's mother / father. You understand your child's desire to see the world, but you are worried about your child's future if he/she does not finish college.
3	You won two tickets to a concert by your favorite musical group. You are calling to invite your friend to go with you even though you know that the concert will be on the night before your friend's final exam in an important class.	You are very excited about your friend's invitation but worried about your exam. You must decide whether or not to accept the invitation to the concert.
4	You lost your good job eight months ago. Since then you have been trying, unsuccessfully, to find a new job. Yesterday you finally received an offer, but the salary is much lower than in your previous job.	You are Student A's spouse. You must help Student A decide whether or not to accept the new job.

2 Practice your role play. Remember to stress words that convey important information.

3 Perform your role play for another pair of students or for the whole class.

Part Three: On the Air

Growing Up Later		
	1970	**2003**
Median age of first marriage in United States	Men: 23.2 Women: 20.8	Men: 27.1 Women: 25.3
Median age of women for first childbirth	22.1	24.8
Young adults living with their parents	47.3%	50.3%

Source: USA Today online, 9-30-2004, "It's time to grow up—later"

A. Prelistening

DISCUSSION

You will hear part of a radio interview about adult children who move back in with their parents. Before you listen, discuss the questions with a partner or in a small group.

- Based on the data in the chart, how has U.S. society changed in the last thirty or so years? Is a similar change happening in other countries you know well?
- What might be the reasons for these social changes?
- When do young adults generally leave home and live independently in your culture?

VOCABULARY PREVIEW

The words and expressions are from the interview. Check (✓) the ones you already know. Check (✓) the others as you work through the activities in Part Three.

_____ adolescence   _____ get (one's) act together (*informal*)

_____ benefits   _____ land on (one's) feet

_____ debt   _____ regroup

_____ emerging   _____ severe

_____ entry-level jobs   _____ skill set

_____ factor   _____ twenty-somethings

B. Listening

MAIN IDEAS

🎧 ① Listen to part of a radio interview with authors Linda Perlman Gordon and Susan Morris Shaffer. Answer the questions or choose the correct words to complete the sentences. Then work with a partner and compare answers.

1. According to Gordon and Shaffer, why do adult children sometimes move back in with their parents?

    Biggest factor: _____

    Another factor: _____

2. The authors say that nowadays adolescence is _____ in earlier generations.

    a. longer than

    b. shorter than

    c. the same length as

3. The authors believe it is _____ for young people to move back in with their parents temporarily.

    a. responsible

    b. irresponsible

    c. disrespectful

4. According to the authors, is there a specific time when children become adults?

    _____

DETAILS AND INFERENCES

🎧 ② Listen again and complete the tasks. Then work with a partner and compare answers.

1. According to Gordon and Shaffer, what is true about many young adults who move back in with their parents these days? Check (✓) all correct statements.

   _____ a. They did not finish university.

   _____ b. Many of them are unemployed.

   _____ c. They are irresponsible.

   _____ d. They have entry-level jobs.

   _____ e. They have few benefits.

   _____ f. Many of them have no insurance.

   _____ g. They have a lot of debt.

2. According to the authors, young adults who move back in with their parents can use this time to _____. Check (✓) all correct answers.

   _____ a. build a house

   _____ b. regroup

   _____ c. build their résumé

   _____ d. learn new skills

3. In Kitty Felde's example about her mother, what can you infer about the situation?

   a. The mother was glad her daughter was living at home.

   b. The daughter wanted to move out.

   c. The mother wanted her daughter to become more independent.

   d. The mother and daughter had a bad relationship.

4. Who probably agrees with the following statements? Write *I* (interviewer) or *A* (authors).

   _____ a. Adolescence is taking longer because society is changing.

   _____ b. Young people are taking too long to grow up these days.

   _____ c. Parents who allow their adult children to move back in are bad parents.

   _____ d. Young adults who move back in with their parents are being financially responsible.

(continued)

5. "To land on your feet" means to

_____ a. fall hard.

_____ b. come out of a bad situation safely.

_____ c. find a job.

_____ d. leave your parents' home.

6. "To get your act together" and "to regroup" mean to

_____ a. reorganize your life.

_____ b. find a job as an actor.

_____ c. write your life story.

_____ d. lie to your parents.

LISTENING FOR LANGUAGE

3 Read about two features of spoken English.

FOCUS ON SOUND
Linking and Blending

Linking means connecting the last sound of one word to the first sound of the next word. In English, this occurs most often when one word ends with a consonant sound and the next word starts with a vowel sound. For example, "savings account" sounds like *savingsaccount,* and "give in" sounds like *givin.*

If the last sound of one word is the same as the first sound of the next word, the identical sounds are said to be *blended* and the two words will sound like one. For example, "bad day" will sound like *badday.*

Linking and blending can make it very hard for English learners to hear where words begin and end, but knowing about these characteristics of spoken English can help you understand many groups of words more easily.

4 Read and say the sentences from the interview. Draw arcs to connect blended and linked sounds. Check your answers with your teacher. Then listen to the sentences and practice saying them. Pay attention to stress and reductions as well as linking and blending. The first item is done for you.

1. There may be more than 4 million people between ages twenty-five and thirty-four who still live at home with Mom and Dad.

2. That seems like an excuse for bad parenting to me.

3. No, it's actually not an excuse for bad parenting.

4. . . . and they're coming out of college with at least twenty thousand dollars' worth of debt.

5. . . . and helping your child to become more adult is something you have to do with every one of your twenty-somethings.

4 Work with a partner. Read any part of the audioscript on page 237. Find and circle four additional examples of linked or blended phrases. Practice saying the phrases out loud with a partner.

C. Real Talk: Use What You've Learned

VOCABULARY REVIEW

1 The new vocabulary from Part Three is listed below. Review the list with a partner. (See Steps for Reviewing Vocabulary on page 6.)

adolescence	entry-level jobs	regroup
benefits	factor	severe
debt	get your act together (*informal*)	skill set
emerging	land on one's feet	twenty-somethings

2 Work in small groups and discuss the questions. Try to use the vocabulary above. Remember to link and blend words in phrases.

1. Review the reasons why many American twenty-somethings are moving back in with their parents after college. Do these same factors exist in other countries or cultures that you know?

2. In your opinion, when does adolescence generally end and adulthood begin? Does the age differ from culture to culture, family to family, or person to person?

3. What are the advantages and disadvantages of living with one's parents after college? What is your preference? Why?

4. What "rules" should parents set for adult children who move back home? Discuss reasonable rules for each area:
   - financial contribution
   - household chores
   - visits from friends

ROLE PLAY

1 Work with a partner. Read the adult child and parent information. Choose roles and prepare a three- to four-minute role play using the vocabulary from Part Three. You may add your own details.

ADULT CHILD

- twenty-three years old
- wants to move back home for a while
- graduated from college one year ago
- was working but quit job; is looking for another one
- wants to save money and travel around the world, then go back to school for an advanced degree

---

PARENT

- takes care of elderly father, who also lives with the family now
- agrees to allow child to move back home for a limited time
- wants to set rules about the child's rent, chores, and other responsibilities while living at home

---

2 Practice your role play. Pay attention to correct stress, reductions, linking, and blending.

3 Perform your role play for another pair of students or for the whole class.

Part Four: In Class

Cultural Adjustment Cycle				
Feeling	**"Honeymoon" Period**	**Culture Shock**	**Gradual Adjustment**	**Adaptation**
	Arrival–2 months	3–6 months	7–12 months	1 year +

Extremely Positive

Extremely Negative

A. Prelistening

DISCUSSION

You will hear a lecture about culture shock. The speaker is the student advisor at a language school. Before you listen, discuss the questions with a partner or in a small group.

- Based on the graph, what are the four stages of the cultural adjustment process? How long does each stage last, approximately? Can you describe how people typically feel at each stage? How do you think they might behave?
- Adaptation to a new culture is easier for some people than for others. What personality traits might account for this?

VOCABULARY PREVIEW

The words and expressions are from the lecture. Check (✓) the ones you already know. Check (✓) the others as you work through the activities in Part Four.

adjust, adjustment	euphoric	rigid
anticipate	factor	stage
anxiety	judgmental	support system
bizarre	minimize	symptoms
come into contact (with)	overreact	

PRETEST

① Close your book. Listen to the lecture once and take notes (write down the important information) in any way you can. Use your own paper.

② Use your notes to write short answers to as many of the questions as possible. Work alone. Don't worry if you can't answer a question. Later you will hear the lecture again.

1. What is culture shock?

   _____

2. What is cognitive dissonance?

   _____

3. What are some of the symptoms of culture shock?

   physical: _____

   mental (behavioral): _____

   emotional: _____

4. What can people do to minimize the symptoms of culture shock?

   _____

5. What psychological factors (characteristics) make some people more or less likely to suffer from culture shock more than others?

   less likely: _____

   more likely: _____

   _____

6. What steps can a person take before arriving in the new culture to minimize the experience of culture shock?

   _____

   _____

B. Listening and Note-Taking

LECTURE ORGANIZATION AND LANGUAGE: SIGNPOSTING

1 Read about signposting, an important organizational aid.

Most good speakers use a technique called *signposting* to inform listeners of what they plan to say or accomplish during their talk. Signposting words and phrases helps listeners predict what they will hear and get ready to take notes. Common signposting techniques include:

- An **announcement** at the beginning of a talk stating what the speaker plans to do or say: "In this lecture I'm going to define 'culture shock' and describe its symptoms."

- **Transitions** and **signal words and phrases** indicating what a speaker will do or say next. General words such as "now," "OK," or "so" are cues that the speaker is moving on. Other phrases tell listeners exactly what the speaker is going to say. "For instance" signals that an example is coming; "on the other hand," signals a contrast; "in short" indicates that the speaker is summarizing or concluding.

- Asking **questions**: A speaker will often use a question to introduce a topic or make a transition. No answer is expected from the listener; the speaker usually goes on to answer the question him or herself.

2 Listen to sentences from the lecture. During the pauses, check (✓) the technique used by the speaker and indicate what the speaker will probably talk about next.

| Sentence | Signal | | | What Speaker Will Talk About |
	Announcement	Transitions/ Signal Words	Question	
1				
2				
3				
4			✓	psychological factors
5				

LECTURE NOTE FORM: TIPS FOR WRITING CLEAR AND USEFUL NOTES

3 Read the tips for writing clear and useful lecture notes.

- Write clearly and make use of all the space on your notebook page. Don't crowd your notes to one side.
- Don't write complete sentences. Instead, use "telegraphic" writing—nouns, verbs, adjectives, and adverbs—to record important information.
- Use abbreviations and symbols to save time as you take notes. (See Appendix 2 on page 221 for a list of common abbreviations and symbols.)
- Start a new line for each new piece of information.
- Outline or indent information as it becomes more specific. In other words, write main ideas next to the left margin; then indent details as they become more specific.

4 Look at the following two sets of example notes from part of the lecture. Which notes are clearer? Why? _____

_____

EXAMPLE A

		CULTURE SHOCK
◯	Def:	
	1. Anxiety when rules we know don't work in new cult.	
	2. Psych def: cognitive dissonance = discomfort when new exp. don't	
	match expect.	
◯	Symptoms	
	1. physical: headaches, overeating, sleep disord.	
	2. fears: cleanliness, shaking hands	
	ex: friend's son, air "smelled funny"	

	CULTURE SHOCK
◯	
	Def: Anxiety when rules we know don't work in new
	culture
	cognitive dissonance = discomfort when new exp. don't
	match expect. (psych def)
	Symptoms
◯	
	1. headaches, overeating, sleep disord.
	2. fears: cleanliness, shaking hands
	ex: friend's son, air "smelled funny"

5 Now look at your pretest notes. Which notes do they resemble more closely, Example A or Example B? What can you do to improve your notes? Write your ideas here:

1. _____

2. _____

3. _____

TAKING NOTES

6 Listen to the lecture again. Add information to your pretest notes. Then use your notes to fill in the missing information in the outline on page 26. Use the cues on the left to guide you.

CULTURE SHOCK

introduction/
review

II. Culture shock

    A. Def:

        1. Anxiety when rules we know don't work in new cult.

        2. Psych def: "Cognitive dissonance" = discomfort when

           new exper. don't match expect.

    B. Symptoms

        1. Physical: headaches, overeating, sleep disord.

        2. Bizarre behav. or fears: cleanliness, shaking hands

           Ex: friend's son thought new country smelled funny

        3.

how to minimize
symptoms
(4 suggestions)

how to prepare
for life in new
culture
(3 suggestions)

7 Compare your notes to the notes in Appendix 4 on page 224.

REVIEWING THE LECTURE

8 Work with a partner or in a small group. Use your lecture notes as you review and discuss the answers to the Pretest questions on page 22.

C. Real Talk: Use What You've Learned

VOCABULARY REVIEW

1 The new vocabulary from Part Four is listed below. Review the list with a partner. (See Steps for Reviewing Vocabulary on page 6.)

adjust, adjustment	euphoric	rigid
anticipate	judgmental	stage
anxiety	minimize	support system
bizarre	overreact	symptoms
come into contact (with)		

2 Work in small groups and discuss the questions. Use the vocabulary above.

1. Are you living in a new place? If so, how long have you lived there? Which stage of the cultural adjustment cycle are you in?

2. Have you ever experienced culture shock? If so, describe your physical, mental, and emotional symptoms.

3. What advice would you give to a person who has never traveled in order to minimize the symptoms of culture shock?

4. How do you usually feel when you come into contact with people who are different from you in nationality, culture, color, religion, etc.?

5. If you are studying in an English-speaking country now, what did you do to prepare in advance for life in this country?

6. Describe your support system in the place where you are learning English. What would you do, for example, if you got into trouble?

QUESTIONNAIRE: FACTORS IMPORTANT TO SUCCESSFUL INTERCULTURAL ADJUSTMENT

1 Work alone. Rate yourself on the following characteristics on a scale of 1 to 5.

Characteristics	Low				High
Open-mindedness	1	2	3	4	5
Sense of humor	1	2	3	4	5
Ability to cope with failure	1	2	3	4	5
Communicativeness	1	2	3	4	5
Flexibility and adaptability	1	2	3	4	5
Curiosity	1	2	3	4	5
Positive and realistic expectations	1	2	3	4	5
Tolerance for differences	1	2	3	4	5
Positive regard for others	1	2	3	4	5
A strong sense of self	1	2	3	4	5

Adapted from questionnaire developed by Laurette Bennhold-Samaan for the Peace Corps, 1996.

2 Calculate your score by adding up your points and dividing by 10. The closer your score is to 5, the easier your cultural adjustment is likely to be.

3 Work in small groups. Compare scores on the questionnaire. Discuss ways that you can minimize the effects of culture shock even if your score is low.

TOEFL® Practice: Synthesizing Listening, Reading, and Speaking

The Internet-based TOEFL exam includes a speaking test in which the test taker must listen to a lecture, read a passage on a related topic, and then answer a question that integrates the lecture and the reading. This section of each Real Talk chapter is designed to help prepare you for the speaking part of the exam and to do well on academic speaking tasks.

1 Read the passage about "reverse culture shock."

When you return to your homeland following an extended sojourn in a foreign country, you may experience some degree of what is called "reverse culture shock" or "reentry shock." Immediately upon returning you may feel excited to be back in familiar surroundings with your family and friends. Once the welcome-home celebrations are over, however, you may find that people are not as eager to look at your photographs and listen to your stories as you are to show and talk about them. Your initial excitement may be replaced with feelings of alienation, irritability, or even hostility toward your family, friends, and home culture. This stage of the reentry process is often more severe than the initial culture shock because it is unexpected.

2 Review your lecture notes. Then use the information from both the lecture and the reading passage to prepare a one-minute oral presentation on the following topic.

- Compare culture shock and reverse culture shock. How are they similar? How are they different?

2

Learning a New Language

Part One: In Person

A. Prelistening

DISCUSSION

You will hear two people talking about how they learned their second languages. Before you listen, discuss the questions with a partner or in a small group.

- Do you enjoy learning languages? Why or why not?

- The pictures above show two types of language learners. Which type do you resemble more closely? Why?

- Are there specific strategies or "tricks" you use to learn English? For example, how do you remember new vocabulary? Share your experience with your classmates.

VOCABULARY PREVIEW

The words and expressions are from the conversation. Check (✓) the ones you already know. Check (✓) the others as you work through the activities in Part One.

_____ comprehensively   _____ flash cards   _____ motivation

_____ easier said than done _____ immigrant   _____ pick up (a language)

_____ fit in with (one's) peers _____ in the habit of   _____ rehearse
                                  (*verb* + -ing)

B. Listening

MAIN IDEAS

JUDY
Native country: Hungary
Second language: English

ANDREW
Native country: United States
Second language: Japanese

🎧 ① Listen to the conversation and fill in the chart. Then work with a partner and compare answers.

	Woman (Judy)	Man (Andrew)
Where they learned		
When they learned (age)		
Main factors in their success		

DETAILS AND INFERENCES

🎧 ② Listen again and read the statements below. Write *J* if a statement is true about Judy, *A* if it is true about Andrew, and *B* if it is true about both of them. Then work with a partner and compare answers.

1. This speaker _____.

_____ a. learned the language because he/she had to

_____ b. learned the language naturally, "organically"

_____ c. studied the language formally

_____ d. learned by talking with a boyfriend/girlfriend

_____ e. was highly motivated

_____ f. believes a lot of language learners don't use the new language as comprehensively as they could

2. Which speaker(s) used the following strategies?

_____ a. made flash cards

_____ b. copied the pronunciation of native speakers

_____ c. translated from the first language into the second language

_____ d. talked to himself/herself in the second language

_____ e. anticipated situations and rehearsed the language he/she would need

LISTENING FOR LANGUAGE

3 Read about the intonation of statements in English.

FOCUS ON SOUND
Intonation of Statements

Authentic spoken language is full of starts and stops, pauses, errors, self-corrections, and mispronunciations. As a result, it is sometimes hard to hear if a speaker has finished expressing an idea or not. The speaker's intonation can be a helpful cue, however. *Intonation* is the way a speaker's voice rises and falls in sentences and questions. If a speaker has finished a thought or statement, the intonation will normally rise slightly just before the end and then glide or drop down. On the other hand, if a speaker has more to say, the intonation at the end will usually rise slightly or stay flat. Judy uses both of these intonation patterns in the first part of the conversation:

- I think one of the key things for me was motivation. . . .

- I wanted to fit in with my peers and really be part of this new society.

4 Listen to segments from the conversation. Pay attention to the intonation of the last word before each blank space. Draw a rising, flat, or falling arrow in the space to indicate the intonation you heard. Then work with a partner and compare answers. Practice reading the segments with the same intonation as the speakers.

Judy: I think one of the key things for me was motivation (1) _____. I really wanted to learn the language well (2) _____. And I had to learn the language well because I was a, an immigrant (3) _____, and uh I needed to learn the language because I couldn't go back to the country I had come from (4) _____.

Andrew: But, uh, I basically found myself in situations where I had to speak it (5) _____, and if you have to speak it, you pick it up usually (6) _____.

Andrew: And so, um, I didn't do any formal training or any formal studies, but it was a matter of every day hearing her speak (7) _____ and I'd pick up several new words every day. I wouldn't take notes, I wouldn't have a study session, it would just be an organic process (8) _____.

Judy: . . . Yeah I would rehearse (9) _____ [Andrew: A ha] ahead of time if I knew the situation I was going to be in (10) _____. And, um, so when I was in the actual situation I had the vocabulary, I had the delivery, and I had the confidence (11) _____.

5 Read about ways that English speakers signal main ideas.

> ## CONVERSATION TOOLS
> ### Signaling Main Points
>
> Written material often begins with a main idea, followed by carefully selected details. Spoken language is more spontaneous. Instead of forming complete ideas ahead of time, speakers may "think out loud" in an unplanned way before reaching their main point. Then, to signal their main idea, they may use expressions like the following:
>
> - The (My) point is . . .
> - What I'm getting at is . . .
> - What I'm trying to say is . . .
>
> - What this means is . . .
> - In other words . . .

6 Listen to Andrew. Which signals does he use? What main points does he make? Fill in the chart. Then work with a partner and compare answers.

Signals	Main Point
1.	
2.	

7 Listen to the conversation again. Note three things you understood this time which you did not understand the first time. Share your notes with a partner.

C. Real Talk: Use What You've Learned

VOCABULARY REVIEW

1 The new vocabulary from Part One is listed below. Review the list with a partner. (See Steps for Reviewing Vocabulary on page 6.)

comprehensively	flash cards	motivation
easier said than done	immigrant	pick up
fit in with (one's) peers	in the habit of (*verb* + -ing)	rehearse

2 Use the vocabulary to complete the sentences. Then work with a partner and compare answers. Comment on the information in the sentences based on your experience or opinion.

1. Learning a new language is not easy. It requires strong

   _____ and lots of practice.

2. If you know you are going to be in a particular situation, it's a good idea to

   make a list of vocabulary you will need and _____

   ahead of time.

3. One way to remember and practice new vocabulary is to make

   _____ and use them to test yourself.

4. Jin-Sook came to the United States at age seventeen as a(n)

   _____ from Korea.

5. As a teenager in a new country, Jin-Sook wanted to learn English quickly in

   order to _____.

6. By talking with his neighbor from Chile, Rick was able to

   _____ several new Spanish expressions every day.

7. To learn quickly, language learners should use their new language

   _____—in every possible situation and even when

   they are thinking to themselves.

8. For most people, learning a language without books or a teacher

   is _____.

9. I don't have many opportunities to use my English. I don't have English-

   speaking friends, and I am not _____ talking to

   strangers.

FIND SOMEONE WHO . . .

Work as a class. Stand up, walk around, and try to find someone who uses each of the language-learning strategies below. Write that person's name in the blank.

Example: Find someone who uses flash cards.
Question: Do you use flash cards?

Find Someone Who . . .	Name
uses flash cards	
repeats new words and phrases out loud	
uses the context to guess the meaning of new vocabulary	
uses gestures or pantomime when he/she doesn't know a word	
looks for native-speaker friends	
listens to music in the new language	
asks speakers of the language for correction	
talks to himself/herself in the new language	
tries to use new words in everyday conversation	
rehearses to prepare for new situations	

DISCUSSION

Work in small groups. Use the vocabulary from Part One as you discuss the questions. Focus on using intonation to signal whether your thoughts are finished or not. Also, use expressions to signal your main ideas as needed.

1. Go over the list of language learning strategies in the Find Someone Who activity. Which of these have you tried or used in the past? Did you find them useful? Why or why not?

2. Do you use any other strategies not mentioned in this lesson?

3. Based on the information in this lesson, are there any new strategies that you plan to try in the future?

Part Two: On the Phone

A. Prelistening

DISCUSSION

You will hear a phone call to an English language school. Before you listen, discuss the following questions with a partner or in a small group.

- How did you choose the English language course or program you are enrolled in now? Check the factors that influenced your decision:

  _____ schedule   _____ teachers

  _____ cost   _____ location

  _____ reputation   _____ type of
                            students
  _____ courses

- If an American asked you to help him or her find a good language school in your native country, how would you help that person find useful information? What advice would you give?

VOCABULARY PREVIEW

The words and expressions are from the conversations. Check (✓) the ones you already know. Check (✓) the others as you work through the activities in Part Two.

_____ accommodate, accommodation   _____ intensive (program)   _____ session

_____ comprehensive   _____ option   _____ tailored to

_____ elective (classes, courses)

B. Listening

MAIN IDEAS

1 Divide into two groups. You will hear a woman calling a language school. Each group will hear a different call. Listen and answer the questions. Then work with your group and compare answers.

1. What is the name of the school? Check (✓) one.

_____ English Language Center

_____ American Language Institute

2. What is the caller's main purpose?

_____

3. When is the caller's nephew arriving?

_____

4. How many different programs does the school offer?

_____

DETAILS AND INFERENCES

2 Remain in separate groups. Listen again with your group and fill in the chart with details from the conversation you heard. (If information is not given, leave the box blank.) Then work with your group and compare answers.

	English Language Center			American Language Institute	
Program	1	2	3	1	2
Type					
Hours per week					
Schedule					
Course length					
Cost					
Types of classes					
Class size					

3 Form pairs consisting of one student from each large group. Tell your partner your answers to Exercises 1 and 2. Then listen and take notes in the chart as your partner gives you information about the other school. Now work together to answer the question:

- Which program(s) would probably be most suitable for the caller's nephew? Why?

LISTENING FOR LANGUAGE

4 Read about thought groups.

FOCUS ON SOUND
Thought Groups

Longer sentences in English are normally divided into smaller chunks or phrases called *thought groups* (or *rhythm groups*). These chunks usually consist of natural units such as the complete subject or predicate or an idiom, phrase, or clause. Each thought group has one or more stressed words, and the intonation rises and falls according to the rules you have learned. (See Focus on Sound on pages 12 and 33.) You will sometimes hear short pauses between thought groups.

5 Listen to segments from the conversations and insert slashes (/) between thought groups. Underline the stressed words. Then work with a partner and compare answers. Practice reading the sentences. The first item is done for you.

1. OK, so <u>first</u> we have our <u>Intensive English</u> / for <u>Academic Purposes</u> program, / which is a <u>ten-week</u> course, / and that's <u>twenty-three hours</u> per <u>week</u>, / <u>nine</u> to <u>three</u> / <u>Monday</u> through <u>Thursday</u> / and <u>nine</u> to <u>twelve</u> on <u>Friday</u>, / and the <u>cost</u> of <u>that</u> / is <u>twenty-seven fifty</u> / for <u>ten</u> <u>weeks</u>.

2. We have an intensive English program, which is our most comprehensive.

3. That covers a grammar class, and a conversation and listening skills class, and a reading and writing class in the afternoon.

4. And the cost for that is eleven hundred and fifty dollars for a four-week session.

5. The third option is the half-day program, and that's twenty lessons per week. This one, there's no classes at all in the afternoon. It's eight hundred and ninety-five dollars for the four-week session, students are in class from nine in the morning till twelve forty-five, and then they're free in the afternoon.

6. **Caller:** Um, and did you say this program was twenty hours a week?

   School Employee: Yes, twenty hours, it's Monday through Thursday from nine to three with no classes on Friday.

6 Read about expressions you can use to check your comprehension.

CONVERSATION TOOLS
Restating or Asking for Clarification

Restating what you think you heard or asking a speaker for clarification are two useful strategies for checking your listening comprehension. For example, in the English Language Center conversation, the caller said: "Elective classes . . . um, <u>do you mean</u> they get to choose what they want?"

You can use the following phrases to restate what you heard or ask for clarification:

- Did you say . . . ?
- In other words, . . .
- Let me make sure I understand this.
- (X) meaning . . .

- (So) what you're saying is . . .
- (Do) you mean . . . ?
- You said . . . ?

7 Listen to both conversations again. Use expressions from Conversation Tools to complete the sentences. Then work with a partner and compare answers. Practice reading the conversations with natural stress, intonation, and thought groups.

CALL 1

1. **Employee:** We have an intensive English program, which is our most comprehensive. That covers 30 lessons per week. OK?

   Caller: Thirty lessons _____ . . . 30 hours?

2. **Caller:** Elective classes . . . um, _____ they get to choose what they want?

3. **Employee:** OK, basically we have two daytime programs, they're both intensive programs.

   Caller: Intensive _____ . . .

4. **Caller:** Just a moment, _____ sessions run ten weeks?

5. **Caller:** Um, and _____ this program was twenty hours a week?

C. Real Talk: Use What You've Learned

VOCABULARY REVIEW

1 The new vocabulary from Part Two is listed below. Review the list with a partner. (See Steps for Reviewing Vocabulary on page 6.)

accommodate, accommodation	intensive (program)	session
comprehensive	option	tailored to
elective (class)		

2 Work in small groups and discuss the questions. Use the vocabulary above. Use expressions from Conversation Tools on page 40 if you need to check your comprehension. Finally, focus on dividing your sentences into natural thought groups.

1. What would be the perfect language program for you? For example:
   - Would it be intensive or part-time?
   - What electives would it offer?
   - How long would the sessions be?

2. Do you feel that your language program is tailored to your needs? For example, if you are a business major, does the program offer a business elective?

3. Does your language school have a website? Did you check it when you were looking for a language program? Was the website comprehensive? That is, did it include all the information you needed to make your decision?

ROLE PLAY

An overseas colleague is coming to work at the North American branch of an international technology company from January 3 to February 14. Clients have complained that it is sometimes difficult to understand this person's accent. The company has agreed to pay up to $500 for this person to take an evening pronunciation course while he or she is in North America.

(continued)

1. Work with a partner and role-play two phone conversations. Take turns being the caller and the school employee who answers the caller's questions. Student A, turn to page 57 for information about pronunciation courses at the American Language Institute. Student B, turn to page 58 for information about pronunciation courses at the English Language Center. Use the recordings in this chapter part as a model for your conversations.

Take notes in the chart on the information your partner gives you.

	American Language Institute	English Language Center
Dates and days		
Times		
Hours per week		
Number of meetings		
Cost		
Course name		
Class size		

2. After your role play, compare programs. Decide which program will be most suitable for the visiting colleague.

Part Three: On the Air

Courtesy of Apple Computer, Inc.

A. Prelistening

DISCUSSION

You will hear a radio show in which a language expert is talking about a common English grammar error. Before you listen, discuss the questions with a partner or in a small group.

- The advertisement in the photo is for Apple Computers. Who is the famous person in the ad?
- What does "Think different" mean? How is it related to the person in the ad?
- The grammar of the slogan is not correct in writing or formal speaking situations. What is the error?

VOCABULARY PREVIEW

The words and expressions are from the radio show. Check (✓) the ones you already know. Check (✓) the others as you work through the activities in Part Three.

_____ endangered species   _____ on the fence   _____ under siege

_____ have an ear for   _____ pet peeve   _____ violation

_____ idiomatic

B. Listening

MAIN IDEAS

1 Listen as language expert Richard Lederer answers a question from a caller on a radio program called "Language Pet Peeves." Answer the question or choose the correct words. Then work with a partner and compare answers.

1. What is the caller's pet peeve about language? _____

2. According to Richard Lederer, using an adjective instead of an adverb is

    a. never correct.

    b. common in certain parts of the United States.

    c. acceptable in certain idiomatic expressions.

    d. incorrect in writing but acceptable in speech.

DETAILS AND INFERENCES

🎧 ② **Listen again and answer the questions or choose the correct words. Then work with a partner and compare answers.**

1. Which two examples of his pet peeve does the caller give?

   a. _____

   b. _____

2. If an expression is *idiomatic*, it is

   a. grammatically correct.

   b. used mostly by well-educated people.

   c. the typical way people speak.

   d. used mainly in writing.

3. In the phrase "go slow," Lederer explains that the word *slow*

   a. is an adjective.

   b. looks like an adjective but is an adverb.

   c. is incorrect.

4. Which of the following are acceptable in spoken English, according to Lederer? Write *Yes* or *No*.

   _____ a. fresh-baked bread

   _____ b. Go slow.

   _____ c. fresh-cut flowers

   _____ d. He speaks real good.

③ **The idioms on the left are from the radio show. Match them with their meanings on the right. If necessary, listen again to hear the idioms in context.**

_____ 1. pet peeve	a. state of being attacked
_____ 2. endangered species	b. undecided
_____ 3. on the fence	c. two errors at the same time
_____ 4. under siege	d. something annoying
_____ 5. double violation	e. have good listening ability
_____ 6. have an ear for (something)	f. close to death or disappearance

LISTENING FOR LANGUAGE

4 Read more about stressed words.

FOCUS ON SOUND
More about Stress

You have learned that content words are normally stressed and function words normally are not, but there are many other guidelines that determine which words are stressed in a phrase or sentence.[1] Here are some of them. In the examples, the stressed words are in capital letters.

Guideline	Example
1. Every thought group has at least one stressed word. If there is more than one, normally one word will be stressed more strongly than the others.	You go past a BAKERY / and you see a SIGN / for fresh-baked BREAD.
2. The *last* content word in a thought group or sentence normally has the strongest stress.	an endangered SPECIES The adverb is under SIEGE. That CONCERNS me.
3. Speakers can change the normal pattern and stress of any word or words they want to emphasize.[2]	*Normal stress pattern:* What is your language pet PEEVE, James? *Modified stress pattern:* What is YOUR language pet peeve, James?
4. Adverbs ending in *-ly* are usually stressed at the end of a thought group or sentence.	Go SLOWLY.
5. Adverbs that tell where (e.g., *here, there*) or when (e.g., *today, this morning*) are normally unstressed at the end.	I bought fresh BREAD today.

5 Listen to the sentences and underline the word with the strongest stress in each thought group. Then work with a partner and compare answers. Practice reading the sentences with natural stress, intonation, pauses, and linking.

Example:

You go past a <u>bakery</u> / and you see a <u>sign</u> / for "fresh-baked <u>bread</u>."

1. And I often wonder / what happened / to "freshly-baked" bread.

2. Yeah, the Apple ad / I think / is "Think different."

---

[1]See Appendix 3 on pages 222–223 for a summary of stress guidelines.
[2]See Focus on Sound: Contrastive Stress on page 92.

3. This is a little bit / on the fence here.

4. Korva, / I think / we say "go slow" / rather than "go slowly."

5. You go to the florist; / do you get fresh-cut flowers / or freshly-cut flowers?

6. I agree / that the adverb / is under siege.

C. Real Talk: Use What You've Learned

VOCABULARY REVIEW

1 The new vocabulary from Part Three is listed below. Review the list with a partner. (See Steps for Reviewing Vocabulary on page 6.)

endangered species	**on the fence**	**under siege**
have an ear for	**pet peeve**	**violation**
idiomatic		

2 Use the vocabulary to complete the sentences. Then work with a partner and compare answers.

1. My language _____ is that many people constantly insert the word *like* in places where it isn't needed and doesn't make sense.

2. Linguists estimate that 175 native American languages are still spoken in the United States. However, almost 90 percent of them are _____. Only a handful of speakers remain and they are surrounded by English speakers.

3. My grandfather _____ languages. He speaks six of them fluently, yet he has never taken a formal language course.

4. Grammarians are _____ about the use of *who* and *whom*. Some think that *whom* is no longer required in conversational English, but others disagree.

5. The word *well* to talk about one's health may be an _____. These days, if you ask people "How are you?" they rarely answer "Very well." More often, the response is "Good" or "Fine."

6. According to grammar books, "He do," "I is," and "They be" are grammatical

_____. However, these forms are perfectly correct in

some dialects of English.

7. *Chill out* is a very common _____ expression that

means "relax," "don't get excited." It is used mainly by young people.

SURVEY

1 Work alone or with a partner. Below are pairs of phrases, one with an adverb and one with an adjective. Ask several English speakers which phrase they would use and record their answers by writing *a* or *b*. Begin your survey like this:

"Excuse me. I'm conducting a survey for my English class. Can I ask you some questions? I'm going to say pairs of phrases and I'd like you to tell me which one you would use."

Expression	Speaker 1	Speaker 2	Speaker 3
a. newborn baby b. newly born baby			
a. slow-moving traffic b. slowly moving traffic			
a. come home safe b. come home safely			
a. dial direct b. dial directly			
a. soft-spoken man b. softly spoken man			
a. quick-drying paint b. quickly drying paint			
a. good-natured person b. well natured person			
a. good adjusted b. well-adjusted			
a. fresh-frozen fish b. freshly frozen fish			

2 Work with your class. Tally the results of the surveys. How many people chose each form?

3 Discuss the following questions in small groups.

1. Which expressions are preferred?

2. What does this survey tell you about the use of adjectives and adverbs in English?

3. Is there a feature of your first language that is changing?

Part Four: In Class

ZITS by Jerry Scott and Jim Borgman.© 2004 ZITS Partnership. King Features Syndicate. Used by permission.

A. Prelistening

QUIZ

You will hear a short lecture about ways that the English language forms new words. Take the quiz on pages 49–50 to see how much you know about English vocabulary. Then check your answers on page 58.

1. In English slang, "uber" probably means
   a. over
   b. above
   c. very
   d. outrageous

2. Approximately how many words does the English language have?
   a. 3 million
   b. 1 million
   c. half a million
   d. It depends on what you count as a word.

3. English evolved from which "mother" language?
   a. Latin
   b. German
   c. Greek
   d. French

4. When a word from one language is "imported" into another language, this process is called
   a. borrowing.
   b. dialecting.
   c. translation.
   d. copying.

5. Approximately what percentage of English words came into English from French or Latin?
   a. 10 percent
   b. 25 percent
   c. 40 percent
   d. 75 percent

(continued)

6. Which of the following is an example of a compound noun?

    a. website

    b. refrigerator

    c. radar

    d. blog

7. Which of the following words comes from the name of the person who invented the food?

    a. hamburger

    b. hot dog

    c. sausage

    d. sandwich

8. In the word *decaffeinated*, which part is the root, or stem?

    a. de

    b. caff

    c. ein

    d. ated

VOCABULARY PREVIEW

The words and expressions are from the lecture. Check (✓) the ones you already know. Check (✓) the others as you work through the activities in Part Four.

_____ blog	_____ metrosexual	_____ Y2K
_____ brainstorm	_____ motel	_____ yuppie
_____ carjacking	_____ personal trainer	_____ 'zine
_____ fridge	_____ smog	

DISCUSSION

Work in small groups and discuss the following questions.

- After looking at the cartoon and taking the quiz, explain what you have learned so far about the ways that English acquires new words.
- How do new words enter your first language? Give examples.

B. Listening and Note-Taking

LECTURE LANGUAGE: COHESION

1 Read about ways that English speakers connect their ideas.

Good lectures have a characteristic called *cohesion*. This means that the parts are connected so that you can recognize whether and how they are related to one another. When a lecture is cohesive, it is easy to take notes on it.

Speakers create cohesion in a variety of ways. Some common techniques are:

- **Unity.** A good lecture, like a good composition, has one central idea supported by clearly related subtopics and details.

- **Repetition of key words.** For example, the lecture in this part is about ways in which the English language acquires new words. The speaker repeats the phrase "new words" more than ten times!

- **Use of synonyms.** Rather than repeating exact words and phrases, speakers often paraphrase or use synonyms. In the lecture, for instance, the speaker uses many synonyms for the words *way* and *acquire* (as in "*ways* in which English *acquires* new words").

- **Use of words from the same "family."** For example, the lecture you'll hear is full of language-related terms such as *word, noun, adjective,* etc.

- **Reference.** Speakers use certain words, especially pronouns, to refer to nouns introduced earlier. In the sentence, "These words are pretty common now, but they didn't even exist ten or fifteen years ago," the phrase *these words* refers to a list of words mentioned in an earlier sentence, and the pronoun *they* refers back to the noun *words* in the same sentence.

- **Transitions.** Transitions show relationship and signal movement from topic to topic. In the lecture, for example, you will hear *one of these . . . another way . . . another process . . . finally . . .* These expressions make it easy to follow the speaker's organization and take notes.

2 Read the following transcripts of speech samples. Then work with a partner and answer the questions.

SAMPLE 1

. . . The Hebrew root *sh-m-r* means "to guard." I mean that's one meaning. Another one is "protect" and even "celebrate." And let me explain that in Hebrew, and also in Arabic, which is a sister language to Hebrew because they both descended from a theoretical proto-Semitic language about five thousand years ago. And I say theoretical because there's no written evidence of it, obviously. It had died out by the time writing was invented. We have three-letter roots that form the basis of most nouns and verbs. And they're just consonants. So *sh-m-r* is just a root and we can make words out of it by adding vowels.

SAMPLE 2

. . . OK so three thousand years ago the English language did not exist. What there was at the time was a language which linguists call proto-Germanic . . . And this language . . . Today we call it German. In other words German was the mother tongue for what was later . . . what eventually became German as well as English, Dutch, Swedish, Danish, and several other European languages. The proof of this is the huge number of similarities in both grammar and vocabulary between German and those other languages . . . For example, they all have definite as well as indefinite articles. Also, if you look at lots of everyday words, you can see that they're almost the same in German and all the languages that descended from it. Take the English word *house,* which is pronounced almost the same in Dutch and German. Or *water,* which is *vater* in Dutch and *wasser* in German.

QUESTIONS

1. Which cohesive devices from the box on page 51 do the speakers use?

2. Which sample is more cohesive (easier to follow)? Why?

③ **Read the thesis sentence from the lecture introduction.**

"And so what I want to do today in this talk is to introduce you to some of the linguistic 'gimmicks,' the techniques that English uses to coin new words."

🎧 **Listen to four other sentences from the lecture. Listen for synonyms for the words** *technique(s)* **and** *coin* **and write them in the chart.**

"Technique(s)"	"Coin"
1. mechanism	1.
2.	2. coining
3.	3.
4.	4.

🎧 **4** Listen to additional sentences from the lecture. Listen for the pronouns on the left. Match them with the nouns they refer to on the right.

_____ 1. one of these   a. stomach

_____ 2. it   b. stummy

_____ 3. some of them   c. blend

_____ 4. others   d. blends

                                            e. words

                                            f. processes

LECTURE NOTE FORM: GRAPHIC LECTURE NOTES

5 Read the explanation about nonlinear, or graphic, methods of taking notes.

> In Chapter 1 on pages 23–24 you learned how to write your notes from the top of the page to the bottom and use indentation or an outline to show the relationship between main ideas and details. Although this is probably the most common way to take notes, there will be times when you may prefer to write your notes in a graphic, or picture, format.
>
> There are many types of graphic organizers. One of the most common ones is the concept map. The topic or central concept is written in a circle in the middle of the page. Main ideas are written on lines extending outward from the center circle, and details are written on lines extending out from the main ideas.

6 The concept map at the top of page 54 shows a student's notes from part of a talk about borrowed words in English. Work with a partner and answer the following questions.

1. What was the talk about?

2. How many main ideas did the talk have?

3. What details were given to support each main idea?

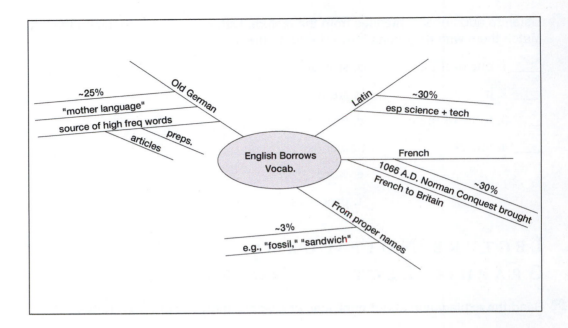

TAKING NOTES

7 Copy the concept map below onto your own paper. Listen to the lecture and take notes on your map. Remember to use abbreviations and symbols. After you listen, rewrite your notes on the map.

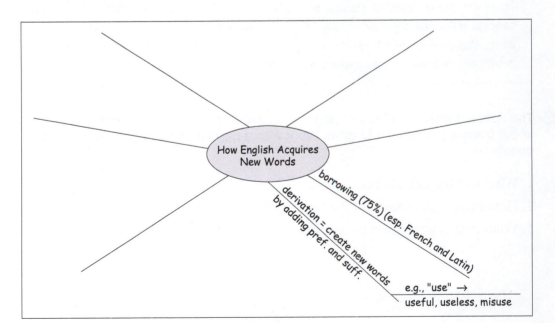

REVIEWING THE LECTURE

8 Work with a partner or in a small group. Use your lecture notes to discuss the following questions.

1. What do we mean when we say that English "borrows" words from other languages?
2. Name, define, and give examples of the six processes that English uses to create new vocabulary.
3. What is the difference in meaning and pronunciation between "race car" and "car race"?

C. Real Talk: Use What You've Learned

VOCABULARY REVIEW

1 The list below contains examples of words resulting from the processes explained in the lecture. Work with a partner. Use a dictionary to define each term.[3] If an item is not in the dictionary, find it on the Internet by searching for "[word] + definition," e.g., "metrosexual + definition."

2 Write or say an original, true sentence using each of the words.

blog	metrosexual	Y2K
brainstorm	motel	yuppie
carjacking	personal trainer	'zine
fridge	smog	

---

[3]Pay careful attention to usage notes such as *colloquial, informal, spoken, nonstandard,* etc. These labels tell you the contexts in which it is appropriate to use words.

WORD CREATION GAME

Work in pairs. Create blended words using the source words and definitions provided. Then check a dictionary to see if your created words exist!

Source Words	Definition	Blended Word
1. brain + maniac	a very smart, scholarly person	
2. chocolate + alcoholic	a person addicted to chocolate	
3. travel + monologue	a description of a trip or journey	
4. rock + documentary	a movie or TV show about a music group	
5. breakfast + lunch	a meal eaten in the late morning	
6. biology + hazard	a biological agent that is dangerous to humans or to the environment	
7. spy + software	computer software that secretly gathers information about people as they use the Internet	

TOEFL® Practice: Synthesizing Listening, Reading, and Speaking

① Read the passage about the word *podcasting.*

What is *podcasting?* It is the streaming of an MP3 or other audio file format to portable players, like Apple's *iPod*, either for play immediately or timeshifted for later listening. . . . The term is a blend of the trade name *iPod* and *broadcasting.*

Broadcast is, obviously, [a compound made] from the roots *broad + cast.* Both are Germanic roots. Of the two, *broad* is older, from the Old English *brád,* meaning "extended in width, wide." The term is found in Old English literature from before 1000. *Cast's* appearance in English dates to around 1230, in the form *casten* and is from the Old Norse *kasta.* Both the Middle English word and its Norse root mean "to throw." So, *to broadcast* means "to spread widely."

Source: Dave Wilton, "A Way with Words," March 4, 2005,
http://www.wordorigins.org/AWWW/Vol04/AWWW030405.html. Used by permission.

② Review your lecture notes. Then use the information from both the lecture and the reading passage to prepare a one-minute oral presentation on the following topic.

• The reading provides an example of how a new word entered the English language. Explain how this example is related to the processes of vocabulary expansion described in the lecture.

EXERCISE 1, PAGE 42

STUDENT A: AMERICAN LANGUAGE INSTITUTE

Dates and days: Option 1: 1/12–2/6, Monday and Wednesday
Option 2: 2/22–3/22, Tuesday and Thursday

Times: 6:30–9:00	**Cost:** $430
Hours per week: 5	**Course name:** Advanced
Number of meetings: 10	**Class size:** Maximum of 12

(continued)

STUDENT B: ENGLISH LANGUAGE CENTER

Dates and days: 1/3–1/31; 2/7–2/28

Monday and Wednesday or Tuesday and Thursday

Times: 6.30–9:00   **Cost:** $350

Hours per week: 5   **Course name:** Intermediate/Advanced

Number of meetings: 8   **Class size:** Maximum of 10

ANSWERS TO THE QUIZ, PAGES 49–50.

1. c
2. b
3. b
4. a
5. d
6. a
7. d
8. b

CHAPTER 3

In the Money

Part One: In Person

A. Prelistening

DISCUSSION

You will hear a retired woman, Mrs. Grant, talking with a young friend about money management. Before you listen, discuss the questions with a partner or in a small group.

- What are the people in the pictures doing to save money? Have you ever done any of these things?

- Can you guess the meaning of the idiom "in the money," which is in the title of this chapter? What are some other idiomatic expressions you know for talking about money?

VOCABULARY PREVIEW

The words and expressions are from the conversation. Check (✓) the ones you already know. Check (✓) the others as you work through the activities in Part One.

_____ brand-new	_____ extras	_____ itemize
_____ coupons	_____ garage sales	_____ live within (one's) means
_____ cut corners	_____ in debt	_____ make ends meet
_____ cut down (on)	_____ interest (*noun*)	_____ stick to a budget
_____ do without		

B. Listening

MAIN IDEAS

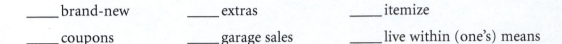 1 **Listen to the conversation. List ten or more money-saving strategies that Mrs. Grant mentions. Then work with a partner and compare lists.**

<u>sewed her daughter's clothes</u>_____   _____

_____   _____

_____   _____

_____   _____

_____   _____

DETAILS AND INFERENCES

2 **Listen again and read the statements below. Write *T* (true) or *F* (false). Then work with a partner and compare answers. Correct all false statements.**

_____ 1. At the time of her husband's death, Mrs. Grant was working full-time in a children's agency.

_____ 2. Mrs. Grant's daughter worked part-time in order to buy a cashmere sweater.

_____ 3. Mrs. Grant never borrowed money.

_____ 4. Mrs. Grant's family did not have a lot of money when she was growing up.

_____ 5. Mrs. Grant has $20,000 in credit card debt.

_____ 6. Mrs. Grant believes it is possible to find high-quality items at garage sales.

_____ 7. According to Mrs. Grant, people should not go grocery shopping when they are hungry.

LISTENING FOR LANGUAGE

3 Read the list of expressions related to money.

CONVERSATION TOOLS
Expressions about Money

cut corners	itemize	make ends meet
cut down (on)	live within (one's) means	stick to a budget
do without		

4 Listen to the short conversations and complete them with expressions from Conversation Tools. Then work with a partner and compare answers.

1. **A:** Guess what! I got a raise at work!

   B: Great! The extra money will help us _____

   so we don't have to borrow any more money from my parents.

2. **A:** Hey Dad. Can I borrow $100 for some concert tickets?

   B: No you can't, Son. It's time for you to learn how to _____.

3. **A:** Do you find it difficult to _____?

   B: Not really. It's easy as long as I pay for everything with cash and don't use

   credit cards.

4. **A:** What's the first step in making a budget?

   B: _____ your expenses. Make a list of every

   single thing you buy for one month.

   (*continued*)

5. **A:** Look at this water bill! It's the biggest we've ever had!

B: I guess it's time to _____ our water use.

6. **A:** How are we going to pay for a new car?

B: Don't worry, we'll find a way. We'll just have to

_____ for a while.

7. **A:** How are you managing since George lost his job?

B: Well, we're living off of my salary and we're

_____ extras like vacations.

5 The idioms on the left are from the short conversations in Exercise 4. Match them with their meanings on the right. If necessary, listen again to hear the idioms in context. (*Note:* Two expressions have the same meaning.)

_____ 1. make ends meet

a. make a list of one's weekly or monthly expenses

_____ 2. live within (one's) means

b. spend what you earn and no more

_____ 3. stick to a budget

c. live without

_____ 4. itemize

d. find ways to save money

_____ 5. cut down (on)

e. have enough money to pay for one's expenses

_____ 6. cut corners

f. reduce one's use of something

_____ 7. do without

6 Read about the intonation of questions in English.

FOCUS ON SOUND
Intonation of Questions

In American English, some types of questions have rising intonation at the end, some have falling intonation, and others have both. Generally, the voice begins to rise or fall on the last stressed syllable in the question. Look at these examples. The stressed syllables are in capital letters.

Question Type	Example
1. *Yes / No*	Have you ever borrowed MOney?
2. *Wh-*	When did Mrs. Grant's HUSband die?
3. Uninverted *Wh-*	Your kids were HOW old at the time?
4. Information tag[1]	That job didn't PAY very much, DID it?
5. Noninformation tag[2]	It was hard for you to live on such a small SALary, WASn't it?
6. Alternative choice	Did you have a JOB at that time, or were you a HOUSEwife?
7. Echo[3]	A BUDget?

7 Listen to the questions in Exercise 6 and repeat them during the pauses. Focus on the rising and falling intonation and on word stress.

8 Work with a partner. Select a set of questions below. Your partner will use the other set. Take turns reading questions and responding. Focus on correct stress and intonation.

SET 1

1. How often do you go shopping for groceries?

2. You're taking how many classes this (quarter, semester, year)?

(continued)

---

[1]The rising intonation at the end means the speaker is asking for information.
[2]The falling intonation at the end means the speaker is showing attention, interest, or sympathy. This kind of construction is not a real question.
[3]"Echo" questions serve the purpose of asking for repetition, clarification, or explanation.

3. That's a very expensive restaurant, isn't it? (*noninformation tag*)

4. Have you heard any news from home?

5. Who's that guy over there?

SET 2

1. Have you ever borrowed money from a friend?

2. You don't have any credit cards, do you? (*information tag*)

3. Do you drive to school or do you walk?

4. When do you want to go shopping?

5. You spent how much money on food last week?

C. Real Talk: Use What You've Learned

VOCABULARY REVIEW

1 The new vocabulary from Part One is listed below. Review the list with a partner. (See Steps for Reviewing Vocabulary on page 6.)

brand-new	extras	itemize
coupons	garage sales	live within (one's) means
cut corners	in debt	make ends meet
cut down (on)	interest (*noun*)	stick to a budget
do without		

2 Use the vocabulary to write five or six interview questions. Use a variety of question types from Exercise 6 on page 63.

Example:

Have you ever been in debt?
Is it hard for you to stick to a budget?
Where can you get help if you have trouble making ends meet?

3 Use your questions to interview an English speaker, if possible. If this is not possible, work with a partner from your class and interview each other. Focus on using correct question intonation.

4 Tell a classmate about the results of your interview. Make complete sentences about the person you interviewed.

Example:

I asked the school secretary if she likes shopping at garage sales, and she said she does not.

ROLE PLAY

1. Work with a partner. Plan role plays based on the two situations. Take turns giving advice. Use vocabulary from Part One.

		Student A	Student B
1		You and Student B are roommates. You didn't stick to your budget this month and you don't have enough money to pay your share of the rent next month.	Tell Student A that you will lend him/her the money for the rent this one time. Then give him/her advice on how to budget or save money.
2		Student B has $1500 in credit card debt. Give him/her advice on how to reduce the debt.	You had some unexpected expenses, and now you have a credit card debt of $1500. You're worried because the interest rate is 18 percent.

2. Practice your role play. Pay attention to the intonation of questions. Then choose one of your role plays and present it to another pair of students or to the whole class.

Part Two: On the Phone

A. Prelistening

DISCUSSION

You will hear a customer talking to a bank employee about different types of bank accounts. Before you listen, discuss the questions with a partner or in a small group.

- What types of bank accounts are you familiar with? Tell what you know about the requirements for opening an account.
- Imagine that you have just moved to a new city. What are some questions you would ask in order to choose a bank?

VOCABULARY PREVIEW

The words and expressions are from the conversation. Check (✓) the ones you already know. Check (✓) the others as you work through the activities in Part Two.

_____ ATM card   _____ interest rate   _____ opening balance

_____ automatic transfer   _____ linked account   _____ savings account

_____ balance   _____ minimum balance   _____ service charge

_____ checking account   _____ money market (account)   _____ waive

_____ debit card

B. Listening

MAIN IDEAS

1. Listen to the conversation and complete the statements. Then work with a partner and compare answers.

1. The caller wants information about _____. Check (✓) all correct answers.

    _____ a. savings accounts

    _____ b. checking accounts

    _____ c. debit cards

    _____ d. the employee

2. The employee gives the customer information about _____ type(s) of savings account(s) and _____ type(s) of checking account(s).

3. At the end of the conversation, the customer

    a. makes an appointment with the employee.

    b. says he will call back after he decides what to do.

    c. asks about the bank's hours of operation.

    d. decides to open a savings account.

DETAILS AND INFERENCES

🎧 ② Listen again and complete the tasks. Then work with a partner and compare answers.

1. Which of the following statements are true about the customer? Write *Yes* or *No*.

    _____ a. He is over eighteen years old.

    _____ b. He has a full-time job.

    _____ c. He is a student.

    _____ d. He will use his social security number for identification.

    _____ e. He is not a permanent resident.

2. How much money does the customer want to deposit?

    a. $2,400

    b. $54

    c. $5,400

    d. $24,000

3. Fill in the missing information about the accounts that the employee describes. If no information is given, leave the space blank.

Account Type	Opening Balance	Service Charge (Fee)	Minimum Balance to Avoid Service Charge	Interest Rate
Basic savings				
Checking				
Basic money market				

4. The service charge on the basic savings account is waived if the customer

    a. keeps at least $300 in the account at all times.

    b. has a linked account.

    c. does both a and b.

    d. does either a or b.

5. With a linked account, $25 is automatically transferred each month from

    a. savings to checking.

    b. checking to savings.

    c. savings to money market.

    d. money market to ATM.

6. The advantage of the money market account is that it has

    a. a free checking account linked to it.

    b. no service charge.

    c. a slightly higher interest rate than the regular savings account.

    d. a much higher interest rate than the regular savings account.

7. Which type of account(s) will the customer probably open, in your opinion? Why?

_____

LISTENING FOR LANGUAGE

3 Read the list of banking terms.

CONVERSATION TOOLS
Banking Terms

ATM card	interest rate	opening balance
automatic transfer	linked account	savings account
balance	minimum balance	service charge
checking account	money market (account)	waive (a fee)
debit card		

4 The items below are excerpts from the conversation. Listen and complete the sentences with banking terms. Some terms are used more than once.

1. **Bank:** So, our basic savings account requires a $300

_____. Otherwise there's a $3 fee each
　　　　　　a

month. If you keep it at at least $300, there'll be no monthly

_____. The opening
　　　　b

_____ is $100. It comes with a
　　　　c

_____, which is just like an
　　　　d

_____ . . .
　　　　e

2. **Customer:** Just to be clear, to avoid the _____ there
　　　　　　　　　　　　　　　　　　　　　　　　a

needs to be $300 in the account at all times?

Bank: That's right, or also the fee is _____ if you
　　　　　　　　　　　　　　　　　　　　b

have a _____ , which is a
　　　　　　　c

_____ , that, that's where they
　　　　d

automatically take a minimum of $25 a month and transfer it from

checking into the savings.

3. **Customer:** What do you mean by "linking"?

Bank: Oh, it means that you set up an _____ each

month from checking to savings, and it can be as little as $25 a month.

4. **Customer:** By the way, what's the _____ on that
　　　　　　　　　　　　　　　　　　　　　　a

_____?
　　　b

Bank: On the savings account you're at .4 percent.

5. **Bank:** But with $5,400 you could also qualify for our basic

_____ account. This one has a $1,000
　　　　a

_____.
　　　b

6. (The customer says he doesn't have a social security number.)

Bank: Oh well, that's all right. You can use your passport and one other form

of ID such as a _____ or your school ID card.

5 Read about word stress in noun compounds and adjective + noun phrases.

FOCUS ON SOUND
Stress in Noun Compounds vs. Adjective + Noun Phrases

A *noun compound* is a noun + noun combination or adjective + noun combination that has a set meaning, so it can usually be found in the dictionary. Normally the first word is stressed, e.g., *CREDIT card, CHECKing account.*[4]

In contrast, adjective + noun phrases (for example *monthly fee*) are not connected as closely in meaning as noun compounds. The first word of the phrase can be easily replaced by a different adjective, e.g., *high fee, annual fee,* etc. In such phrases, both words are normally stressed: *MONTHly FEE.*

Keep in mind that these are guidelines, not rules. There is variation from speaker to speaker. For example, the customer in the recording stresses the first word of compound nouns more clearly than the bank employee does. Also, a speaker may "break" one of these guidelines to stress other information in the sentence.

6 For each banking term that you wrote in Exercise 4, place a mark or marks (') over the word(s) that you predict will be stressed. Listen again. Repeat the pronunciation and check your predictions. (*Remember:* There may be variation between speakers.) Then read the segments with a partner.

C. Real Talk: Use What You've Learned

VOCABULARY REVIEW

1 The new vocabulary from Part Two is listed below. Review the list with a partner. (See Steps for Reviewing Vocabulary on page 6.)

ATM card	interest rate	opening balance
automatic transfer	linked account	savings account
balance	minimum balance	service charge
checking account	money market (account)	waive (a fee)
debit card		

---

[4]See Appendix 3 on page 222 for a summary of stress guidelines.

2 Use the banking terms to write seven questions to ask a bank employee. With a partner, practice asking your questions. Focus on using correct stress and linking.

Example:

Can I get an ATM card if I open a checking account?

1. _____
2. _____
3. _____
4. _____
5. _____
6. _____

ROLE PLAY

1 Work with a partner. Role play a conversation in which a university student calls a bank to get information about different types of accounts. (Assume that you are in an English-speaking city.) Pay attention to the pronunciation of noun compounds and adjective + noun phrases.

STUDENT A

You are a visiting scholar. You have $800 to put into a savings account. You will be working on campus, so you will also have money to put into a checking account. Ask about:

- different types of accounts
- monthly fees
- interest rates

(Try to use some of the questions you wrote in Exercise 2 above.)

STUDENT B

You are the bank employee. Give your partner information about:

- a basic savings account with a fee of $3 per month that can be waived if the student also opens a checking account
- the interest rate on the savings account (.7 percent)
- a money market account with an opening deposit of $1,000, a minimum balance of $800, and an interest rate of .4 percent

2 Switch roles. Do the role play again with a different partner.

3 If you are in an English-speaking country, call a local bank and get information about different types of accounts. Take notes on the information you hear. In class, compare your notes with a classmate's to find out which bank offers better services.

Part Three: On the Air

A. Prelistening

DISCUSSION

You will hear a radio interview about lending money. Before you listen, discuss the following questions with a partner or in a small group.

- In Shakespeare's play *Hamlet,* the character Polonius gives the following advice to his daughter, Ophelia: "Neither a borrower nor a lender be, for loan oft loses both itself and friend." What do you think this quotation means? Do you agree with Polonius's advice?

- In your family, community, or culture, where do people normally go if they need to borrow money? Do they go, for example, to a bank, a family member, a friend, one's employer?

- Study the following sentences. Explain the difference in use between *borrow, lend,* and *loan.*

  - I borrowed $10 from my roommate.

  - Sorry, I can't lend / loan you any more money.

  - We will need a loan in order to buy a new car.

VOCABULARY PREVIEW

The words and expressions are from the interview. Check (✓) the ones you already know. Check (✓) the others as you work through the activities in Part Three.

_____ appropriate	_____ kiss (something) off (*informal*)	_____ loan (*noun, verb*)
_____ come up short	_____ laid off	_____ payback (*noun*)
_____ deadline	_____ lend	_____ pay back (*verb*)
_____ end up		

B. Listening

Culture Note

Small Claims Court

A *small claims court* is a state court that resolves disputes involving relatively small amounts of money, typically between $2,000 and $10,000. In this type of court adversaries appear without lawyers and present their side of the story before a judge. They may invite witnesses, but there are no lawyers and no jury. The final decision is made by the judge.

MAIN IDEAS

1. Listen to an interview with Michelle Singletary, author of the column "The Color of Money" for the *Washington Post* newspaper. Write brief answers to the questions. Then work with a partner and compare answers.

1. What is Singletary's "number one rule" for lending money to people you know?

_____

2. What question does Singletary ask before agreeing to loan someone money?

_____

3. According to Singletary, what should you do if you lend someone a large amount of money?

_____

4. What is the purpose of the "pot of money" that Singletary and her husband created?

_____

DETAILS AND INFERENCES

🎧 ② Listen to segments from the interview. Pause between segments and answer the questions. Then work with a partner and compare answers.

SEGMENT 1

What does Singletary mean?

    a. You should lend people money.

    b. You shouldn't lend people money.

    c. Sometimes it's OK to lend people money.

SEGMENT 2

By "let it go," Singletary means

    a. lend to family members only.

    b. lend money without expecting to get it back.

    c. refuse to lend money to anyone.

SEGMENT 3

Singletary would probably lend money to someone who . . . (*Check (✓) all that apply.*)

_____ a. couldn't pay the rent because of an unexpected expense.

_____ b. got laid off.

_____ c. wanted money for an expensive car.

_____ d. needed money to pay college tuition.

_____ e. lost money in a card game.

SEGMENT 4

According to Singletary, if you lend someone a lot of money, what information should the loan contract specify?

    a. _____

    b. _____

SEGMENT 5

In this context, "documentation" probably means

    a. a passport.

    b. information about bank accounts.

    c. a loan contract.

"Kiss the money off" means

    a. accept the fact that you will not get the money back.

    b. kiss the money for good luck before you lend it to someone.

    c. go to court to get back money you lent someone.

LISTENING FOR LANGUAGE

3 Read about the pronunciation of phrasal verbs.

FOCUS ON SOUND
Stress and Linking in Phrasal Verbs

Phrasal verbs are verb + preposition combinations.[5] There are several grammatical categories of phrasal verbs in English. *Inseparable* phrasal verbs consist of a verb followed directly by a preposition (or two). Normally the first preposition is stressed, e.g., *sit DOWN, cut DOWN on*. *Separable* phrasal verbs can have an unstressed pronoun or a stressed noun between the verb and preposition or a stressed noun after the preposition, e.g., *pay (you) BACK, pay JIM back, pay back JIM*.

If the preposition begins with a vowel, it will be linked to the preceding verb or object: *end UP, catch UP on*.

4 Listen to phrasal verbs and practice saying them. Pay attention to the stressed words.

INSEPARABLE	SEPARABLE
1. need back	1. lend (it) out
2. end up	2. give (it) back
3. come out of	3. get (your money) back
4. give back	4. put (it) down
5. catch up on	5. pay (you) back
	6. kiss (the money) off

---

[5]Some phrasal verbs consist of verb + adverbial particles. These will not be discussed here.

5 Study the list of phrasal verbs related to money.

CONVERSATION TOOLS
Phrasal Verbs Related to Money

Verb	Meaning[6]	Example
cut back, cut down on	reduce the use of something	1. Ahmet cut back on entertainment in order to save money. 2. You need to cut down on your spending.
cut out	eliminate	3. Students have to cut out unnecessary expenses.
do without	live without	4. It's hard for me to do without a car.
get by	survive	5. While Mr. Smith was unemployed, the family got by on Mrs. Smith's salary.
pay back	return money you borrowed	6. I'll pay you back after the first of the month.
pay off	finish paying for something	7. The Diaz family recently paid off their house.

6 Work with a partner. Predict which words will be stressed and linked in the example sentences above. Then listen to the sentences. Repeat them with precise stress, reductions, intonation, and linking.

---

[6]Some items have idiomatic meanings as well. For example, *cut it out* means "stop it."

C. Real Talk: Use What You've Learned

VOCABULARY REVIEW

① The new vocabulary from Part Three is listed below. Review the list with a partner. (See Steps for Reviewing Vocabulary on page 6.)

appropriate	end up	lend
come up short	get by	loan *(noun, verb)*
cut back / down on	kiss (something) off *(informal)*	payback *(noun)*
cut out		pay back *(verb)*
deadline	laid off	pay off
do without		

② Work as a class. Make questions with the phrases in the left column. Stand up, walk around, and try to find someone who answers *Yes*. Write that person's name in the blank. Write only one name for each question. Don't write a name more than once.

Example:

Do you pay off your credit card every month?
Have you borrowed money and paid it off?

Find Someone Who . . .	Name
pays off his/her credit card every month	
has been **laid off**	
can't **do without** a cell phone	
is **getting by** on a part-time salary	
has borrowed money and **paid it off**	
has **cut out** something in order to save money	
is trying to **cut back** on meals in restaurants	
has **come up short** on money at a restaurant	
has lent money without expecting to get **paid back**	
needs to **catch up on** paying bills	

DISCUSSION

Work in small groups and discuss the following questions. Try to use the phrasal verbs from this chapter.

1. Have you ever borrowed money? From whom? Did you pay it back?
2. Have you ever lent money to anyone? To whom? Did you get it back?
3. Do you think it is appropriate to ask a borrower how he/she will spend the money before you agree to give this person a loan?
4. Before lending a large amount of money to anyone, Singletary requires people to sign a contract stating the amount of the loan and the deadline for paying it back. What is your opinion of this?

ROLE PLAY

1 Work with a partner. Choose a role and perform a three- to five-minute role play in which one person asks the other for a loan.

STUDENT A

You are a friend, family member, or colleague who wants to borrow some money from Student B. Explain how much you need to borrow and why you need it.

STUDENT B

A family member, friend, or colleague comes to you and asks for a loan. Ask the person questions to decide if you will lend the money. If you agree to the loan, be sure to ask how your partner plans to repay it. Decide if you will ask him or her to sign a contract.

2 Add new details to the situation. Practice your role play once or twice. Then perform your role play for another pair of students or for the whole class.

Part Four: In Class

U.S. Credit Card Facts	
8	Average number of credit cards per person
$8,562	Amount of credit debt carried by the average American
18.9%	Average credit card interest rate
$1,000	Amount the average U.S. household pays in finance charges per year
40%	Percentage of Americans who pay their credit card bills in full each month
3 billion	The number of solicitations sent out by credit card companies each year

Sources: http://www.fool.com/ccc/secrets/secrets.htm
http://ask.yahoo.com/ask/20040209.htm

A. Prelistening

DISCUSSION

You will hear part of a lecture about credit card debt. Before you listen, discuss the questions with a partner or in a small group.

- Examine the facts in the chart. What general observations can you make about the use of credit cards in the United States?
- Do you have any credit cards? How many? How do you use them?
- The following are typical ways that people in the United States pay for their college education. If you are a college student or college graduate, which of these methods have you used?

a. parents

b. loans

c. scholarship (grant)

d. personal savings

e. work

VOCABULARY PREVIEW

The words and expressions are from the lecture. Check (✓) the ones you already know. Check (✓) the others as you work through the activities in Part Four.

_____ accumulate   _____ go into debt   _____ "plastic" (*informal*)

_____ bankruptcy   _____ grant(s)   _____ revolving balance

_____ double (*verb*)   _____ impact   _____ segment

_____ go broke (*informal*)   _____ labor market   _____ student loan(s)

B. Listening and Note-Taking

LECTURE NOTE FORM: TAKING NOTES ON NUMBERS AND STATISTICS

① Read about ways to take clear, concise notes on numbers and statistics that you hear in lectures.

- Use mathematical symbols. For example, use + or ↑ for "increase," use < for "less than," use > for "more than, " etc.[7] Use = for any form of the "be" verb.

  Lecture: "The amount of consumer debt in the United States is more than 2 trillion dollars."
  Notes: *U.S. consumer debt => $2 trillion*

- If a year is given, write it first, followed by a colon.

  Lecture: "In 2003, 313,000 Americans paid their taxes with a credit card."
  Notes: *2003: 313K Amer. paid taxes w/ credit card.*

- If several facts are given for the same year, write the year first, then list the facts on separate lines and indent them equally.

  Lecture: "In 1992, 42 percent of students borrowed money for college, and they left college with an average debt of 9,000 dollars."
  Notes: *1992: —42% of st. borrowed money for coll.*
  —Left coll. w/ $9K debt

  (continued)

---

[7]See Appendix 2 on page 221 for a list of abbreviations and symbols.

- If two years are compared, list the topic of the comparison first, then list the years on separate lines underneath.

Lecture: "In 2001, 70 percent of young American adults had credit cards. By 2004, the amount had risen to 96 percent."

Notes: % of young adults w/ credit cards:

2001: 70%

2004: 96%

2 Read the sentences and rewrite them in note form, following the tips above. The first one is done for you. Then work with a partner and compare answers.

1. "The average credit card debt among 25 to 34 year olds in 2001 was 4,008 dollars."

   2001: Av. cred. card debt among 25–34 yr. olds = $4,008

2. "In 1993, the U.S. savings rate was 5.9 percent. Ten years later, it had fallen to 1.3 percent."

   _____

   _____

3. "In 2002, the average salary for males was 35,487 dollars and for females, 30,093 dollars."

   _____

   _____

4. "In 2004, the average fee for a late credit card payment was 39 dollars. It was just 10 dollars in 1996."

   _____

   _____

LECTURE LANGUAGE: EXPRESSIONS FOR INCREASE AND DECREASE

3 Read about ways to express the concepts *increase* and *decrease,* which are commonly used with numbers and statistics.

Verbs and phrases that have the same or similar meanings as the words *increase* and *decrease* are commonly used with numbers and statistics.

Examples	Comments
In the last decade costs for necessities like food and housing **have increased** faster than workers' salaries.	• Synonyms for **increase** include: **rise, go up, jump, skyrocket**. • **Jump** and **skyrocket** mean that the increase was fast, sudden, or extreme.
Due to inflation, real family income has **decreased** in the past decade.	• Synonyms for **decrease** include: **crash, decline, go down, fall, plunge, plummet, shrink**. • **Crash, plummet**, and **plunge**, indicate that the decrease was rapid, sudden, or steep. • **Shrink** is used metaphorically to talk about a decreasing *amount* of something, e.g., money.
College tuition increased **by** $4,000 last year. Tuition at private universities has increased **from** $18,500 **to** $22,300 since 2002.	• **By** is used for the *amount* of the increase or decrease. • **From** indicates the starting amount. • **To** indicates the ending amount.
The amount of money available for scholarships was **halved** between 2001 and 2003.	• **Halve** means "cut in half." • Similar verbs are **double** (2x), **triple** (3x), and **quadruple** (4x).

4 Listen to sentences from the lecture about credit card debt among college graduates. Pause the recording after each item. Take notes using the techniques and expressions from Exercises 1 and 3.

1. _____

2. _____

3. _____

4. _____

5. _____

6. _____

5 Work with a partner. Compare notes. Then use the notes to restate the sentences you heard.

TAKING NOTES

6 Before you listen to the lecture about credit card debt, study the sample budget for a recent college graduate earning $36,000 a year.

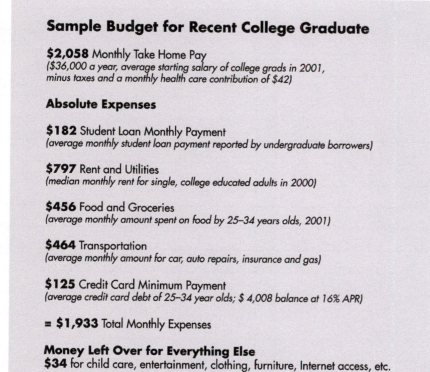

Sample Budget for Recent College Graduate

$2,058 Monthly Take Home Pay
($36,000 a year, average starting salary of college grads in 2001, minus taxes and a monthly health care contribution of $42)

Absolute Expenses

$182 Student Loan Monthly Payment
(average monthly student loan payment reported by undergraduate borrowers)

$797 Rent and Utilities
(median monthly rent for single, college educated adults in 2000)

$456 Food and Groceries
(average monthly amount spent on food by 25–34 years olds, 2001)

$464 Transportation
(average monthly amount for car, auto repairs, insurance and gas)

$125 Credit Card Minimum Payment
(average credit card debt of 25–34 year olds; $ 4,008 balance at 16% APR)

= $1,933 Total Monthly Expenses

Money Left Over for Everything Else
$34 for child care, entertainment, clothing, furniture, Internet access, etc.

Source: "Generation Broke: The Growth of Debt Among Young Americans" by Tamara Draut and Javier Silva. Borrowing to Make Ends Meet Briefing Paper #2, October 2004, http://www.demos-usa.org/pubs/Generation_Broke.pdf

Listen to the lecture and take notes on your own paper. Use what you have learned about lecture note form, language, and organization. Then use your notes to complete the outline. Use the cues on the left to guide you.

	I. Intro
	Topic:
description	Recent coll. grads:
facts	II. Facts
year	• 1992-2001:
	av. cred. card debt ↑ 55%, = $4,008 per household
	bankruptcy rate ↑ 19%
year	•
definition	•
central question	
reasons	1.
	2.
	3.
past	
present	

loan stats		yr.	% borrowed	av. debt at grad.
		1992		
	◯			
result				
example				
4th reason (2 parts)	◯			
		4.		

REVIEWING THE LECTURE

8 Work with a partner or in a small group. Use your notes to discuss the questions.

1. Describe the segment of the U.S. population that this lecture is about.

2. Describe the financial situation of today's typical college graduates. Use statistics from the lecture.

3. What is a "revolving balance"? Why is it a bad thing to have?

4. What are the four causes of rising debt levels among recent college graduates?

5. What has happened to the cost of living in the last decade, and how does this affect recent college graduates?

6. How did the employment situation of college graduates change in the decade before this lecture was recorded?

7. Discuss the cause and the effect of rising student loan debt.

8. Why is it easy for young adults to accumulate credit card debt?

C. Real Talk: Use What You've Learned

VOCABULARY REVIEW

1 The key vocabulary from Part Four is listed below. Review the list with a partner. (See Steps for Reviewing Vocabulary on page 6.)

accumulate	go into debt	"plastic" (*informal*)
bankruptcy	grant(s)	revolving balance
double (*verb*)	impact	segment
go broke (*informal*)	labor market	student loan(s)

2 Use the vocabulary above to fill in the blanks. Then work with a partner and compare answers.

1. For the past three years the _____ has been tight. There haven't been enough good jobs.

2. My grandmother never pays for anything with _____. She always uses cash.

3. Naomi has a _____ of more than $4,000 on her credit cards. The monthly interest charges are more than $100.

4. Gregory paid for college with a combination of _____

   and _____. It will take him eight years to repay the loans.

5. Last year more than one million people declared _____. Most of them got into debt by overspending on credit cards.

6. The fastest-growing _____ of the U.S. population is people in their 50s and 60s—the so-called "baby boomers."

7. Instead of paying my bills one by one, I like to _____ them throughout the month and then pay them all at once.

8. The easy availability of credit has had both a positive and a negative

   _____ on the way Americans spend money.

9. Martin bought an expensive sports car and now he is

_____ trying to pay for it.

10. Recently the price of gasoline has almost _____ , so many people are buying smaller cars with better fuel economy.

DISCUSSION

In small groups, discuss the questions. Use the key vocabulary.

1. If you use credit cards, do you pay them off each month, or do you have a revolving balance? What is the interest rate on the credit cards you use?

2. Have you ever accumulated more debt than you were able to pay off?

3. In your native country or culture, is bankruptcy an option for people who cannot pay their debts? If not, what happens to such people?

4. Compare your budget to the sample budget on page 83. Which of your expenses are similar, and which are different? Which additional expenses do you have?

5. Suppose you had no money for luxuries. What could you do if you wanted something extra, such as tickets to a concert?

PRACTICE WITH STATISTICS

Work with a partner. Student A, look at the information below. Student B, look at the information on page 88. Follow the directions.

STUDENT A

1. Make sentences based on the information. Use the expressions from page 82. Your partner will take notes.

1. South Korea—total purchases made with credit card	1998: $53 billion	2002: 519 billion
2. U.S. personal savings rate	1993: 5.9%	2003: 1.3%
3. Americans who pay taxes with a credit card	1999: 53,300	2003: 313,000
4. Average cost of tuition at a public university	2002: $9,338	2005: $10,818

Sources: 1. and 2. : http://www.pbs.org/wgbh/pages/frontline/shows/credit/more/world.html
3. and 4. : http://moneycentral.msn.com/content/Savinganddebt/Managedebt/P95340.asp

Take notes on Student B's sentences.

2 Make sentences based on this information. Your partner will take notes.

1. Number of credit and debit cards in France	Debit: 39 million	Credit: 9 million
2. Average cost of tuition at a private U.S. university	2002: 24,851	2005: 28,769
3. U.S. fast food purchases made with credit cards	2002: $6.1 billion	2003: $12.9 billion
4. Total amount of U.S. revolving debt	January 1994: $313 billion	January 2004: $753 billion

Sources: 1. http://www.pbs.org/wgbh/pages/frontline/shows/credit/more/world.html
2. http://www.princetonreview.com/college/finance/articles/save/costcollege.asp
3. http://www.cardweb.com/cardtrak/news/2004/december/21a.html
4. http://www.consumersunion.org/pub/0513%20FACTS%20ABOUT%20CREDIT%20CARD%20DEBT.pdf

Take notes on Student A's sentences.

3 Student A and Student B: Using your notes, reconstruct your partner's sentences. Have your partner check your sentences.

TOEFL® Practice: Synthesizing Listening, Reading, and Speaking

1 Read the passage about the advantages of owning credit cards.

A U.S. government study conducted in 2001 found that most college administrators viewed credit card usage by students as something positive. They cited the advantages of using a credit card for establishing credit, medical or family-related emergencies, making travel arrangements and reservations, payment conveniences such as shopping by telephone and the Internet, and cashless transactions. The report showed that 77 percent of students used their credit card for routine personal expenses and 67 percent of students used it for occasional or emergency expenses. The survey also reported that most students used their credit cards responsibly.

Source: "Credit Card Usage Among College and University Students,"
http://www.ericdigests.org/2003-2/credit.html

2 Review your lecture notes. Then use the information from both the lecture and the reading passage to prepare a one-minute oral presentation on the following question.

- For college students, what are the advantages and disadvantages of owning credit cards?

CHAPTER 4
Memories

Part One: In Person

A. Prelistening

DISCUSSION

You will hear several people talking about their sensory memories. Before you listen, discuss the questions with a partner or in a small group.

- Describe the picture. What is the woman looking at? What might she be remembering? Have you ever had a similar experience?

- Our five senses—smell, sight, sound, taste, and touch—can trigger powerful memories. Do you know why or how this happens?

VOCABULARY PREVIEW

The words and expressions are from the speakers' descriptions of their sensory memories. Check (✓) the ones you already know. Check (✓) the others as you work through the activities in Part One.

_____ bring back (a memory)   _____ take (someone) back

_____ evocative (of something)   _____ transport (someone) back

_____ remind (someone) of (something)   _____ trigger (a memory or association)

B. Listening

MAIN IDEAS

1 Listen to the audio segments and take notes in the chart. Then work with a partner and compare answers.

Segment	Sense	Memory
1		Speaker 1: Speaker 2:
2		
3		
4		

DETAILS AND INFERENCES

2 Listen again. Mark the statements *T* (true), *F* (false), or *U* (unknown because there is not enough information). Then work with a partner and compare answers. Correct all false statements.

SEGMENT 1

_____ 1. Sawdust smells like cut wood.

_____ 2. The second speaker enjoys the smell of cigarette smoke.

_____ 3. The second speaker's father is dead.

_____ 4. The speaker got a job in Tobago after university.

_____ 5. Tobago probably has a warm climate.

_____ 6. The speaker probably has a lot of purple and green clothes.

_____ 7. As a child, the speaker enjoyed building with blocks.

_____ 8. The speaker probably grew up in Los Angeles.

_____ 9. The speaker is about fifty years old.

_____ 10. The texture of the baseball was both rough and smooth.

LISTENING FOR LANGUAGE

③ Read about ways that English speakers can change the basic stress pattern.

FOCUS ON SOUND
Contrastive Stress

You have learned (Chapter 1, Part Two, page 12) that in the basic sentence-stress pattern for English, content words are usually stressed while function words are not. You also learned (Chapter 2, Part Three, page 45) additional guidelines governing stress, such as the fact that the last content word of a sentence or thought group is normally stressed.[1]

By now you have probably noticed many exceptions to the guidelines in earlier chapters. The fact is that speakers can choose to stress any word(s) they want in order to emphasize them. Consider this example from the recording:

Speaker 1: (Talks about how the smell of sawdust reminds her of her father.)

Speaker 2: You know what reminds me of MY father?

Although pronouns are not normally stressed, Speaker 2 stresses the pronoun "my" to emphasize the contrast between the two speakers' memories.

④ Listen to the examples of basic stress and contrastive stress. Repeat each sentence after the speaker. Then work with a partner and fill in the meaning of the contrastive stress.

_____

[1] See Appendix 3 on page 222 for a summary of stress guidelines.

Basic Stress	Contrastive Stress	Meaning of Contrastive Stress
1. Speaker 1: I have a question.	Speaker 2: **I** have a question, too.	Not only Speaker 1 but also Speaker 2 has a question.
2. Speaker 1: Joe will e-mail you tomorrow.	Speaker 2: Tell Joe to **CALL** me tomorrow.	
3. Speaker 1: Hannah will bring the coffee to the meeting.	Speaker 2: No, **MARK** will bring the coffee.	
4. Lynn has a doctor's appointment tomorrow.	**CATHY** has a doctor's appointment **TODAY**.	
5. Please put the chair here.	And please put the table **THERE**.	

5 Read the questions. Then listen to the same sentence read with different stress each time. Match the question with the sentence you hear.

Example:

You hear: "No, please put it HERE."
This answer matches the question: "Do you want me to put the box over there?"

a. Did Jack's father plant flowers in the spring? _____

b. Did Brian's mother plant flowers in the spring? _____

c. Did Jack's mother plant flowers in the summer? _____

d. Did Jack's mother cut flowers in the spring? _____

e. Did Jack's mother plant fruit trees in the spring? _____

C. Real Talk: Use What You've Learned

VOCABULARY REVIEW

1 The new vocabulary from Part One is listed below. Review the list with a partner.

bring back (a memory)	take (someone) back
evocative (of something)	transport (someone) back
remind (someone) of (something)	trigger (a memory or association)

2 Use the vocabulary to complete the sentences. (*Note:* Some items have more than one correct answer.)

1. My grandmother wore a perfume called White Shoulders. Whenever I smell that perfume, it _____ the memory of my grandmother even though she died almost twenty years ago.

2. For many people, the smell of popcorn is _____ of movie theaters because popcorn is always sold at movie theaters, and it tastes wonderful.

3. There's a candy bar called Three Musketeers that _____ of my childhood whenever I eat it.

4. The taste of fresh milk _____ to the time when I spent a summer working on a farm.

DESCRIBING MEMORIES

Work in small groups. Take turns describing memories that are triggered for you by the senses of sight, sound, smell, taste, and touch. As you speak, use a variety of expressions from the box. Focus on using the basic stress pattern. As you listen to your classmates, respond to them and try to use contrastive stress.

Example:

A: Whenever I eat a doughnut, I think of my mother. She LOVES them.
B: That's funny. MY mother HATES doughnuts.

Part Two: On the Phone

A. Prelistening

DISCUSSION

You will hear a couple arguing about forgetting something. Before you listen, discuss the questions with a partner or in a small group.

- Look at the list below. Have you ever forgotten any of these things? Check the items that apply to you. Then tell your partner(s) what happened.

_____ your keys in the car
_____ someone's birthday
_____ to give someone a message
_____ to pay a bill on time
_____ to pick someone up when expected
_____ an important appointment
_____ to return a library book or a rented movie
_____ other: _____

- Have you ever had an argument with another person because one of you forgot something? What did each person say? How did the argument end?

VOCABULARY PREVIEW

The words and expressions are from the conversation. Check (✓) the ones you already know. Check (✓) the others as you work through the activities in Part Two.

_____ absentmindedness   _____ (have something) on (one's) mind

_____ (it's not) the end of the world (*informal*)   _____ scatterbrain (*informal*)

_____ make it up to (you)   _____ slip (one's) mind

B. Listening

MAIN IDEAS

1 Listen to the conversation and answer the questions. Then work with a partner and compare answers.

1. Why is the wife upset?

   _____

2. What is the husband's excuse?

   _____

3. What does the husband plan to do in order to avoid the same problem in the future?

   _____

4. How do the speakers feel at the end of the conversation? How do you know?

   _____

DETAILS AND INFERENCES

🎧 ② **Listen to the conversation again and answer the questions. Then work with a partner and compare answers.**

1. Who forgot to do the following things recently? Mark *W* for the wife, *H* for the husband, or *N* for neither of them.

   _____ a. pick up their child at the game

   _____ b. return rented videos on time

   _____ c. remember spouse's birthday

   _____ d. give important messages

   _____ e. get dinner ready

2. Which of the following statements are probably true? Check (✓) them. How do you know?

   _____ a. Joseph is the couple's daughter.

   _____ b. The wife is calling from her car.

   _____ c. Joseph plays soccer.

   _____ d. The husband doesn't write down messages.

   _____ e. They are both busy people.

   _____ f. The argument will continue later.

LISTENING FOR LANGUAGE

③ **Read about the ways English speakers use their voices to convey strong emotions.**

FOCUS ON SOUND
Using the Voice to Express Emotions

English speakers express strong feelings such as anger, embarrassment, enthusiasm, and surprise by changing their voices in specific ways. These include:

- increased volume (loudness)
- stronger stress and higher pitch on key words
- greater rise or fall at the end of statements or questions

In the recording, these features become more and more obvious as the husband and wife become angrier with each other. As soon as the husband apologizes, however, the speakers' pitch decreases and the stress pattern returns to normal.

4 Listen to the conversation again. Raise your hand in places where the speakers show strong emotion. Lower your hand when the speakers calm down.

Examples:

Wife: What?!! Howard, you didn't tell me! (*anger*)

Wife: We've got to do something about this . . . (*calming down*)

5 Read about language for concluding an argument.

CONVERSATION TOOLS
Apologizing, Reconciling, Forgiving

What usually happens after an argument?

- One person apologizes, or the two people apologize to each other.
- They make up, or *reconcile*. That is, they say or offer to do something nice for one another.
- They forgive each other (or not!).

The following expressions are commonly used for these three functions.

Apologizing	Reconciling	Forgiving
I apologize.	How can I make it up to you?	I forgive you.
(Please) forgive me.	Let me make it up to you.	That's OK.
I'm (so / very / terribly) sorry.	Tell you what: I'll . . .	That's all right.
It's my fault.	Let's work this out.	Don't worry about it.
I didn't mean to do it.	I feel really bad about this.	Forget about it.
It won't happen again (I promise).		

6 Work with a partner. Turn to the audioscript of the conversation on page 252. Do the following tasks.

1. Circle the expressions the husband and wife use to apologize, reconcile, and forgive one another. Then replace the expressions you circled with other expressions from the chart.

2. Take the roles of the husband and the wife. Read the entire audioscript out loud with the new expressions you inserted. Focus on using your voices to express different feelings.

C. Real Talk: Use What You've Learned

Vocabulary Review

1 The new vocabulary from Part Two is listed below. Review the list with a partner.

> absentmindedness
> (it's not) the end of the
>   world (*informal*)
> make it up to (you)
>
> (to have something) on (one's) mind
> scatterbrain (*informal*)
> slip (one's) mind

2 Use the vocabulary to complete the sentences. Then work with a partner and compare answers.

1. I'm worried about my father's _____. Last week while I was visiting he left the stove on and his front door unlocked.

2. It's not _____ if you fail this test; you can take it again next week.

3. **A:** You look stressed out. What's wrong?

   B: Oh, I've got a hundred things _____, and I don't have enough time to do everything.

4. **A:** Did you call the phone company about the mistake in our bill?

   B: Oops, it _____. I'll do it now.

5. This is the third time you've lost your glasses, you _____!

6. I know I forgot your birthday, but I promise I'll _____ next week. I'll take you to the best restaurant in town!

Role Play

1 Work with a partner. Role-play at least two of the scenarios on page 99. Use the new vocabulary above and expressions for apologizing, reconciling, and forgiving in Conversation Tools on page 97.

Scenario	Student A	Student B
1	You had a problem in one of your college classes. The professor offered to meet you one afternoon to give you extra help. You made an appointment with her, but you forgot to go. You feel terribly embarrassed. Call the professor, apologize, and explain.	The professor
2	The brother	Your brother's girlfriend called and asked you to give him a message saying she couldn't meet him for dinner as planned because she had to work late. You forgot to give him the message. As a result, he waited for her at the restaurant for over an hour. Now he is very upset with you.
3	Your neighbor frequently borrows things from you and forgets to return them. For example, she's had your vacuum cleaner for a week and one of your CDs for two weeks. Also, she owes you thirty-five dollars for babysitting. You decide to confront her.	The neighbor
4	The best friend	You told your best friend a secret: You have a crush on your classmate. Your friend told one other person, who told another person, and someone told the classmate. You are furious with your friend and have a big argument about it.

2 Practice your role plays. Remember to use variations in volume, word stress, pitch, and intonation to express strong emotions.

3 Perform a role play for another pair of students or for the whole class.

Part Three: On the Air

A. Prelistening

PARTNER ACTIVITY: TEST YOUR MEMORY

You will hear part of a radio interview with Dr. Mel Levine, professor of pediatrics at the University of North Carolina Medical School. Before you listen, conduct the following short experiments. You will need a watch or clock with a second hand.

Dr. Mel Levine working with a child

1 Work with a partner. Choose a set of directions and read them to your partner. Do not read your partner's directions.

> **STUDENT A**
>
> a. Say to your partner: "Name as many animals as you can in 30 seconds. I'm going to count. Are you ready? Begin."
>
> b. Count the number of animals your partner lists in 30 seconds.
>
> c. After 30 seconds, tell your partner to stop. How many animals did your partner list?
> _____

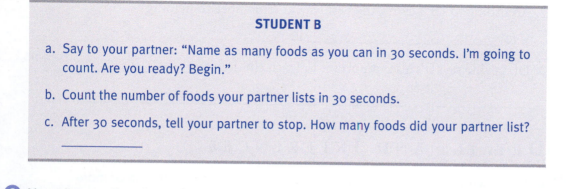

2 Now discuss the questions with your partner:

1. Did you use any kind of system or trick to help you name as many items as possible in 30 seconds? Explain.

2. Complete the sentence according to your own ideas and experience: "The best way to remember something is to _____."

VOCABULARY PREVIEW

The words and expressions are from the interview. Check (✓) the ones you already know. Check (✓) the others as you work through the activities in Part Three.

_____ describe   _____ modify

_____ elaborate   _____ picture (*verb*)

_____ extend   _____ recode

_____ filing system   _____ transform

B. Listening

MAIN IDEAS

1 Listen to the interview. Complete the sentences. Then work with a partner and compare answers.

1. In the first part of the interview, Dr. Levine's advice is targeted at

   a. parents.

   b. children.

   c. teachers.

   d. anyone who has memory problems.

(continued)

2. According to Dr. Levine, the best way to remember something

   is to _____ it.

3. Dr. Levine says it's also important to teach children to _____

   _____ .

DETAILS AND INFERENCES

🎧 **2** **Listen again and complete the following tasks. Then work with one or more partners and compare answers.**

1. Which of the following are examples of ways to transform, or recode, information, according to the interview? Check (✓) all correct answers.

   _____ a. describe it in words

   _____ b. make a picture of it

   _____ c. memorize it

   _____ d. think of examples of it

   _____ e. repeat it over and over

   _____ f. say it in another language

2. Dr. Levine suggests that if information comes in visually, you should

   _____ .

3. Dr. Levine suggests that if information comes in verbally, try to

   a. _____

   b. _____

   c. _____

   d. _____

4. According to Dr. Levine, "The more you _____ information, the more effectively it gets filed in memory." Check (✓) all that apply.

   _____ a. picture

   _____ b. extend

   _____ c. elaborate

   _____ d. decode

   _____ e. modify

5. The thirteen-year-old in Dr. Levine's example named the following animals: cow, chicken, turkey, pig, lion, tiger, giraffe, elephant, rhino, spider, ant, bee. Which "folders" was this child using? _____

_____

6. According to Dr. Levine, which of the following is the correct sequence of activities for students to follow before an exam?

    a. study, take a shower, go to sleep

    b. sleep, get up early, study

    c. take a shower, study, go to sleep

    d. get up early, take a shower, study

7. "Instant replay" is a sports term,[2] but in this context, Dr. Levine is talking about

    a. the recycling of information during sleep.

    b. good dreams.

    c. the best way to study for an exam.

    d. happy memories.

LISTENING FOR LANGUAGE

3 Read about *metaphor,* a type of comparison.

CONVERSATION TOOLS
Metaphors

There are many ways of comparing two things in English. One is by using comparative language; for example, "It's **easier** for me to remember numbers than names." Another type of comparison uses the words *like* or *as:* "He has a memory **like** an elephant." A third type of comparison, called *metaphor,* is less direct. Metaphors often use the verb *be* to imply similarity, for example in the famous line from Shakespeare, "All the world's a stage, and all the men and women merely players."[3]

Writers and speakers sometimes use an *extended metaphor.* That is, they suggest a metaphor and refer to it in different ways throughout the speech or piece of writing.

---

[2]"Instant replay" is the immediate repeated broadcast, on television, of action in a sports event.
[3]From *As You Like It* 2.7.

🎧 **4** Listen to a segment from the interview and answer the questions. Then work with a partner and discuss your answers.

1. According to Dr. Levine, memory is like a _____.

2. Which other words are part of this metaphor? _____

_____

C. Real Talk: Use What You've Learned

VOCABULARY REVIEW

1 The new vocabulary from Part Three is listed below. Review the list with a partner. (See Steps for Reviewing Vocabulary on page 6.)

describe	extend	modify	recode
elaborate	filing system	picture (*verb*)	transform

2 Dr. Levine uses all the verbs in the chart to describe strategies for remembering information. Work with a partner. State which verbs are synonyms.

DISCUSSION

Work in small groups. Use vocabulary from Part Three and information from the interview to answer the following questions.

1. How do you prefer to learn: visually, aurally (by hearing), kinesthetically (by touching and doing), or through a combination of all three? Did you ever have a problem in school because of the way you prefer to learn?

2. Which of Dr. Levine's list of recoding strategies have you used? Which ones have worked best for you? Give examples. Which new strategies will you try to use in the future?

3. A friend is having trouble remembering information for a test. Which of Dr. Levine's memory strategies would you advise the student to use for each of the following things:
   - the plot of a novel
   - the major rivers of the United States
   - a list of plants and their characteristics
   - the effects of stress
   - a list of English vocabulary words

4. Dr. Levine compares memory to a filing system. Do you think this is a good metaphor for describing memory? Why or why not?

5. What other metaphors can you think of to describe the way memory works?

OUT-OF-CLASS ACTIVITY

① Repeat the 30-second animal-naming test from Exercise 1 on page 100 with three people of different ages. Try to test at least one child. Record the results in the table below.

Name	Age	Number of Animals

② In class, report your results and discuss them with your classmates. Were the results different for people of different ages? Do the findings confirm or contradict what you learned in the listening? Explain.

Part Four: In Class

A. Prelistening

DISCUSSION

You will hear a lecture about memory improvement strategies. Before you listen, discuss the following questions with a partner or in a small group.

- Why is the student in the cartoon worried? Do you have the same problem?
- Which of the following types of information are often hard for you to remember? Check them.

_____ names	_____ vocabulary in a new language
_____ numbers	_____ appointments
_____ directions to a place	_____ where you put things
_____ events in history	_____ mathematical formulas
_____ shopping lists	_____ other: _____
_____ sequences of steps (e.g., how to use an electronic device, how to cook something)	

- Do you ever use memory "tricks" to help you remember the things you checked? Describe your methods.

VOCABULARY PREVIEW

The words and expressions are from the lecture. Check (✓) the ones you already know. Check (✓) the others as you work through the activities in Part Four.

_____ enhance	_____ mind's eye	_____ systematic
_____ facilitate	_____ recall	_____ target word
_____ method	_____ sequence	_____ visualize

B. Listening and Note-Taking

LECTURE ORGANIZATION: DESCRIBING A PROCESS OR TECHNIQUE

1 Read about describing a process or a technique.

> One of the most common features of lectures is a description of a process or technique. The following nouns tell you that a speaker is describing a process.
>
> | | | |
> |---|---|---|
> | method | process | steps |
> | phases | sequence | system |
> | procedure | stages | technique |
>
> These words are often combined with words that show a sequence, for example, *the first / second / third step.*

2 Listen to part of the lecture introduction and answer the following question.

Which technique will the lecture describe? _____

LECTURE LANGUAGE: HYPOTHETICAL SITUATIONS

3 Read about hypothetical situations.

> Listeners are sometimes asked to imagine themselves in a hypothetical (imaginary) situation. For example: *Let's suppose that you have a new friend, and you want to remember her phone number.* The speaker uses this imaginary example as a way of introducing the main point: how to remember someone's phone number.
>
> Here are phrases that can be used to signal a hypothetical situation. Note that a dependent (noun) clause comes after them.
>
> • (Let's) suppose/imagine/pretend/say (that) . . .[4]
>
> • What if . . .?

---

[4]*Let's* and *that* are optional.

🎧 ④ **Listen to four hypothetical situations. Complete the sentences with the missing signal phrases.**

1. _____ you have a new friend and you learn that your friend's phone number is 934-1971. And _____ that, coincidentally, you were born in 1971.

2. OK, so _____ you are a student in a language class and you're trying to learn a new word.

3. So _____ that you're studying English and one of the words on your vocabulary list is the word *expeditious*.

4. OK. So now _____ that it's a week later and you have a vocabulary test the next day.

⑤ **Work with a partner and compare answers. Then restate each sentence with a different signal phrase.**

TAKING NOTES

🎧 ⑥ **Listen to the lecture and take notes on your own paper. Use what you have learned about lecture form, language, and organization. Then rewrite your notes in the space. Use the cues on the left to guide you.**

	I. Intro
◯	A. Previous lec.: Memory works by transforming info
topic	B. This lec.:
	C. Def:
examples	
mnemonic technique	II. Keyword method
	A. History: Dev'd 30 years ago by R. C. Atkinson
	B. Purpose:
	C. Ex: *kaposzta* (Hungarian)
◯	

	III. Steps
1st step	A. Choose key word
3 characteristics	1. Charac. of good key word
	2. Ex: *kaposzta* → cop
2nd step	B.
	1. contains key word + target meaning, i.e., cop + cabbage
	2.
	3.
example	4.
3rd step	C.
how to study	
conclusion	

REVIEWING THE LECTURE

7 Work with a partner or in a small group. Use your lecture notes to discuss the questions.

1. What are mnemonics?
2. What was the original purpose of the keyword method?
3. What are the three characteristics of a good keyword?
4. What are the three steps in the keyword method?
5. How can you use the keyword method to study for a vocabulary test?

C. Real Talk: Use What You've Learned

VOCABULARY REVIEW

1 The new vocabulary from Part Four is listed below. Review the list with a partner. (See Steps for Reviewing Vocabulary on page 6.)

enhance	mind's eye	systematic
facilitate	recall	target word
method	sequence	visualize

2 Work in small groups and discuss the questions. Use the new vocabulary whenever possible.

1. Describe your procedure(s) for learning new vocabulary up to now. What sequence do you follow? Do you think your technique(s) is (are) useful?
2. Have you ever consciously used visualization to facilitate your memory? Did it help you remember?
3. The keyword method was developed to help students learn vocabulary, but can you think of other types of information (e.g., see the list on page 104) that could be recalled using this system?

PRACTICING THE KEYWORD METHOD

1 Work in small groups. Follow the steps in the keyword method to learn the target words in the left column.

Word	Definition	Keyword
doodad (*noun*)	small and unnecessary object whose name you have forgotten or do not know	
genial (*adj*)	cheerful, kind, and friendly	
plummet (*verb*)	suddenly and quickly decrease in value or amount; to fall suddenly from a high place	
quibble (*noun*)	complaint or criticism about something that is not very important	
kowtow (*verb*)	be too eager to obey or be polite to someone who has more power than you or who has something you want	
truncate (*verb*)	make something shorter than before	
trapezoid (*noun*)	geometric figure with four sides, only two of which are parallel	

2 Your teacher will give you a test on the words. Use the keyword method to study.

3 After the test, discuss your experience with the keyword method. Did it help you remember the new words? Do you think you will use the method again in the future?

FOLLOW-UP

1 If possible, work with a partner who does not speak your first language. Teach each other three words from your language. Use the keyword method to remember the words your partner teaches you. Three days from now, test each other on the words.

2 Use the keyword method to study for your next vocabulary test. Write in a journal or report orally about your experience and the effectiveness of the method.

TOEFL® Practice: Synthesizing Listening, Reading, and Speaking

1 Read the passage about keywords.

> In an experimental study, students were asked to learn the Spanish word *pestana*, meaning "eyelash." One group was given the key word *pest*, which sounds like *pestana* but is not related to it in meaning.
>
> The second group consisted of subjects who were allowed to select their <u>own</u> keywords. Given free choice, they tended to choose the key phrase *paste on*, which not only sounded like the target word but also had a meaningful association (as in to *paste on* false eyelashes). This suggested that keywords that are related to the keyword in both sound and meaning might be preferable for long-term retention of target vocabulary.
>
> Source: "About Memory," http://www.memory-ey.com/mnemonics/keyword_language.htm
> Used by permission of The Memory Key.

2 Review your lecture notes. Then use the information from both the lecture and the reading to prepare a one-minute oral presentation on the following topic.

- Summarize the characteristics of a good keyword. Demonstrate how you would apply these principles if you were trying to teach an English speaker some words in your first language.

5
Body Trends

Part One: In Person

A. Prelistening

DISCUSSION

You will hear a discussion between parents and their daughter about getting a tattoo. Before you listen, discuss the questions with a partner or in a small group.

- What is your opinion of the tattoo in the photo?
- If you really wanted a tattoo, would you get one even if your family was against it?

VOCABULARY PREVIEW

The words and expressions are from the discussion. Check (✓) the ones you already know. Check (✓) the others as you work through the activities in Part One.

____ fit in

____ for a change

____ for one thing . . . for another (thing) . . .

____ get tired of (something or someone)

____ give (someone) a hard time

____ on (one's) own

____ think (something) through

B. Listening

MAIN IDEAS

 ① Listen to the discussion and answer the questions. Then work with a partner and compare answers.

1. What kind of tattoo does Jennifer want? _____

2. Do her parents approve or disapprove? _____

3. Is Jennifer going to get what she wants? _____

DETAILS AND INFERENCES

② Listen again and and complete the tasks. Then work with a partner and compare answers.

1. How old is Jennifer, probably? How do you know?

2. Fill in the chart with some of Jennifer's arguments for and her parents' arguments against getting a tattoo.

Jennifer's Arguments	Parents' Arguments
1. Tattoos are cool.	1. They don't care what other kids are doing.
2.	2.
3.	3.
4.	4.
5.	5.
6.	6.

3. At the end of the conversation, what does Jennifer propose getting instead of a tattoo? _____

4. In your opinion, which of the following adjectives describe each parent's reaction to Jennifer's request? Why do you think so?

angry	firm	patient	tolerant
critical	humorous	sarcastic	uninterested

Mother: _____

Father: _____

LISTENING FOR LANGUAGE

3 Read about language for maintaining open communication between speakers.

CONVERSATION TOOLS
Expressing Support or Understanding

In the conversation, the mother said, "Jennifer, honey, I understand how you feel. You want to be cool and you want to fit in. But a tattoo just isn't something we can support, OK?"

The mother says "I understand how you feel" as a way of showing her daughter that she supports and understands her, even though she disagrees with her. Then she restates her daughter's point of view, indicating that she is listening carefully. The effect of the mother's utterance is to reduce tension and keep the discussion friendly.

Other expressions used in this way are the following:

- I know what you mean.
- I hear / know what you're saying.
- I hear you.
- I'm with you.

4 Work with a partner. Tell your partner about a time when you felt angry, hurt, or upset. Your partner should express support and restate what you said in his or her own words.

C. Real Talk: Use What You've Learned

VOCABULARY REVIEW

1 The new vocabulary from Part One is listed below. Review the list with a partner.

fit in	give (someone) a hard time
for a change	on (one's) own
for one thing . . . for another (thing) . . .	think (something) through
get tired of (something or someone)	

2 Use the vocabulary to complete the sentences.

1. **Mother:** Please get off the phone. I want you to get started on your homework.

   Teenage daughter: Why do you always _____ about talking on the phone? I get my homework done and I always get good grades. Why can't I talk with my friends?

2. We've eaten at that Italian restaurant a dozen times. Why don't we go out for Indian food _____?

3. **Son:** I'm going to look for a part-time job.

   Father: Have you _____? How are you going to have enough time to work, study, and play sports?

4. **A:** Wow! You painted your room red! That color is pretty intense.

   B: I know, but if I _____ it, I'll just paint over it.

5. **Parent:** What's bothering you, honey? Are you having trouble at school?

   Child: Not really. It's just that I'm the only kid in the ninth grade who doesn't have a cell phone. I feel like I don't _____.

6. **A:** Are you going to Africa with a group?

   B: No. I'm going _____.

7. **Question:** Why are health-care costs rising so dramatically?

Answer: Because _____, people are living longer in general, and _____, new technologies and medicines cost a lot of money.

DISCUSSION

Work in small groups. Use the vocabulary from Part One as you discuss the questions.

1. Why is it so important to Jennifer to have a tattoo? Did you feel the same way at her age?

2. If you were Jennifer's parents, would you allow her to get a tattoo? Why or why not?

3. In your opinion, at what age or stage of life are children old enough to make their own decisions about their bodies?

4. Are tattoos and other forms of body decoration, such as piercing, common in your culture or society? Explain.

5. How would you describe the different communication styles of Jennifer's mother and father? How do they compare with the way your parents or other family members talked to you?

ROLE PLAY

1 Work in pairs or groups of three. Plan a three- to four-minute role play like the conversation between Jennifer and her parents. The child wants something and asks for the parents' (or one parent's) approval. The parent or parents respond. Decide who will take which role.

2 Choose from one of the following situations or create your own scenario.

- joining the military
- dropping out of school
- going overseas to study
- getting a part-time job while still in school
- getting a car
- piercing, tattooing, or having plastic surgery
- moving out to live with friends in an apartment

3 Practice your role play. Use expressions for showing support and understanding and the Part One vocabulary. In addition, use your voice to convey strong emotions. (See Chapter 4, Part Two, page 96).

4 Perform your role play for another pair or group of students or for the whole class.

Part Two: On the Phone

A. Prelistening

Culture Note

Polls

In the United States, it is common for the government and for businesses to collect information by hiring polling organizations such as Gallup or Harris to do telephone surveys or polls for them. News organizations like CNN and NBC also conduct polls. When conducting a poll or survey, the polling company interviews people from across the country by phone. They try to select a "representative sample," consisting of people of all ages, geographical locations, ethnic groups, income levels, etc. The results of such interviews are used to gather information about trends in politics, public opinion, and consumer behavior.

DISCUSSION

You will hear a telephone survey about beauty. Before you listen, discuss the following questions with a partner or in a small group.

- Have you ever participated in a phone survey? What was it about? What questions were asked? How much time did it take?
- Who would benefit from a public opinion survey about beauty? What kinds of questions might be asked?

VOCABULARY PREVIEW

The words and expressions are from the telephone survey. Check (✓) the ones you already know. Check (✓) the others as you work through the activities in Part Two.

_____ all in all

_____ conduct a poll

_____ demographic information

_____ elective surgery

_____ get ahead

_____ on the whole

_____ run (something) by (someone)

B. Listening

MAIN IDEAS

1 Listen to the telephone survey and answer the questions. Then work with a partner and compare answers.

1. This poll is mainly about _____

_____.

2. Which of the following topics does the poll taker ask questions about? Listen for the poll taker's questions and check (✓) all that apply.

_____ a. the importance of beauty in our society

_____ b. the woman's estimation of her own attractiveness

_____ c. the woman's estimation of her husband's attractiveness

_____ d. experience with elective cosmetic or plastic surgery

_____ e. whether the woman will have plastic surgery in the future

_____ f. the woman's opinion of body piercing and tattoos

_____ g. how much money the woman spends each year on beauty products

DETAILS AND INFERENCES

2 Listen again. Circle the woman's answers to the survey questions.

Question	Answer
1.	a. very important
	b. fairly important
	c. not too important
	d. not at all important
	e. no answer or no opinion
2.	a. beautiful or handsome
	b. attractive or above average
	c. average
	d. somewhat below average
	e. unattractive
	f. no answer or no opinion
3.	a. satisfied
	b. wish to be more attractive
	c. no answer or no opinion
4.	a. yes, pleased
	b. no, not pleased
	c. no answer or no opinion
5.	a. has had plastic surgery
	b. has not had plastic surgery
	c. no answer or no opinion
6.	a. would consider plastic surgery
	b. would not consider plastic surgery
	c. no answer or no opinion

3 Complete the woman's demographic information. (Leave blank if the information is not given.)

Age: _____

Income: _____

Marital status: _____

LISTENING FOR LANGUAGE

4 Read about the intonation of items in a series.

FOCUS ON SOUND

Intonation of Items in a Series

In sentences or questions containing lists of items joined by *and* or *or,* each item in the list is a separate thought group. Each thought group except the last one will have rising intonation beginning on the most heavily stressed word. The last thought group will have falling intonation.

Example:

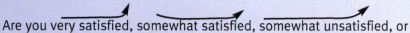

Are you very satisfied, somewhat satisfied, somewhat unsatisfied, or

unsatisfied?

5 Listen to some of the survey questions. Repeat each question after the speaker.

1. Would you say it is important, fairly important, not too important, or not at all important?

2. Would you say you are beautiful or handsome, attractive or above average, average, somewhat below average in attractiveness, or unattractive?

3. Are you satisfied with how attractive you are, or do you often wish you could be more attractive?

4. All in all, would you say you are generally pleased with the way your body looks, or not?

5. Have you ever had elective or cosmetic surgery to improve the appearance of some part of your body, or not?

6 Study ways of signaling a generalization.

7 Work with a partner. Choose three of the topics below and ask your partner opinion questions about them. Then respond to your partner's questions. Use expressions from Conversation Tools in both questions and answers.

Example:

Question: In general, do you like the weather in [Miami]?

Answer: I like it for the most part, although I don't like the humidity.

- the weather in your city
- a movie, song, or fashion
- a recent government decision or law
- a restaurant or type of food
- your job or work
- the place where you live
- other: _____

C. Real Talk: Use What You've Learned

VOCABULARY REVIEW

The new vocabulary from Part Two is listed below. Review the list with a partner.

all in all	get ahead
conduct a poll	on the whole
demographic information	run (something) by (someone)
elective surgery	

ROLE PLAY

1. Work with a partner. Use the survey form below and take turns playing the role of the poll taker and the respondent in the phone conversation. (*Remember:* You may choose not to answer any question by saying "I'd rather not answer that" or "I'd rather not say.")

Question	Answer
1. How important do you think a person's physical attractiveness is in our society today in terms of his or her happiness, social life, and ability to get ahead?	Very important Fairly important Not too important Not at all important
2. If you had to describe yourself to someone who didn't know you, how would you describe your physical appearance?	Beautiful or handsome Attractive or above average Average Somewhat below average in attractiveness Unattractive
3. All in all, are you satisfied with how attractive you are, or do you often wish you could be more attractive?	Satisfied Wish to be more attractive
4. All in all, would you say you are generally pleased with the way your body looks, or not?	Yes, pleased No, not pleased
5. Have you ever had elective cosmetic or plastic surgery to improve the appearance of some part of your body, or not?	Yes No
6. Would you consider elective cosmetic or plastic surgery to improve the appearance of some part of your body, or not?	Yes No

2 The poll in this lesson is based on an actual Gallup poll conducted on September 15, 1999.[1] Work in small groups. Look at the questions on page 123 and the results of the poll below. Discuss any results that interest or surprise you.

1. 76% very important or fairly important; 23% not too important or not important at all

2. 8% beautiful or handsome; 34% attractive or above average; 54% average; 2% below average

3. 76% satisfied; 23% not satisfied

4. 72% yes; 27% no

5. 2% yes; 98% no

6. 19% yes; 81% no

Part Three: On the Air

A. Prelistening

DISCUSSION

You will hear a radio interview with a woman who had plastic (cosmetic) surgery. Before you listen, discuss the questions with a partner or in a small group.

- What are the benefits and risks of having plastic surgery?

- Do you know anyone who has had plastic surgery? Why did this person have it?

---

[1]"Americans Agree That Being Attractive Is a Plus in American Society," September 15, 1999, http://www.gallup.com/poll/content/content/?CI=3601.

VOCABULARY PREVIEW

The words and expressions are from the interview. Check (✓) the ones you already know. Check (✓) the others as you work through the activities in Part Three.

_____ boost (one's) self-esteem

_____ bump (*noun*)

_____ dot-commers

_____ fired up

_____ not in great shape

_____ The (hand)writing is on the wall.

_____ washed out

B. Listening

> **Culture Note**
>
> *Age discrimination* is the unfair treatment of a person or group on the basis of age. Young people and the elderly are the most common targets of this type of discrimination; people in these age groups often face problems with employment or housing. Age discrimination is illegal in the United States, but it does happen because it is very difficult to prove in court.

MAIN IDEAS

1 Listen to the interview and answer the questions. Then work with a partner and compare answers.

1. How old is Maria?

   _____

2. What kind of work does she do?

   _____

3. What kind of surgery did Maria have?

   _____

4. Why did she have it?

   _____

DETAILS AND INFERENCES

🎧 ② Listen again and complete the tasks below. Then work with a partner and compare answers.

1. Fill in the following chart with facts and phrases about Maria before and after her surgery.

	Before Surgery	After Surgery
General appearance	washed out	
Eyes		
Nose		
Self-esteem		fired up

2. Read the statements below. Check (✓) the true ones. Correct the false ones.

_____ a. Maria's company is doing well.

_____ b. Maria is unemployed right now.

_____ c. Maria had trouble getting her current job because of her age.

_____ d. Maria had surgery to reduce the size of her nose.

_____ e. Maria has seen young people take jobs away from older workers.

3. "Dot-commers" are often

a. in their twenties.

b. Maria's age.

c. middle-aged.

d. ready to retire.

LISTENING FOR LANGUAGE

3 Read about different ways of saying "yes."

CONVERSATION TOOLS
Affirmative Answers

English has many ways of saying "yes." Maria, the woman interviewed in the radio segment, says "absolutely" a number of times. This word indicates that she is very certain about her answer. Affirmative answers can also be neutral or weak, indicating that the speaker is not certain about the response.

Strong	Neutral	Weak
Absolutely	Yes	I guess / suppose / think so.
Definitely	Yeah	Possibly (yes)
Certainly	Um hmm	Maybe / Perhaps
No question about it.		
There is no doubt in my mind.		

4 Listen to several exchanges between the interviewer and Maria. Write the words from the chart above that Maria uses in her responses.

1. (2 answers) _____

2. _____

3. _____

4. _____

5 Write three *yes/no* questions to ask a partner about the topic of the radio interview, plastic surgery. Take turns asking and answering the questions. For affirmative answers use expressions from the chart in Conversation Tools.

Example:

Question: Is cosmetic surgery becoming more common in your country?
Answer: Definitely.

1. _____

2. _____

3. _____

C. Real Talk: Use What You've Learned

VOCABULARY REVIEW

1 The new vocabulary from Part Three is listed below. Review the list with a partner.

boost (one's) self-esteem	not in great shape
bump (*noun*)	The (hand)writing is on the wall.
dot-commers	washed out
fired up	

2 Work with a partner. Read the sentences and restate them by replacing the underlined expressions with expressions from the box.

1. Mr. Assad's company is <u>not doing well.</u>
2. <u>There are signs that the company will soon fail.</u>
3. Jackie looked <u>pale and tired</u> after working a sixty-hour week.
4. Joe had surgery to correct the <u>irregularity</u> in his nose.
5. After her cosmetic surgery, Mrs. Linden felt <u>enthusiastic.</u>
6. Silicon Valley is full of <u>twenty-two-year-old kids</u> starting high-tech industries.
7. Many people say that their plastic surgery <u>helped them to feel more confident.</u>

DISCUSSION

Work in small groups. Discuss the questions. Use the Part Three vocabulary and a variety of affirmative answers.

1. What is your opinion of what Maria did? In her place, would you have done the same thing? Why or why not?
2. Who has plastic surgery in your culture or country? Is it common among men as well as women?
3. Examine the chart of the number of cosmetic surgery procedures performed in various countries in 2003. Is your native country on the chart? Are you surprised by any of the rankings? Do you see any patterns or trends?

Number of Cosmetic Surgery Procedures, Top 15 Countries, 2003		
Country	Percentage of Procedures World wide	Rank
United States	16.35	1
Mexico	9.64	2
Brazil	9.00	3
Canada	6.01	4
Argentina	5.96	5
Spain	5.49	6
France	4.82	7
Germany	3.84	8
Japan	3.79	9
South Africa	3.50	10
Great Britain	3.15	11
South Korea	2.79	12
Taiwan	2.51	13
Italy	2.24	14
Belgium	1.99	15

Source: ISAPS Statistics 2003, International Society of Aesthetic Plastic Surgery

Part Four: In Class

A. Prelistening

DISCUSSION

You will hear part of a lecture about body image perceptions in men. Before you listen, discuss the questions with a partner or in a small group.

- What is your reaction to the male images above? Do they look "normal" to you? Are they attractive?

- In your culture, what do people mean when they say a woman is *feminine* or a man is *masculine*? Do the terms refer to behavior, physical appearance, or both?

- Two examples of *body image disorders* are bulimia and anorexia. What do you know about these eating problems? Are you aware of any other such disorders?

VOCABULARY PREVIEW

The words and expressions are from the lecture. Check (✓) the ones you already know. Check (✓) the others as you work through the activities in Part Four.

_____ account for	_____ disorder(s)	_____ slim
_____ analyze (data)	_____ distorted	_____ steroid abuse
_____ bodybuilding	_____ in short	_____ with respect to
_____ bulked up		

B. Listening and Note-Taking

LECTURE ORGANIZATION AND LANGUAGE: RESEARCH REPORTS

Reports about research are often divided into four parts. Study the chart with information about the content and typical language of each part.

Part	Content	Typical Language[2]
1. Introduction	Background information regarding previous research or what researchers already know The purpose of the current research or the question being studied (the hypothesis)	• Dates • Past or present perfect tense verbs • Present tense verbs or conditional • Question
2. Method	(In social science research) A chronological list of steps or a description of what the researchers did A description of *subjects*—i.e., the humans who participate in research studies	• Key words: *method, methodology, procedure, steps, process, stage*[3] • Transitions of chronological order: *first, next*, etc. • Key words: *subjects, participants* (in the study)
3. Results	A report about what the researchers learned or discovered	• Nouns: *results, findings* • Verbs: (The researchers) *found / learned / discovered / found out. . .*; (The study/ research) *showed . . .* • Statistics (numbers, percentages, etc.)[4] • Expressions of comparison / contrast

(continued)

---

[2]Language used to present this information can vary widely.
[3]See Chapter 4, Part Four, page 107.
[4]See Chapter 3, Part Four, page 80.

Part	Content	Typical Language
4. Discussion	The researchers' interpretation of the study results, e.g., reasons, explanation	• Expressions of cause and effect[5] • Modals of possibility: *may, might, could* • Stative verbs: *seem, appear* • Verbs: The research (study) *suggests / implies / indicates . . .*
	Conclusions drawn from the results Suggestions for future research	• Future tense • Modals of suggestion / obligation: *should, ought to*

🎧 **2** Listen to sentences from the lecture. Indicate which part they probably came from: Introduction, Method, Results, or Discussion. List the cues that helped you choose your answer. Then work with a partner and compare answers.

Sentence	Part	Cues
1		
2		
3		
4		
5		
6		
7		
8		

LECTURE LANGUAGE: EXPRESSIONS OF CONTRAST

3 Read about some ways of talking about differences.

> You may already be familiar with many expressions for discussing differences. The expressions below may be less familiar. They are often found in academic writing and speaking. They are used less often in conversation. Study the examples. Notice the grammatical function of each expression of contrast: verb, noun, conjunction, etc.
>
> *(continued)*

---

[5]See Chapter 7, Part Four, pages 187–188.

Examples:

- The results of the current study **contrast with** the results found by earlier researchers.
- Some people are able to eat as much as they want, **yet** they do not gain weight easily.
- Two percent of the respondents in a poll said they had had plastic surgery, **whereas** 98 percent stated that they had not.
- Few participants in the poll had plastic surgery. **In contrast / Conversely,** the majority of respondents said they would consider having plastic surgery in the future.
- Researchers found several **significant differences** between the groups.

4 Read the following paraphrases of sentences from the lecture. Replace the underlined expressions of contrast with the new expressions above. Some items have more than one correct answer.[6]

1. What the researchers found were two <u>important contrasts</u> between the Western and the Eastern groups.

   _____

2. The Western men saw themselves as skinny and underdeveloped, <u>but</u> the Taiwanese men were basically satisfied with the way they looked.

   _____

3. The Western men guessed that women preferred a male body that was about 30 pounds, or 14 kilos, more muscular than average. <u>However,</u> when the researchers asked actual Western women to choose the male body they liked, they chose an average body, without added muscle.

   _____

4. <u>On the other hand</u>, the Taiwanese men guessed that women would prefer an average body, similar to their own.

   _____

5. The traditional role of Western men has changed over the last generation. This <u>is different from</u> Chinese culture, where there's been much less of a change in the traditional family structure.

   _____

---

[6]In writing, the answer choices are limited by punctuation. For example, the words *but* and *yet* are normally preceded by commas. In speaking, these rules obviously do not apply.

TAKING NOTES

🎧 ⑤ Listen to the lecture and take notes on your own paper. Divide your notes into four main parts: Introduction, Method, Results, and Discussion. Then rewrite your notes in the space. Use the cues on the left to guide you.

topic	I. Intro
	A. Previous topic: Body image disorders in women
	B. This lec. topic: Body image disord. in men
	1. 1-2% of Western men have it
	2. Expressed as:
	a. obsession w/ bodybuilding
	b. use of steroids
	3. Contrast: East Asian cultures: (a) + (b) rare
new study	II. New study:
where	A.
research	
question	
subjects	
method	III.
	A.
	B.
	1.
	2.
	3.
	4.
	C. Also asked women to choose ideal body

results		IV. Results: 2 sig. diffs.
interpretation		
conclusion		C. Findings suggest:
discussion		V. Why? 3 hypotheses
1st hypothesis		
2nd hypothesis		
3rd hypothesis		

REVIEWING THE LECTURE

6 Work with one or more classmates. Use your notes to discuss the questions.

1. How common are body image disorders in Western and Taiwanese men, respectively?

2. What question did the researchers from McLean Hospital investigate?

3. What were the steps in their method?

4. What four questions did they ask subjects?

5. Which body type did the Western subjects consider ideal? Which one did the Taiwanese subjects choose?

6. Which body type did the two groups of female subjects choose?

7. What do the study results suggest about Western and Taiwanese men's body images?

8. What three hypotheses did the researchers propose to account for the study results?

C. Real Talk: Use What You've Learned

VOCABULARY REVIEW

1 The new vocabulary from Part Four is listed below. Review the list with a partner.

account for	disorder(s)	slim
analyze (data)	distorted	steroid abuse
bodybuilding	in short	with respect to
bulked up		

2 Read the information about steroid use. Complete the sentences with vocabulary from the box.

1. _____ is a serious problem not only among adult males but also, surprisingly, among adolescents. In 2002, the National Institute for Drug Abuse (NIDA) conducted a survey in which teens were asked if they had ever used steroids; 2.5% of 8th graders, 3.5% of 10th graders, and 4% of 12th graders reported that they had.[7]

---

[7]National Institute on Drug Abuse. "NIDA InfoFacts: High School and Youth Trends," http://www.drugabuse.gov/Infofax/HSYouthtrends.html. Bethesda, MD: NIDA, NIH, DHHS.

2. Adult male users of steroids often suffer from low self-esteem and a
_____ body image. They spend countless hours in
weight training and _____, but no matter how
_____ they become, they never feel satisfied with their
physiques.

3. Steroid use is common among both male and female college students.
_____ female students, surveys have shown increased
steroid use among swimmers, basketball players, and runners.

4. Steroid use can _____ many undesirable side effects,
including liver damage, aggression, depression, hyperactivity, acne, baldness, and
paranoia.

5. _____, there is no doubt about the serious health risks
associated with steroids, yet use of these drugs is increasing among males and
females.

DISCUSSION

**Work in small groups. Use expressions of contrast from the box on page 133 and
the Chapter 5 vocabulary as you discuss the following questions.**

1. If the McLean Hospital study were conducted with male subjects from your
   home country or culture, what do you predict the results would be? Would the
   men answer like the Western men or the Taiwanese men in the study?
2. Which of the three hypotheses (definition of masculinity, media influence, or
   traditional roles of men and women) might explain the results you predicted for
   your country or culture?

RESEARCH REPORT

1 Search on the Internet or in a library for an article on body image disorders in boys,
girls, men, or women. (Useful search terms include "body image disorders," "steroid
abuse," "body dysmorphic disorder," or "BDD.") *Note:* Do not select an article from
a commercial site. Look for information from news (e.g., the BBC or *Psychology
Today* magazine) or academic (university or government organization) sources.

2 Prepare a three- to five-minute oral report in which you summarize the article.
Describe or define the disorder and refer to the research you read about. If
possible, include information about research methods, results, and the
interpretation of the results.

TOEFL® Practice: Synthesizing Listening, Reading, and Speaking

1 Read this passage from the McLean Hospital study described in the lecture.

> The McLean researchers concluded their research report with a disturbing question: Can Chinese (Taiwanese) men's attitudes concerning their body image "continue to resist the influences of Western culture?" An examination of similar studies of female body image suggests a discouraging answer to this question. Studies in Hong Kong, Polynesia, and Fiji all revealed dissatisfaction, following a period of exposure to Western media, in women who had previously been content with their bodies. "These observations raise the prospect that Western notions of male body image may also be invading Chinese (Taiwanese) culture," the researchers state.
>

2 Review your lecture notes. Then use the information from both the lecture and the reading to prepare a one-minute oral presentation on the following question:

- What was the basic finding of the McLean hospital study with respect to body image perception among Taiwanese men? If the study is repeated in ten years, how are the results likely to be different? Why?

CHAPTER 6

Discoveries

Part One: In Person

A. Prelistening

BACKGROUND

Two of the greatest scientific achievements in the history of space exploration occurred in December and January of 2003–4: the landing on the planet Mars of the Exploration "rovers," mobile robots designed for scientific exploration. One rover, named *Spirit*, landed in a location called Gusev Crater. The other rover, *Opportunity*, landed on the opposite side of Mars in a place called Meridiani.

Mars rover on Mars surface

The rovers, which had been expected to operate for a period of only about six months on the rocky Martian surface, continued functioning, sending back photographs and data about Mars's geography and soil. The discoveries made by these two robots have caused great excitement in both the scientific community and the general public.

DISCUSSION

You will hear part of a conversation between a space engineer and a young student. Before you listen, discuss the questions with a partner or in a small group.

- What do you know about the planet Mars?
- Do you remember hearing that the NASA rovers had landed on Mars in 2004? What was your reaction to this event?
- Do you think people will ever live on Mars?

VOCABULARY PREVIEW

The words and expressions are from the conversation. Check (✓) the ones you already know. Check (✓) the others as you work through the activities in Part One.

_____ conducive   _____ gut feeling   _____ mineral(s)

_____ distinctive   _____ habitable   _____ mission

_____ drop in the bucket   _____ microbes   _____ site

B. Listening

MAIN IDEAS

🎧 ① Listen to the conversation and answer the questions. Then work with a partner and compare answers.

1. In the 2003–4 missions, what were the Mars rovers looking for?

   _____

2. What did they discover?

   _____

3. Why is this discovery important?

   _____

4. What will be the next step in the exploration of Mars?

   _____

DETAILS AND INFERENCES

🎧 ② **Listen again and answer the questions. Then work with a partner and compare answers.**

1. What discovery proved that there was once water on Mars?

    a. a mineral called hematite

    b. unusual rock formations

    c. microbes in ice near the poles

    d. bacteria in the soil

2. The scientist believes that there _____ microscopic organisms in Martian ice.

    a. are

    b. aren't

    c. could be

    d. couldn't have been

3. He believes that in the future, people _____ live on Mars.

    a. will

    b. might

    c. won't

    d. can't

4. A "gut feeling" is a

    a. secret.

    b. guess.

    c. proof.

    d. problem.

5. A "drop in the bucket" is a

    a. large share.

    b. total.

    c. tiny amount.

    d. unknown quantity.

(continued)

6. "Columbus of the twenty-first century" means a modern

    a. genius.

    b. scientist.

    c. entrepreneur.

    d. explorer.

LISTENING FOR LANGUAGE

3 Read about the pronunciation of modals of possibility.

FOCUS ON SOUND

Modals of Possibility; Past Unreal Conditionals

The conversation includes many modals of possibility in both the present/future and past forms. It also has examples of the past unreal conditional with *would*. Study the following keys to the pronunciation of these structures.

Form	Pronunciation
Present / future forms: *May / could / might* + base form of the verb Example: We *might find* that Mars *could be* a place where people *could live* in the future.	1. *Could* is pronounced /kʊd/. The "l" is silent. 2. The modal and verb are stressed, e.g., *míght líve*.

Past forms:
May / might / could / would + *have* + past participle
 	
Examples:
Meridiani *may have been* the site of a lake millions of years ago.
 	
The spirit of exploration has always taken us places where we've never been before. Otherwise, we never *would have discovered* Antarctica or gone to the moon. . .
	1. Would is pronounced /wʊd/. The "l" is silent.
	2. *Have* is reduced to /əv/ or /ə/.
	3. The modal and the participle are stressed, e.g.,
	  • may have found → `may /əv/ or `may/ə/ found
	  • might have been → `might /əv/ or `might/ə bɪn/
	  • could have lived → /`kʊdəv/ or /`kʊdə/ lived
	  • would have discovered → /`wʊdəv/ or/`wʊdə / discovered

4 Listen to sentences from the conversation and fill in the missing words. Work with a partner and compare answers. Then practice pronouncing the sentences with correct stress and reductions.

1. At Meridiani, they discovered a mineral called hematite which can only be formed in the presence of water, which leads to the possibility that Meridiani _____ the site of a lake millions of years ago.

2. Whether there are tiny microbes hidden hundreds of feet deep in what _____ ice near the poles—that's a possibility.

3. Well, these discoveries are important because they're the first small steps in discovering whether another planet is, or _____ in the past, habitable. And so we _____ that Mars _____ a place that people _____ in the future . . .

4. The next step is to find, uh, to maybe go back to the same places or to go some other places where there _____ water, and then to do some more sophisticated chemical analysis of the soil to find out what kind of minerals there are, and are they conducive to, _____ in the past conducive to life being there in the past.

5. Otherwise, we never _____ Antarctica or gone to the moon or any of the other places that people have explored throughout history.

5 Read about ways of expressing skepticism.

CONVERSATION TOOLS
Expressing Skepticism

Skepticism means an attitude of doubt about whether something is true, correct, or good. In the conversation, the student expresses skepticism when she says, "Come on. You don't really think that people are going to live on Mars, do you?"

This comment has several features that indicate the speaker is skeptical. One is the phrase *come on*.[1] The second is the use of the tag question *do you?*, and the third is the speaker's intonation.

Below are additional phrases that English speakers use to express skepticism.

- You don't really believe/think . . . (do you?)
- You don't honestly / seriously think . . . (do you?)
- I can't believe you think . . .
- You can't be serious.
- I find that hard to believe / imagine.
- That's ridiculous.

[1]See *Real Talk 1*, Chapter 8, Part One: In Person, page 82.

6 Have you ever heard of "urban myths" or "urban legends"? They are stories that have been told and retold so many times that most people are sure they are true, though many of them are not. Below is a list of urban myths. Work with a partner. Read a myth to your partner. Your partner will respond with an expression of skepticism. Take turns.

Example:

A: We use only 10 percent of our brains.
B: I find that hard to imagine.

1. There are alligators in the sewers beneath New York City.
2. If you swallow a piece of gum, it will take seven years to pass through your digestive system.
3. If you put a tooth in a glass of Coca-Cola overnight, the tooth will dissolve.
4. Hair and fingernails continue to grow after a person's death.
5. During the tsunami of December, 2004, elephants rescued forty-two people.
6. If you shave your hair, it will grow back darker and thicker.
7. You can avoid paying for traffic tickets if you have an international driver's license.
8. If you drop something on the floor, you can pick it up and eat it if it's on the floor for less than five seconds.

C. Real Talk: Use What You've Learned

VOCABULARY REVIEW

1 The new vocabulary from Part One is listed below. Review the list with a partner.

conducive	gut feeling	mineral(s)
distinctive	habitable	mission
drop in the bucket	microbes	site

2 Use the vocabulary to complete the sentences.

1. In 2005 NASA sponsored a highly successful

    _____ to the planet

    Saturn. The spacecraft, called *Cassini,* made

    discoveries about Saturn's rings, including the

    presence of a second moon.

2. The *Cassini* spacecraft sent pictures to earth which revealed

_____ signs of water vapor on Saturn's moon

Enceladus.

3. Despite the presence of water vapor, it is not likely that Saturn could ever be

_____. It is far too cold, for one thing.

4. Research showed that a higher intake of the _____

zinc (Zn) improved children's mental skills.

5. Research by French scientists showed that young

children may have a _____

for geometry. With no training, the children were able to

select one image that was different from five others

that illustrated the same principle of geometry.

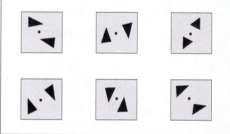

Which image does not belong?

6. There are millions of _____ on

human hands. Most are harmless, but some can cause

disease. That is why it's essential to wash your hands frequently.

7. Mt. Vesuvius in southern Italy was the _____ of a

volcanic eruption in the year C.E. 79. Scientists today are studying papyruses

found in a villa nearby which contain the writings of ancient Greek and

Roman philosophers.

8. The environment of Earth's moon is not _____ to

human life. There is no water and no atmosphere.

9. The amount of money available for cancer and AIDS research is a

_____ compared to the amount of money needed to

find a cure for these diseases.

Discussion: The Pros and Cons of Space Exploration

Your teacher will assign you to one of two groups, either for (pro) or against (con) future space exploration.

1 With your group, list all the arguments you can think of that support your assigned position.

"Pro" Example:

The desire to explore is an innate human characteristic that has led us to many important discoveries on earth.

"Con" Example:

Sending robots and satellites into space creates pollution.

Focus on the correct pronunciation of modals and try to use phrases for expressing skepticism.

2 Form new, smaller groups consisting of two students from the "pro" side and two students from the "con" side. Discuss your respective arguments for and against space exploration. Again, try to use the new language from this lesson as you speak.

3 With the whole class, discuss your real opinion of the advantages or disadvantages of space exploration.

Part Two: On the Phone

My Family

A. Prelistening

DISCUSSION

You will hear two people talking about a family connection. Before you listen, discuss the questions with a partner or in a small group.

- Use a dictionary to look up the word *genealogy*. Is this something you are interested in? What about other people from your family or culture?
- Does your family have a family tree? Who made it? Do you have a copy?
- Have you ever used the Internet to try to find or get in touch with family members you've never met?

VOCABULARY PREVIEW

The words and expressions are from the conversation. Check (✓) the ones you already know. Check (✓) the others as you work through the activities in Part Two.

_____ as sharp as a tack   _____ Google™ (someone) (*verb, informal*)

_____ coincidence   _____ (someone's) head is spinning

_____ detective   _____ high school reunion

_____ genealogy   _____ obsession

B. Listening

MAIN IDEAS

1 Listen to a conversation between a man named Brent Knoop and a woman named Rose Green. Then work with a partner and compare answers.

1. Where is Brent from? What is he doing in Rose's town?

   _____

2. Have Brent and Rose ever met before? _____

3. What do they discover during the conversation? _____

   _____

4. How did Brent find Rose? _____

   _____

DETAILS AND INFERENCES

🎧 ② **Listen again and complete the tasks. Then work with a partner and compare answers.**

1. Fill in the missing names on the diagram.

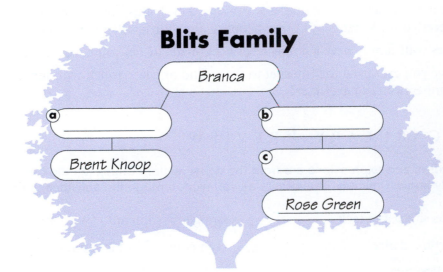

Blits Family

Branca

a. _____

Brent Knoop

b. _____

c. _____

Rose Green

2. Complete the sentences with names from the diagram.

a. _____ and _____ had the maiden name Blits.

b. _____ and _____ were first cousins.

c. _____ and _____ are first cousins once removed.

d. _____ was Rose's great grandmother.

3. Complete the sentences. Use your own words to explain the meaning of the expressions.

a. When Rose says "My head is spinning," she means she is _____.

b. When Brent says his mother is "as sharp as a tack," he means she is

_____.

3 Read about pronunciation changes that occur in connected speech.

FOCUS ON SOUND
Reduced Consonant Clusters; Syllable Deletions

Reduced consonant clusters

A consonant cluster is a group of consonant sounds pronounced with no intervening vowel sound. For example, the word *strange* has two clusters: *str* at the beginning and *ng* (pronounced /ndʒ/) at the end. Clusters also occur frequently across word boundaries, e.g., *first name* or *huge family*.

English speakers often reduce complex clusters by dropping one or more sounds. Some examples from the recording are:

sound, pronounced /saʊn/
didn't, pronounced /dɪnt/
first name, pronounced /fərs neɪm/

Syllable deletion

In some long words, unstressed syllables are deleted. Some examples are:

chocolate /tʃɑklɪt/
different /dɪfrənt/
family /fæmli/
interesting /ɪntrɪstɪŋ/
several /sɛvrəl/

These and other sound changes you have learned about can make it difficult to understand rapid spoken English.

4 Listen to phrases and short sentences. Circle the reduced consonant clusters.

1. This may sound strange.

2. your mother's first name

3. my grandmother

4. try to find people

5. on my next visit

6. You found me.

7. don't know

8. He left for work.

🎧 **5** Listen and write the sentences you hear. Use conventional spelling.

1. _____

2. _____

3. _____

4. _____

5. _____

6. _____

7. _____

C. Real Talk: Use What You've Learned

VOCABULARY REVIEW

1 The new vocabulary from Part Two is listed below. Review the list with a partner.

as sharp as a tack	Google™ (someone) (*verb, informal*)
coincidence	(someone's) head is spinning
detective	high school reunion
genealogy	obsession

2 Use the vocabulary to complete the sentences. Then work with a partner and compare answers.

1. My eighty-six-year-old grandfather has trouble walking, but his mind

   is _____.

2. Have you ever tried to _____ yourself on the Internet? Did you get any "hits"?

3. By _____, Fred ran into an old high-school classmate at the library. He hadn't seen her in years.

4. After six hours of reading numbers and facts on a computer screen, Melinda's

   _____.

5. Sasha graduated from high school in 2000. His ten-year _____ will be in 2010.

6. My cousin became interested in _____ and started recording and videotaping all the older members of our family.

7. Researching family history has become an _____ with him. He spends all his free time doing it.

8. My cousin is quite a skilled _____. By looking at old records and interviewing people all over the country, he has been able to find branches of our family that we didn't know existed.

DISCUSSION

Work in small groups. Use expressions from the vocabulary box on page 150 as you discuss the answers to the questions.

1. Have you ever made an interesting discovery regarding someone in your family?

2. As an adult, have you ever met family members that you had never heard of before? How did you meet them?

3. If you met someone with the same family name as yours, what questions would you ask to discover if you're related?

4. How does your mother language describe family relationships, compared to English? For example, does the language have a term for a first cousin once removed? Does the vocabulary indicate the closeness or importance of family relationships in your culture?

ROLE PLAY

1 Work with a partner. Role-play one or both of the scenarios. Use the Part Two vocabulary from the box on page 150 as well as expressions of skepticism from Conversation Tools on page 143.

Scenario	Student A	Student B
1	You are at home when you receive an unexpected phone call from a person who might be your cousin.	Your hobby is genealogy. After searching on the Internet you have discovered the name of a person who may be a close cousin of yours. Call and try to find out if you are related.
2	You work as a cashier in a bakery. When a customer pays with a credit card, you are very surprised to see that he/she has the same unusual family name as you.	You have come into a bakery to buy a cake. When it is your turn to pay, you use a credit card. The cashier acts very surprised to see your name and explains that he/she has the same (unusual) name. You begin exchanging family information with the cashier to find out if you are related.

2 Practice your role plays.

3 Perform a role play for another pair of students or for the whole class.

Part Three: On the Air

man's ring

man using metal detector

A. Prelistening

DISCUSSION

You will hear an interview segment from a radio program called *The Motley Fool.* Before you listen, discuss the following questions with a partner or in a small group.

- Have you ever seen or used a metal detector? Tell about your experience.
- Examine the ring in the picture. What do you think it's made of? How much do you think it's worth?
- Can you guess how the ring and the metal detector in the pictures are related to one another?

VOCABULARY PREVIEW

The words and expressions are from the interview. Check (✓) the ones you already know. Check (✓) the others as you work through the activities in Part Three.

_____ appraise

_____ come out of the woodwork (*informal*)

_____ fake

_____ initials

_____ investment grade

_____ run-of-the-mill

_____ sapphire(s)

B. Listening

MAIN IDEAS

1 Listen to the program hosts, brothers David and Tom Gardner, talking to a caller named Doug. Answer the questions. Then work with a partner and compare answers.

1. What did Doug find? _____

2. How did he find it? _____

_____

3. Where is it now? _____

DETAILS AND INFERENCES

🎧 ② Listen again and complete the tasks. Then work with a partner and compare answers.

1. Which of the following statements are true about the ring? Check (✔) all that are true.

   _____ a. It was large.

   _____ b. It had one sapphire and several diamonds.

   _____ c. It had the owner's initials in it.

   _____ d. It was appraised at $80.

   _____ e. It belonged to the program host.

2. Which of the following statements are true about Doug? Check (✔) all that are true.

   _____ a. He got the metal detector for his birthday.

   _____ b. The ring was the first thing he found.

   _____ c. At first he didn't know that the ring was valuable.

   _____ d. He tried to find the owner of the ring.

   _____ e. In the end he sold it for $15,000.

3. The expressions on the left are from the conversation. Match them with their meanings on the right. If necessary, listen again to hear the expressions in context.

   _____ 1. fake   a. ordinary

   _____ 2. run-of-the-mill   b. not real

   _____ 3. investment grade   c. appear unexpectedly and in large numbers

   _____ 4. come out of the woodwork d. very valuable

LISTENING FOR LANGUAGE

③ Read more about reduced forms.

FOCUS ON SOUND
Changing Final /ɪŋ/ to /ɪn/; More Reductions

The sound that is spelled *ing* is usually pronounced as /ɪŋ/. There are dialects of English, however, where this final sound is often pronounced /ɪn/, especially in casual speech. For example, in the conversation you heard Doug pronounce *coming* as *comin'*/ ˈkʌmɪn/.

In addition, the following reductions, pronounced by the speakers in the conversation, are common in most dialects of English:

- *Going to* is pronounced *gonna* / ˈɡʌnə/
- *Of* is reduced to /ə/, e.g., *kind of* is pronounced *kinda* / ˈkaɪndə/
- *Because* is reduced to *cuz* /kʌz/
- *Would* is contracted to *'d* /əd/, even after nouns, e.g., *people would* → *people'd*

4 Listen to sentences from the interview. Write the missing words. Use conventional spelling. Then work with a partner and compare answers.

1. **Host:** Are we _____ some background ukulele there?

   Doug: No, that's actually my other phone, but I'm

   _____ ignore it for right now.

2. **Doug:** . . . and I really _____ thought it was fake

   because it was as big as it was.

3. **Host:** What were the initials?

   Doug: Oh, I'm sorry I honestly don't remember.

   Host: _____ I lost a ring in South Bend, Indiana . . .

4. **Doug:** I figured if I gave too much information I'm sure

   _____ out of the woodwork to claim it.

5 Read about digressing and returning to the topic.

CONVERSATION TOOLS
Digressing and Returning to the Topic

To digress means to abandon one topic and begin speaking about something unrelated. Digression signals include the phrases *by the way* or *that reminds me*. Digressions also occur when a speaker is interrupted.

To return to one's original topic after a digression, a speaker can use one of the following signals:

- At any rate, . . .
- (To get) back to (what I was saying) . . .
- Anyway, . . .
- In any case, . . .

🎧 **6** Listen to part of the interview again and answer the questions.

1. Who digresses, Doug or the hosts? _____

2. What is the topic of the digression? _____

3. Which words does Doug use to return to the topic? _____

4. Which words does one of the hosts use? _____

7 Work in small groups. Practice digressing and returning to the topic as follows:

- Each student tells a story about something interesting that he or she did recently.

- The other members of the group interrupt and ask unrelated questions, causing the speaker to digress.

- The main speaker uses signals from the box to return to the topic of his or her story.

Example:

Speaker 1: Last weekend I went to the movies with my friend Jake. We wanted to see the new James Bond movie, and . . .

Speaker 2: Did you drive or take the bus?

Speaker 1: The bus. Anyway, when we got to the theater, the line was really long, so . . .

C. Real Talk: Use What You've Learned

VOCABULARY REVIEW

1 The new vocabulary from Part Three is listed below. Review the list with a partner.

appraise	investment grade
come out of the woodwork	run-of-the-mill
fake	sapphire(s)
initials	

2 Write a one-page story about a great discovery similar to Doug's. (Your story does not have to be true.) Use vocabulary from the box above in your story, but instead of writing the words, leave blanks for another student to fill in. Write the correct answers on the back of your paper.

Example:

Last week I found a gorgeous _____ bracelet in the washroom of a restaurant where I was having dinner with my friend Paula. At first I was sure the stone was _____ because it was so huge. . .

3 Exchange papers with a partner. Fill in the blanks in each other's stories with words from the box above. Then check your answers by looking on the back of your partner's paper.

DISCUSSION

Discuss the following questions with a partner or in a small group.

1. Have you ever found an object that turned out to have great value?
- What was the object?
- How did you find it?
- What was its value?
- Did you keep it?
2. Doug put an ad in the newspaper to try to find the owner of the ring he found. In his place would you have done the same thing?

ROLE PLAY

Imagine that Doug placed this advertisement in the newspaper. Role-play phone conversations between Doug and several people calling to claim the ring.

> **Found:** in South Bend, Indiana: Large man's ring. Call Doug at **555-3493** to claim.

1. Form groups of five, if possible. Your teacher will assign you a role to play. Student A will be Doug. Students B–E will be callers wanting to claim the ring.
2. Read the information on the next page for your role. Try not to read anyone else's information, and do not share your information with anyone else.
3. Sit in a circle with the people in your group. Take turns phoning "Doug" to claim the ring. Answer his questions. Begin like this:

    Doug: Hello?

    Caller: Hello, my name is _____. I'm calling about your ad in the paper. I lost a ring . . .

    Doug: Can you tell me what it looks like and where you lost it? etc.

4. After everyone has called, "Doug" will call back the true owner of the ring and give him or her the good news.

STUDENT A: DOUG

The ring you found has one large diamond and three sapphires. The ring itself is made of silver. Inside the ring are the initials KD. You found it in South Bend, Indiana.

As each person calls you about the ring, ask him or her to describe the ring they lost. Also ask where they lost the ring.

Ask each person for a name and phone number, thank each one for calling, and say that you will call back if the ring belongs to him or her.

STUDENT B: CALLER 1

Your name is Zeta (or Zaman) Halabi. You lost a gold woman's ring with a large round diamond last summer at the zoo in South Bend.

STUDENT C: CALLER 2

You lost a large man's ring at a park in South Bend, Indiana. The ring was made of gold and had several small diamonds. Your name is Sylvia (Sylvio) Franco.

STUDENT D: CALLER 3

Your name is Katherine (or Karl) Dempsey. You lost a large man's ring in a park in South Blend, Indiana. The ring is made of silver, and it has one large diamond and three sapphires. Your initials, KD, are on the inside of the ring.

STUDENT E: CALLER 4

You lost a large man's silver ring while you were on a picnic by Lake Michigan, near South Blend, Indiana. The ring had two large sapphires. Your name is Max(ine) Pennington, and your initials are on the inside of the ring.

Part Four: In Class

A. Prelistening

You will hear a talk about Christopher Columbus. What do you know about this explorer? Take the quiz and find out. Mark the statements *T* (true) or *F* (false). You will hear the answers in the lecture.

Q U I Z

_____ 1. Christopher Columbus was Spanish.

_____ 2. Columbus believed he could reach Asia by sailing west.

_____ 3. At the time of Columbus's voyage, uneducated people still believed the earth was flat.

_____ 4. Queen Isabella of Italy financed Columbus's voyage.

_____ 5. Columbus first landed on an island in the Caribbean.

_____ 6. Columbus was the first European to set foot on the shores of North America.

_____ 7. Columbus brought African slaves to the New World.

_____ 8. Columbus introduced Christianity to the New World.

VOCABULARY PREVIEW

The words and expressions are from the lecture. Check (✓) the ones you already know. Check (✓) the others as you work through the activities in Part Four.

_____ ancestor(s)	_____ funding	_____ legacy
_____ claim (*noun*)	_____ give / take credit	_____ resist
_____ commodities	_____ initiate	_____ set foot (in / on)
_____ finance	_____ kidnap	_____ take into account

B. Listening and Note-Taking

LECTURE ORGANIZATION: MAKING ASSERTIONS AND PROVIDING PROOF

1 Read about the ways English speakers commonly organize true statements—
assertions—and supporting evidence.

An *assertion* is a generalization that a speaker believes to be true. For example, some people assert that Christopher Columbus was born in the Italian city of Genoa. Others are certain that he was from Catalonia in Spain. If you wanted your listener to believe one of these statements or the other, you would have to provide proof to support your position.

The following types of details are commonly used to prove an assertion:

- Facts and statistics
- The opinions of experts
- Examples and anecdotes

A speaker can choose to begin with an assertion and follow it with the supporting details. It is equally correct, but less common, to begin with the proof and conclude with the assertion.

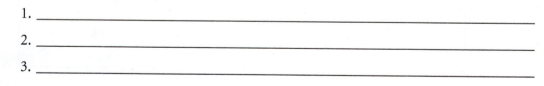

2 Listen to segments from the lecture. Write the assertions in your own words.

1. Assertion: _____

   _____

2. Assertion: _____

   _____

3. Assertion: _____

   _____

LECTURE LANGUAGE: SIGNALING PROOF

3 Study the list of signals for introducing proof.

Many expressions can introduce the details used to prove an assertion. Here are a few of them:

To introduce an expert opinion

- According to X, . . .
- X says / points out / argues that . . .

Rhetorical questions

- How do we know this?
- What proof do we have of this?

Other expressions

- We know this because / from . . .
- This was proven / shown when . . .
- On the basis of X, (historians) know that . . .
- The evidence is clear that . . .
- Records show / demonstrate / prove that . . .

4 Listen to the segments from Exercise 2 again. Write the words which introduce the proof.

1. _____

2. _____

3. _____

Work with a partner. Student A, look at the information below. Student B, look at the information on page 166. Tell the information to your partner, using expressions for making assertions and providing proof. Take notes on the information your partner tells you.

STUDENT A

Assertion:

In 1492, educated people already knew that the earth was round.

Evidence:

1. The Monastery of St. Catherine in the Sinai peninsula has a religious statue painted five hundred years before Columbus, showing Jesus ruling over a spherical (round) earth.

2. Already in the tenth century, Arab scientists had described the earth as a sphere with 360 degrees of longitude and 180 degrees of latitude.

TAKING NOTES

6 Examine the map of Columbus's voyages. Listen to the lecture and take notes on your own paper. Use what you have learned about lecture form, language, and organization. Then rewrite your notes in the space. Use the cues on the left to guide you.

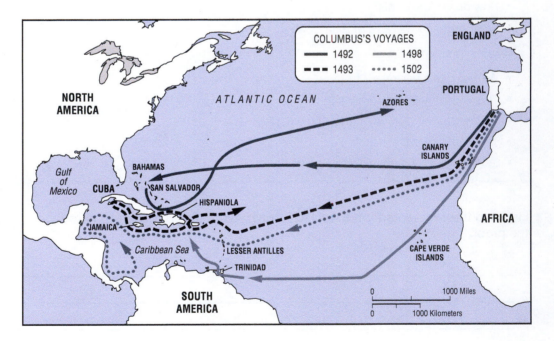

topic		I.
4 facts		1492 sailed
	○	
2 discoveries		II. Americans give C. credit for:
1st assertion		III. Both beliefs = false
proof		
	○	
2nd assertion		
proof		
3 positive accomplishments		IV. What did C. accomplish?
	○	
result		

(continued)

3 negative accomplishments	V.
◯	
conclusion	VI.

REVIEWING THE LECTURE

7 Work with a partner or in small groups. Use your notes to discuss the questions.

1. What are some commonly known facts about Christopher Columbus?

2. Which discoveries do Americans give Columbus credit for?

3. What evidence is there that Columbus did not make these discoveries?

4. What are three of Columbus's positive accomplishments?

5. How did Columbus pay for his voyages to the New World?

6. In what ways did the arrival of Columbus hurt the Native American population?

C. Real Talk: Use What You've Learned

VOCABULARY REVIEW

1 The key vocabulary from Part Four is listed below. Review the list with a partner.

ancestor(s)	funding	legacy
claim (*noun*)	give / take credit	resist
commodities	initiate	set foot
finance	kidnap	take into account

2 Work in groups of four. Each student asks the questions in one of the following boxes. The other students take turns answering.

STUDENT A

1. How did you get the funding to pay for this English course?

2. Are you generally open to change, or do you resist it?

3. Do you remember to take into account the cost of tips and taxes when you travel?

STUDENT B

1. What country or area of a country did your ancestors come from?

2. Have you ever set foot in that place?

3. Tell about an important legacy you received from a relative, friend, or teacher.

STUDENT C

1. What are some commodities that your native country exports or imports?

2. What are some important projects that your country needs to finance at this time? Where do you think the money is going to come from?

3. Are political kidnappings common in your country?

STUDENT D

1. Do you believe the claim that Columbus was a great historical hero?

2. Who is generally given credit for discovering or establishing your native country?

3. Who or what initiated your country's industrial or modern development?

SURVEY

1. If possible, survey one or more Americans and ask them the following questions. Take notes on their responses.

1. Who discovered America?

2. What do you know about Christopher Columbus?

2. When you finish the survey, share the results with your classmates by completing the tasks.

1. Compile the answers to the first question. Figure out the percentage of people surveyed who said Columbus discovered America. Discuss: Are you surprised by this result?

2. Make a list of the answers to the second question. Compare the information you heard with the information from the lecture. Discuss: Generally, do you think the people you surveyed were well informed about Columbus and his activities?

TOEFL® Practice: Synthesizing Listening, Reading, and Speaking

1 Read the passage about the legacy of Columbus.

> In recent decades Columbus has become a controversial figure in the view of many Americans. Some, particularly Native Americans, hold him responsible for European exploitation of the western hemisphere, slavery in the Caribbean, and the deaths of many thousands of indigenous people.
>
> Others continue to celebrate Columbus's undeniable impact on Western civilization. He is regarded as the discoverer of the Americas because it was his voyages that made Europeans aware of the vast land masses to the west. His discoveries forged a bond between Europe, America, and Africa that continues to this day.

2 Use information from both the lecture and the reading to prepare a one-minute oral presentation on the following question:

- Which of Columbus's positive or negative accomplishments had the greatest impact on history, in your opinion? Why?

EXERCISE 5, PAGE 162

STUDENT B

Assertion:

Viking explorers reached the shores of North America 500 years before the time of Columbus.

Evidence:

1. In 1960, archeologists discovered the remains of a Viking settlement on the island of Labrador in Canada. They were able to date the settlement to the year 1000 by means of tools and other objects found at the site.

2. Two ancient poems describe the exploration and settlement of North America by Viking sailors. In 1837 a Danish historian named Carl Christian Rafn studied the poems and concluded that they were true.

CHAPTER 7

Law and Order

Part One: In Person

A. Prelistening

BACKGROUND

The U.S. Constitution specifies that a person accused of a crime has a right to a trial before "a jury of his peers." In a criminal trial (as opposed to a civil one[1]), a jury consists of twelve citizens who listen to the evidence and then determine whether the accused person is guilty or innocent. Other key participants in a trial are the judge, who rules on questions of law and procedure (but not guilt or innocence), the lawyers (or *attorneys*), and witnesses. In criminal cases, there is an attorney for the defense and an attorney for the prosecution.

By law, every U.S. citizen (with a few exceptions) must be available for jury duty. In a trial, the lawyers for the two sides choose the members of the jury from a large pool of potential jurors. A typical jury trial lasts from one to three days, though some cases may last weeks or, in rare cases, months.

---

[1] Civil trials generally involve disputes about money, rights, personal injury, or ownership. The loser in a civil case must pay the winner an amount of money determined by the jury. The loser does not serve time in jail.

DISCUSSION

You will hear a woman talking about jury duty. Before you listen, discuss the questions with a partner or in a small group.

- Have you ever seen a trial in the United States, or have you seen an American movie or television program that had a courtroom scene? Describe what these experiences taught you about the U.S. justice system.
- What questions do you have about the U.S. criminal justice system? Make a list.

VOCABULARY PREVIEW

The words and expressions are from the conversation. Check (✓) the ones you already know. Check (✓) the others as you work through the activities in Part One.

_____ (aggravated) assault	_____ fleabag hotel	_____ nod off
_____ (be) arrested	_____ foreman	_____ open and shut case
_____ case (*noun*)	_____ guilty	_____ prosecutor
_____ (be) charged with (a crime)	_____ jail	_____ resist arrest
_____ defense (attorney)	_____ judge	_____ testify
_____ deliberation (room)	_____ jury	_____ trial
_____ deny	_____ jury duty	_____ witness
_____ down and out	_____ long-winded	_____ witness stand
_____ evidence		

B. Listening

MAIN IDEAS

🎧 ❶ Listen to the conversation and take notes on the key information below. Then work with a partner and compare answers.

The defendant: _____

The victims / witnesses: _____

The charge: _____

The verdict: _____

DETAILS AND INFERENCES

🎧 ② Listen again, answer the questions, and complete the tasks. Then work with a partner and compare answers.

1. How did the speaker feel about the defendant? How do you know?

   _____

2. Describe the defendant. Use at least four adjectives.

   _____

3. What unusual thing happened during the trial?

   _____

4. Check (✓) the statements that are true about the U.S. justice system, based on the information in the talk. Correct any false statements.

   _____ a. An accused person is allowed to speak in his or her own defense.

   _____ b. The attorney who represents the accused person is called a prosecutor.

   _____ c. After the lawyers present their cases, the judge gives the jury instructions about the law.

   _____ d. Jury members can disregard the law if they all agree to do so.

   _____ e. The judge is present during jury deliberations.

   _____ f. Only college graduates are permitted to serve on a jury.

   _____ g. In the deliberations room, the first thing the jurors do is to elect a foreman or forewoman.

5. Listen to the following idioms and expressions in context and write their meanings:

   a. down-and-out (*adj*): _____

   b. fleabag hotel: _____

   c. long-winded: _____

   d. an open-and-shut case: _____

LISTENING FOR LANGUAGE

3 Read about one variety of spoken American English.

FOCUS ON SOUND
Southern American English (SAE)

Linguists who study accents divide the United States into six major accent regions.[2] Among these accents, Southern American English, or SAE, is one of the most difficult for learners of English to understand. The speaker in this chapter part is from Louisiana, and her speech illustrates a number of features typically found in SAE. These include reduction of consonant clusters[3], pronunciation of the *-ing* ending as *-in'*,[4] and many variations in the pronunciation of vowels and diphthongs. Here are just a few:

- The diphthong /ay/ as in "time," side," and "trial," loses the /y/ and is pronounced as a simple vowel, i.e., /tɑɪm/➔/tɑm/

- The sound /eɪ/ as in "way," "case," and "jail" changes to a diphthong resembling /aɪ/ as in "life."

- The sound /a / before an /r/, as in "charge," heart," and "sorry" sounds more like /o/.

- Some short vowels are pronounced as diphthongs. For example, "man" sounds a bit like /meyən/, "did" sounds like /diyəd/, and "call" sounds like /kawəl/.

4 Listen to phrases and sentences from the recording. Pause after each phrase or sentence and write it on the line.

1. _____

2. ___. . . and so_____

3. _____

4. ___. . . the o- and_____

5. _____

6. _____

7. _____

---

[2]North, West, Midland, Mid-Atlantic, South, and New England. Source: PBS, "Do You Speak American?", http://www.pbs.org/speak/speech/mapping/map.html.
[3]See Chapter 6, Part Two, page 149.
[4]See Chapter 6, Part Three, pages 154–155.

5 Read about ways of expressing sympathy in English.

CONVERSATION TOOLS
Expressing Sympathy

In the recording, the speaker expresses sympathy or compassion for the defendant in the following sentences:

- "He was a very poor witness, **bless his heart**." (This expression is used mainly in the South and by older Americans.)
- "He was pretty pathetic, **poor fellow**." (*Variations:* poor man, poor guy)
- "We all kind of **felt sorry for him**."
- "In a way, **my heart went out to him**."

The following sentences show examples of additional expressions of sympathy or compassion:

- "I really **felt (bad) for** the injured officer. It looked like he was in a lot of pain."
- "I **pitied** my neighbor when her son was injured in a motorcycle crash."

6 Read the true story about a crime. Then work with a partner and use at least four of the expressions from the box above to talk about the people in the story. (Remember that you can also form negative statements using the expressions.)

Example:
I really feel sorry for the boy's girlfriend.

Drive-Thru Hold-Up

CLEVELAND; A teenage boy and his girlfriend were in the boy's car in the drive-thru line of a fast-food restaurant in a small town in Ohio. While waiting in line, the boy got out of his car, walked to the driver's side window of the car ahead of his, pointed what appeared to be a gun in his pocket (it was really his fingers), and demanded cash.

The occupants of the car in front had only enough money to pay for their food and offered the robber a skateboard instead. The teenage robber then began yelling and cursing at his victims, saying he didn't want a skateboard. He walked back to his own car and got in on the driver's side. At that point, the victims called 911. The police arrived quickly and surrounded the robber's car. A police officer recognized the teen as a Cleveland (Ohio) resident whom he had ticketed earlier in the week for driving without a license.

Despite the presence of several officers, the suspect refused to get out of the car and fought the officers as they attempted to remove and arrest him. His frightened girlfriend was not arrested.

Source: http://www.dumbcrooks.com/old-dumbcrooks-site/

C. Real Talk: Use What You've Learned

VOCABULARY REVIEW

1 The new vocabulary from Part One is listed below. Review the list with a partner.

(aggravated) assault	feel sorry for (someone)	long-winded
(be) arrested	fleabag hotel	nod off
case (*noun*)	foreman	open-and-shut case
(be) charged with (a crime)	guilty	prosecutor
defense (attorney)	(my) heart went out to (someone)	resist arrest
deliberation (room)	jail	testify
deny	judge	trial
down and out	jury	witness
evidence	jury duty	witness stand

2 Work in small groups. Choose one of the topics below and discuss it in detail, using as much of the new vocabulary in the box as possible. Then listen to your classmates and place a check (✓) next to each vocabulary item they use.

a. Describe the justice system in a country you know well. Describe the participants and the steps involved in a trial and compare them with what you have learned about the justice system in the United States.

b. Tell about an experience you have had with the legal system, either in the U.S. or in another country.

c. Tell about a crime or a trial you observed or know a lot about.

INTERVIEW / RESEARCH

1 If possible, interview at least one person who has served on a jury in the United States. (If this is not possible, search the Internet or newspaper for interesting court cases and read them.) Ask the person questions about his or her jury service and take notes on the following points:

• the type of trial (criminal or civil) _____

• the charge _____

• the defendant _____

- evidence and witnesses _____
- the judge's instructions _____
- the jury's deliberation process _____
- the verdict _____

2 In class, work with a partner or small group. Tell each other about the cases you heard or read about. Use your notes to provide details from the interview or research.

VIEWING COURTROOM SCENES IN MOVIES

1 With your classmates, watch a movie about a criminal trial. Two classic films are *Twelve Angry Men* (1957), which provides a fascinating view into what happens during jury deliberations; and *Inherit the Wind* (1960), about a teacher who was brought to trial for teaching the theory of evolution in 1925. (Additional lists of courtroom scenes in films may be found by performing an Internet search for "courtroom dramas" or "law-related movies.")

2 Answer the questions regarding the movie or scene you watched; use the Part One vocabulary in the box on page 172 and expressions of sympathy from Conversation Tools on page 171, if appropriate.

1. What was the title of the movie?
2. Who was the defendant and what was the charge? Did you feel sorry for him or her?
3. Which lawyer did a better job, in your view—the defense attorney or the prosecutor?
4. What evidence was presented at the trial?
5. Were the witnesses believable?
6. What is your opinion of the judge?
7. Did the jury deliberate seriously? Did anything unusual happen during deliberations?
8. What was the result? Do you think it was fair?

Part Two: On the Phone

A. Prelistening

DISCUSSION

You will hear a conversation between a police detective and the witness to a crime. Before you listen, discuss the questions with a partner or in a small group.

- What do you know about the job of a police detective?
- Have you ever witnessed a crime? Were you interviewed by the police? What did you tell them?

VOCABULARY PREVIEW

The words and expressions are from the conversation. Check (✓) the ones you already know. Check (✓) the others as you work through the activities in Part Two.

_____ accelerate	_____ end up	_____ make (of a car)
_____ approach	_____ hit-and-run accident	_____ speed (*verb*)
_____ crosswalk	_____ investigate / investigation	_____ suspect
_____ detective		

B. Listening

MAIN IDEAS

🎧 ① Listen to the phone conversation and answer the questions. Then work with a partner and compare answers.

1. What type of crime did the witness see? _____

2. Who committed the crime? _____

3. Who was the victim? _____

4. What did the suspect do in the end? _____

DETAILS AND INFERENCES

🎧 ② Listen again and complete the tasks. Then compare answers with a partner.

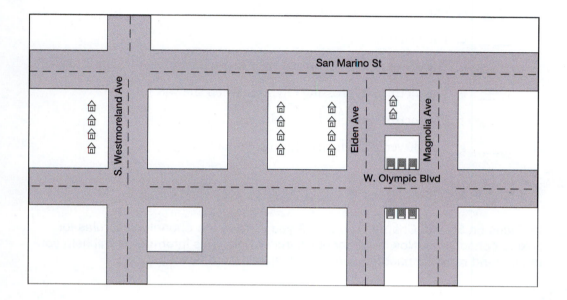

1. Draw the following items on the map of the intersection of Elden and Olympic.

   a. the witness's car just before the accident

   b. the route of the van before, during, and after the accident

   c. the location of the victim at the time of the accident

   d. the location of the victim after the accident

2. According to the witness, are the following statements true, false, or unknown? Mark them *T*, *F*, or *U*.

_____ a. The witness was a passenger in a stopped car.

_____ b. The driver of the van was a man.

_____ c. The van was speeding.

_____ d. The driver of the van turned right to avoid running through a red light.

_____ e. The victim was crossing Olympic when she was hit.

_____ f. The victim was killed immediately.

_____ g. The driver knew he had hit the woman.

LISTENING FOR LANGUAGE

3 In Focus on Sound, Chapter 1, page 18 you learned the phonological rules for linking consonants. Now read about linking vowels. This information will help you understand rapid, connected speech and speak more fluently.

FOCUS ON SOUND
Linking Vowels

When one word ends in a diphthong and the next word begins with a vowel, English speakers most often link the sounds by inserting /y/ or /w/. Study the following guidelines.

Linking with /y/ occurs after:	Linking with /w/ occurs after:
/iy/ He ͡ʸ is late.	/uw/ Who ͡ʷ are you?
/ey/ They ͡ʸ aren't here yet.	/ow/ No ͡ʷ answer.
/ay/ I ͡ʸ understand.	/aw/ How ͡ʷ is she?
/ɔy/ The boy ͡ʸ ate it.	

4 Listen to phrases with linked vowels. Write the phrases.

1. _____   5. _____

2. _____   6. _____

3. _____   7. _____

4. _____

5 Practice pronouncing the phrases in Exercise 4 with proper linking between vowels.

CONVERSATION TOOLS
First Impressions, Second Thoughts

People often form ideas or opinions and then change their minds after a period of consideration. In the recording, for example, you heard the witness say, "*Originally* I thought she [the victim] was going east to west on Elden, but *on second thought,* I mean, if she was doing that and the van hit her, she couldn't have . . . ." Notice the way the speaker marked his first impression and later thought. Ways of signaling these functions include:

To signal the original thought

- **At first / Originally / Initially / To begin with,** I thought the light was red.

To signal the later thought

- After **going over it in my mind,** I decided the light must have been green.
- I've been **thinking it over,** and now I realize I was mistaken.
- **On second thought,** I think there was someone in the crosswalk.
- I can't stop **going back and forth** about the accident. I'm not sure what happened first.

6 Work with a partner. Take turns listening and speaking. Use the expressions from Conversation Tools above to make statements about your original and later impressions or ideas on a list of topics. Take notes on your partner's sentences in the chart below. Student A, turn to page 178 for your list of topics. Student B, turn to page 192.

Example:

Topic: a movie you have seen

"A while ago I saw the movie *Crash*. At first I thought it was really strange and confusing. But I've been going over it in my mind, and now I realize it was actually very clever. There was a strange connection among all the characters. You never knew which way the relationships were going to go."

Topic	Original Idea	Later Idea
Example: the movie *Crash*	strange, confusing	clever
1.		
2.		
3.		

TOPICS FOR STUDENT A
1. something you studied (a language, a musical instrument, etc.)
2. a person you know
3. a product you bought or wanted to buy, e.g., a car

C. Real Talk: Use What You've Learned

VOCABULARY REVIEW

1 The new vocabulary from Part Two is listed below. Review the list with a partner.

accelerate	end up	make (of a car)
approach	hit-and-run accident	speed (*verb*)
crosswalk	investigate / investigation	suspect
detective		

ROLE PLAY

1 Work with a partner. Role-play the two accident scenarios on the next page. Use the illustrations that show the outcomes of two hit-and-run accidents. The detective should call the witness and ask questions. The witness should provide information about the driver, the car, and the sequence of events in the accident. Use vocabulary from the box above and expressions from Conversation Tools, page 177.

Scenario	Student A	Student B
1	You are a witness to the accident illustrated in Scene 1.	You are a police detective looking for information about the accident.
2	You are a police detective looking for information about the accident illustrated in Scene 2.	You are a witness to the accident.

2 Practice your role plays.

3 Choose one role play and perform it for another pair of students or for the whole class.

Scene 1

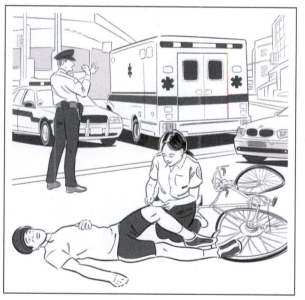

Scene 2

YOU BE THE JUDGE

1 Work in groups of four or five. Imagine that the driver of the white van in the hit-and-run accident discussed in the phone conversation was caught and brought to trial. The jury has found him guilty of criminal hit-and-run driving. You are the judge who must decide on his punishment. Read the additional information about the driver below. It may or may not influence your decision.

DRIVER INFORMATION

- The driver was a forty-five-year-old man with a wife and three young children.
- He had a valid driver's license.
- He did not know the victim and says he did not see her in the intersection.
- He had two beers with lunch on the day of the accident.
- He was talking on a cell phone when the accident happened.
- He was speeding in order to get through the intersection before the light turned red. When he realized he was too late, he turned right to avoid driving through the red light.

2 Choose one person to present your group's decision to the class. Include the reasons for your decision.

Part Three: On the Air

A. Prelistening

DISCUSSION

You will hear a report about a proposed city ordinance (law) that would prevent people in the city of Atlanta, Georgia, from asking other people for money in public, a practice known as *panhandling*. Before you listen, discuss the questions on the next page with a partner or in a small group.

- What causes some people to ask strangers for money?
- How do you feel or react when a stranger asks you for money?

VOCABULARY PREVIEW

The words and expressions are from the interview. Check (✓) the ones you already know. Check (✓) the others as you work through the activities in Part Three.

_____ competitor

_____ curb

_____ empower/empowerment

_____ erode

_____ generate

_____ infuriate

_____ keep (someone) away from (somewhere)

_____ menacing

_____ ordinance

_____ sweep (something) under the rug

_____ threaten

_____ violation

B. Listening

MAIN IDEAS

1 Listen to the report and answer the questions. Then work with a partner and compare answers.

1. According to Danny, the homeless man, why do people panhandle?

   _____

2. What would the proposed city ordinance do?

   _____

DETAILS AND INFERENCES

2 Listen again and complete the tasks listed on page 182. Then work with a partner and compare answers.

1. Fill in the missing information in the chart.

Speaker	For or Against the Ordinance?	Reason
Murphy Davis, Open Door		
Tony Singfield, Martin Luther King Campaign for Economic Justice		
Lamar Willis, City Council member		
A.J. Robinson, Central Atlantic Progress		

2. Mark the statements *T* (true) or *F* (false).

_____F_____ a. Danny Solomon is a chef at McDonald's.

_____T_____ b. If the ordinance is passed, police could arrest people for panhandling.

_____F_____ c. Panhandling has cost Atlanta $3 billion in lost conventions and tourism.

_____T_____ d. Lamar Willis believes free speech can be limited if it benefits the government.

_____T_____ e. Other U.S. cities have passed laws making panhandling illegal.

3. "Sweep (something) under the rug" means

a. clean the house.

b. hide a problem.

c. put something in the wrong place.

d. solve a problem cleverly.

LISTENING FOR LANGUAGE

3 Read about stress in words with suffixes.

FOCUS ON SOUND

Stress in Words with Suffixes

Adding a suffix to a word can affect the word in one of three ways.

Influence of Suffix	Examples from Recording	Similar Suffixes
1. Some suffixes are "neutral." They don't affect the stress pattern of the base word.	HOMEless THREATening emPOWerment	-able, -al, -er, -ful, -ing, -less, -ly, -ment, -ness
2. Some suffixes cause the final syllable to be stressed.	conventionEER	-aire, -eer, -ese, -esque, -ique
3. Some suffixes cause the stress in the root word to move to the syllable just before the suffix.	eCOnomy ⟶ ecoNOmic CRIminal ⟶ criminaliZAtion	-al, -eous, -graphy, -ial, -ic, -ion, -ious, -ity, -tion

4 Look at the list of words. Predict where the stress will fall and place a mark (′) over the syllable. Then listen, repeat, and check your predictions. The first item is done as an example.

1. courágeous
2. questionnaire
3. ridiculous
4. photography
5. educational
6. unhappiness
7. indecision
8. neighborhood
9. destiny
10. Lebanese
11. critique
12. homogeneous
13. reality
14. legislation
15. illegal
16. menacing

5 Work with one or more classmates. Think of at least three additional words that fit each pattern described in the chart in Focus on Sound above.

C. Real Talk: Use What You've Learned

VOCABULARY REVIEW

1 The new vocabulary from Part Three is listed below. Review the list with a partner.

competitor	keep (someone) away from (somewhere)
curb	menacing
empower/empowerment	ordinance
erode	sweep (something) under the rug
generate	threaten
infuriate	violation

2 Work with a partner. Read the statements and respond with your opinion. Tell your partner if you strongly agree, agree, have no opinion, disagree, or strongly disagree with each statement. Explain your answer.

1. I find panhandlers menacing.
2. It infuriates me when strangers beg me for money.
3. The presence of panhandlers threatens the economic growth of an area.
4. A ban on panhandling would violate some people's freedom of speech.
5. Sometimes it is necessary to curb people's freedom of speech.
6. The proposed ordinance against panhandling is cruel.
7. Any city that does not ban panhandling will lose tourists and convention business to its competitors.
8. Police should be empowered to arrest people for panhandling.
9. A government has the right to keep people away from any place it chooses.
10. The city where we live sweeps the problems of poor people under the rug.
11. Panhandling in this neighborhood is eroding people's quality of life.
12. Raising taxes is the best way for a government to generate money for needed programs.

ROLE PLAY:
A CITY COUNCIL MEETING

In the United States, city governments, often called councils, are elected by the citizens, and city council meetings are generally open to the public. You and your classmates are going to role-play a city council meeting in which arguments for and against a ban on panhandling in your town are heard. Follow the steps below.

1. Choose the following roles:
   - Five or six members of the city council, e.g., mayor, secretary, treasurer, parliamentarian, and representatives of various city neighborhoods
   - Speakers representing downtown business groups who favor the ban
   - Supporters of rights for the poor, who are against the ban
   - Citizens of the town, both for and against the ban

2. Follow these procedures:
   a. The mayor opens the meeting and announces the purpose: to hear arguments for and against an ordinance banning panhandling in the downtown area.
   b. Speakers in favor of the ban explain their reasons.
   c. Speakers against the ban explain their reasons.
   d. Citizens are called on to ask questions and voice their opinions.
   e. Members of the city council vote on the ordinance.
   f. The mayor announces the results.

Note: No one may interrupt a person who is speaking. The parliamentarian calls on speakers and enforces the "no interrupting" rule.

Part Four: In Class

A. Prelistening

You will hear part of a college lecture about some causes of crime. Before you listen, discuss the questions with a partner or in a small group.

- What causes some people—and not others—to commit crimes?

- What is the difference between violent crime and "white-collar" crime?

- Who commits the majority of crimes in a country you know well? Consider the following factors: age, gender, social class, economic class, and educational level.

VOCABULARY PREVIEW

The words and expressions are from the lecture. Check (✓) the ones you already know. Check (✓) the others as you work through the activities in Part Four.

_____ aboriginal	_____ erosion	_____ perspective
_____ capital, capitalist	_____ homogeneous	_____ property
_____ comprise	_____ manifestation	_____ social constructs
_____ Death Row	_____ migration	_____ sociologist
_____ disorganization	_____ norms	

B. Listening and Note-Taking

LECTURE ORGANIZATION: CAUSE AND EFFECT

Read the information on page 187 about the organization of lectures which discuss the causes and/or effects of a social problem like crime.

Discussions of problems often include one or more of the following types of information:

- a description of the problem or situation
- the causes of the problem (reasons)
- the results of the problem (effects)
- the solution or solutions to the problem

Speakers can combine and organize these elements in many ways. For instance, a talk may deal only with causes or only with effects; a problem may have one cause and several effects or a number of causes leading to one major effect; the speaker may or may not present solutions.

As you have learned, good speakers will indicate which topics they plan to discuss, and in what order, in their introduction.

2 Listen to the lecture introduction and answer the questions. Then work with a partner and compare answers.

1. What is the speaker's main focus in this talk?

   a. causes   b. effects   c. solutions   d. all of the above

2. What form will your notes take? Sketch a quick outline on your own paper.

LECTURE LANGUAGE: EXPRESSIONS OF CAUSE AND EFFECT

3 Study the information about expressions of cause and effect.

English has dozens of ways of talking about causes and effects. Some expressions can be confusing because they sound alike. In addition, either the cause or the effect may be mentioned first.

Examples:

cause(s)	*effect*
Greed and easy access to money	may **result in** white-collar crime.

effect	*cause(s)*
Most often, white-collar crime	**is the result of** greed and easy access to money.

To hear the difference between causes and effects, focus on the following:

- active or passive verbs, e.g., *cause* versus *is caused by*
- prepositions, e.g., *result in* versus *be the result of*
- synonyms for *cause*, e.g., *lead to, result in*

4 Work with a partner. Read the following sentences and study their structure. Underline the expressions of cause or effect. Label the causes and effects. Notice which comes first. The first item is done as an example.

　　　　　　　cause　　　　　　　effect
1. Lack of attention <u>causes</u> many car accidents.

2. Her success as a dancer is the result of hard work, good luck, and knowing the right people.

3. The love of money is the root of all evil.[5]

4. Over 80 percent of the residents of the area are immigrants. Therefore, most children starting school do not speak English as their first language.

5. In some cities, homelessness is a manifestation of very high housing costs.

6. The parents were relieved to learn that their daughter's reading problem was caused by nothing worse than weak eyesight.

7. Because of poor sanitation, there were frequent outbreaks of cholera, dysentery, and typhoid fever in the refugee camp.

8. If children are not given sufficient love and affection as babies, they are likely to have difficulty forming close, trusting relationships as they grow up.

5 Read the segments from the lecture and predict which expressions of cause/effect from Exercise 4 fit in the blanks. Then listen to the recording and see if you predicted correctly.

1. The first is the structural-functionist perspective. This proposes that crime, and especially increases in crime, are a _____ social disorganization . . .

2. There's still a great deal of migration to the western provinces [of Canada], _____ we would expect the west to be less organized . . . , for there to be less shared values and ideas, and _____ there will be more crime.

3. This is the conflict theory, based on the original ideas of Karl Marx, in which crime is _____ the conflict between the classes in any society. In other words, crime _____ inequality.

4. So it could well be that _____ aboriginal peoples are at the bottom of the class structure, they tend to be unfairly treated by the legal system.

---

[5]From the New Testament of the Bible.

TAKING NOTES

🎧 ⑥ Listen to the first two causes of crime that the speaker discusses. Take notes on your own paper. Use what you have learned about lecture form, language, and organization. Then rewrite your notes in the space. Use the cues on the left to guide you.

		TWO CAUSES OF CRIME
topic		
1st theory		I. Structural-functionist perspective
causes of crime	◯	A. ↑ crime result of
		•
		•
		•
origin of theory		
		C. If theory is correct → crime will occur when there's rapid social change, e.g.,
examples of social change		
example– country **where is crime?**		D.
reason		
	◯	
other countries		E.
examples		
1st theory– conclusion		F.
2nd theory		II.
origin		
cause of crime		
		C. Laws created by people w/ power → protect their interests
examples		

(continued)

		D. Law treats diff. classes differently
examples	◯	• Canada: 12% of prison pop = aboriginals, but abor = 4% pop
2nd theory– conclusion		

REVIEWING THE LECTURE

7 Work with a partner or in small groups. Use your notes to discuss the questions.

1. What are the causes of crime, according to (a) the structural-functional theory, and (b) the conflict theory?

2. In Canada, is the crime rate higher in the east or in the west? Which theory accounts for the difference? Explain.

3. How does the structural-functional theory explain the relatively low crime rate in Japan and Korea?

4. Restate the examples which show how the legal system treats people of different economic classes differently.

C. Real Talk: Use What You've Learned

VOCABULARY REVIEW

1 The new vocabulary from Part Four is listed below. Review the list with a partner.

aboriginals	erosion	perspective
capital, capitalist	homogeneous	property
comprise	manifestation	social constructs
Death Row	migration	sociologist
disorganization	norms	

2 Complete the sentences with words from the box on page 190. Then work with a partner and compare answers.

1. _____ have suggested several theories to help us understand the causes of crime.

2. The structural-functionist _____ proposes that increases in crime are the result of social _____.

3. According to one theory, crime is the result of a loss of shared _____ and an _____ of social control.

4. In Canada there is still a great deal of _____ to the western provinces.

5. We expect countries that are quite _____ to have lower crime rates.

6. According to Karl Marx, crime is a _____ of the conflict between the classes in any society.

7. Laws are _____. They're created by the members of a society, and they can change.

8. Laws work to the advantage of people who have a great deal of _____ or _____.

9. In Canada, 12 percent of people in prisons are _____.

10. In the United States, blacks _____ 41 percent of the prisoners on _____.

DISCUSSION

Work in small groups and discuss the questions. Use the vocabulary from the box on page 190 whenever possible. Use a variety of cause-and-effect expressions.

1. Does either theory that the lecturer presents explain the occurrence of crime in the area where you live? Explain.

2. Does either theory show a clear or practical way to prevent crime?

3. In your view, what are some other possible causes of crime?

TOEFL® Practice: Synthesizing Listening, Reading, and Speaking

1 Read the passage about the increasing crime rate in China.

China's crime rate has been increasing since the late 1970s when the country embarked on economic reforms. In the early 1980s, the reported crime rate was 90 crimes per 100,000 people. By the late 1990s, this had jumped 45 percent, to 131 per 100,000, according to United Nations figures.

Professor Liu Jianchong of Rhode Island College in the United States, an expert on the subject of crime in China, says the economic boom has created a large income gap between the rich cities and the impoverished rural areas, where more than 900 million Chinese live. As the cities grow richer, rural residents migrate to them in search of work. However, under China's residency system, they are denied many benefits of city life, including schools for their children and health care. Crime has exploded in these frustrated populations.

Source: "China Confronts Rising Crime in a Fast-Track Economy,"
http://english.chosun.com/w21data/html/news/200503/200503010031.html

2 Use the information from both the lecture and the reading to prepare a one-minute oral presentation on the following topic:

- Explain how the example of China supports the sociological theories presented in the lecture.

EXERCISE 6, PAGE 177

TOPICS FOR STUDENT B

1. a public figure, such as a politician or actor
2. a place where you have stayed, visited, or lived
3. a custom from a different country

8

Lights, Camera, Action!

Part One:
In Person

A. Prelistening

DISCUSSION

You will hear part of an interview with a young film producer named Rachel Miller. Before you listen, discuss the questions with a partner or in a small group.

- What do you know about the work of a film producer? For example, what is the role of a producer? How do producers spend their working time?

- If you wanted to become a film producer, what kind of training do you think you would need to get?

- How do movies get made? What are the steps? Share your knowledge or your questions about this process.

VOCABULARY PREVIEW

The words and expressions are from the interview. Check (✓) the ones you already know. Check (✓) the others as you work through the activities in Part One.

_____ at the end of the day

_____ be in the right place at the right time

_____ broad (humor)

_____ cast

_____ fall apart

_____ flop (*noun, verb*)

_____ genres

_____ gritty

_____ guaranteed

_____ iffy (*informal*)

_____ intern (*verb*)

_____ juggle

_____ multitasking

_____ put all (one's) eggs in one basket

_____ a short (*noun*)

_____ take a shot (at)

_____ a thriller

_____ topical

B. Listening

MAIN IDEAS

🎧 **1** Listen to the interview and check (✓) each main topic that is discussed. Then work with a partner and compare answers.

_____✓ 1. how a producer is different from a director

_____✓ 2. how Ms. Miller trained to become a producer

_____ 3. the process of creating a short film

_____✓ 4. how movies get made

_____ 5. why the movie *The Island* was unsuccessful

_____✓ 6. what producers do in order to get a film made

_____✓ 7. Ms. Miller's current projects

_____✓ 8. The characteristics that enable producers to do many things at the same time

DETAILS AND INFERENCES

🎧 **2** **Listen again, answer the questions, and complete the tasks. Then work with a partner and compare answers.**

1. List three things Ms. Miller did to prepare for her career as a movie producer.

   a. _high school_

   b. _____

   c. _____

2. According to Ms. Miller, the most important factor in producing a successful movie appears to be

   a. luck or chance.

   b. having the right "formula."

   c. famous stars.

   d. getting a studio to distribute it.

3. Ms. Miller says the film *The Island* "flopped." This means that

   a. it was a huge hit.

   b. it made a hundred million dollars.

   c. it earned very little money compared to what it cost to make.

   d. it got bad reviews from professional movie critics.

4. What does a producer do to "fight" for a project?

   _____

5. Fill in the missing information concerning the projects Ms. Miller is working on now. List each movie genre or theme and the adjectives she uses to describe it.

Genre/Theme	Adjectives
1.	broad, fun, smart
2. teen boys and grief	
3.	
4.	
5.	
6.	

6. What do all of Ms. Miller's projects have in common?

a. _____

b. _____

7. List three characteristics that a producer needs to have, or things a producer needs to do, in order to juggle many projects at the same time.

a. _____

b. _____

c. _____

LISTENING FOR LANGUAGE

🎧 ③ The speaker uses a number of expressions related to the theme of luck or chance. Listen to a section of the interview again and fill in the missing expressions. Then work with a partner and compare answers. Discuss the meaning of each expression.

A movie is _____, _____,
  1   2

_____, hard work, being _____
  3

_____. It's about getting that material to the producer or
  4

the director who will _____ at it. And, who'll stay with the
  5

project and fight for the project. And someone to champion you. And it's about . . .

nothing is _____ in this business. There's no formula to
  6

make a fantastic movie. For example, *The Island*, which cost a hundred million

dollars to make, starring Scarlett Johanssen and Ewan McGregor, Dreamworks

made it, and it flopped. And it only made 10 mil-, 12 million dollars the opening

weekend. So everything is _____ in this business.
  7

And for a producer, it's about _____,
  8

about having ten projects, so if one falls apart, one might go and one might be in this

stage and one might be in this stage. . . .

4 Study the information in the box about additional expressions for talking about luck, opportunity, or chance.

> ## CONVERSATION TOOLS
> ### Chance, Opportunity, and Luck
>
> The following idiomatic expressions were used in Exercise 3:
>
> - (be) in the right place at the right time
> - take a shot (at something)
> - (something is) iffy
> - (not) put all (one's) eggs in one basket
>
> Here are a few more idioms related to chance, opportunity, and luck. Notice how they are used in context.
>
> - After working for a large production company for three years, Ms. Miller felt ready to **take a chance** and start her own company.
> - We **missed the boat** when we decided not to buy that house. The value has gone up by $50,000 in less than six months.
> - Don't **miss out on** this fantastic opportunity! Shop today and save 10 percent on every item in the store.

5 Match each expression on the left with its meaning on the right. Some expressions have similar meanings.

EXPRESSIONS	MEANING
_____ 1. be in the right place at the right time	a. miss a good opportunity
_____ 2. take a shot (at)	b. invest all your time, effort, and money in just one thing
_____ 3. iffy	c. do something that may be risky
_____ 4. put all your eggs in one basket	d. uncertain
_____ 5. take a chance	e. be somewhere just when something lucky happens
_____ 6. miss the boat (when)	
_____ 7. miss out (on)	

6 Work in pairs. Use expressions from the Conversation Tools box on page 197 to complete the imaginary conversation between Ms. Miller and a young film student.

Student: So have you had a chance to read my script?

Ms. Miller: Yes, I have. It's an interesting story. How'd you come up with it?

Student: Well, it's based on something that I actually saw. I just happened to

_____. It made such a powerful

₁

impression on me that I knew I had to write about it.

Ms. Miller: I agree that it's a powerful story, but . . .

Student: So will you produce it?

Ms. Miller: Well, I have to think about it. Controversial stories like this are always

_____. You never know how the public is going to

₂

respond. Plus you have no experience, and investors don't like to

_____ on an unknown. So it's going to be hard to raise

₃

money. On the other hand, I'd hate to _____ the chance to

₄

produce something really different. It could be a big hit.

Student: So you'll _____ at it?

₅

Ms. Miller: I'll tell you what. I'm working on about eight projects right now. I can't

_____, you know. I'm really busy for

₆

the next three weeks, but after that, I'll make some calls and see if anyone's

interested.

7 Work with a partner. Role-play the conversation in Exercise 6.

C. Real Talk: Use What You've Learned

VOCABULARY REVIEW

1 The new vocabulary from Part One is listed below. Review the list with a partner.

at the end of the day	gritty	put all (one's) eggs in one basket
be in the right place at the right time	guaranteed	
	iffy (*informal*)	a short (*noun*)
broad (*humor*)	intern	take a chance (on)
cast	juggle	take a shot (at)
fall apart	miss out on	a thriller
flop (*noun, verb*)	miss the boat (*informal*)	topical
genres	multitasking	

2 Work in groups of four or five. Use the vocabulary above to discuss the topics and questions.

1. What's your favorite movie? Why do you like it?

2. List as many film genres as you can. Which is your favorite? Why?

Example:

My favorite film genre is mystery, especially the suspenseful old black-and-white movies by Alfred Hitchcock.

3. What are some other jobs that require juggling schedules and multitasking? Do such jobs appeal to you?

4. Tell about a time when . . .
   - you were in the right place at the right time
   - you missed out on the chance to do something interesting
   - you put all your eggs in one basket
   - something you worked on really hard flopped

5. Internships are common in many professions in North America. Are such learning opportunities common in other places? Have you ever been an intern?

RESEARCH: MOVIE INDUSTRY JOBS

1 Have you ever looked at the long list of credits at the end of a movie and wondered what all those people do? Below is a partial list of movie industry jobs. Choose one job and do research to find out what this person does.

director	gaffer	set dresser
cinematographer	key grip	costume designer
art director	dolly grip	costumer
editor	best boy	make-up artist
stunt coordinator	foley artist	hairdresser
line producer	ADR editor	dialogue coach
continuity person	music mixer	unit publicist
film loader	FX coordinator	production caterer
steadicam operator	matte artist	negative cutter
production sound mixer	location manager	day player
boom operator	property master	story editor

2 Report your findings to the class. Take notes on your classmates' reports.

3 Choose a job you might like to have. Tell the class why it interests you and why this might be a good job for you.

Part Two: On the Phone

A. Prelistening

DISCUSSION

You will hear a typical recorded announcement from a movie theater. Before you listen, discuss the questions with a partner or in a small group.

- Movie theaters in North America seldom have people answer their phones anymore. Instead they use recorded messages to provide information about the movies showing. What kind of information would you expect to hear in this type of recording?

- Have you ever called a movie theater for information? What did you want to find out? Who answered—a person or a recording? Did you get the information you needed?

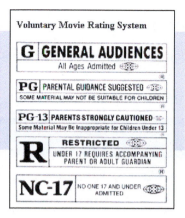

VOCABULARY PREVIEW

The words and expressions are from the recorded announcement. Check (✓) the ones you already know. Check (✓) the others as you work through the activities in Part Two.

_____ bargain matinees   _____ rated (G, PG-13, R)   _____ showtime

_____ late show   _____ running time   _____ subtitles

_____ Q and A (*informal*)   _____ screen (*verb*)

B. Listening

MAIN IDEAS

1 Read the list of topics below. Check (✓) the ones you predict you will hear in the recorded announcement. Then listen to the recording to verify and correct your predictions.

_____ theater name   _____ film running times

_____ theater location   _____ ticket prices

_____ movies currently showing   _____ information about online ticket sales

_____ movies showing next week   _____ parking information

_____ showtimes   _____ food sold at the theater

_____ film ratings

DETAILS AND INFERENCES

🎧 ② **Listen again and do the exercises below. Then work with a partner and compare answers.**

1. Fill in the missing information.

You are a / an . . .	You want to see . . .	Day/time of day	Showtime	Ticket price
1. 21-year-old student	*Batman Begins*	Wednesday evening		
2. 62-year-old man	*March of the Penguins*	Sunday bargain matinee		
3. Adult woman	*Stealth*	Saturday late show		
4. Adult woman	*Stealth*	Monday early evening		
5. 10-year-old child	*March of the Penguins*	Friday late afternoon		

2. Match the name of the movie with details about it. Some items have more than one correct answer.

_____ 1. *The Edukators*

_____ 2. *Batman Begins*

_____ 3. *Stealth*

_____ 4. *March of the Penguins*

a. There's a special late show on Saturday night.

b. It is rated PG.

c. There is no screening on Thursday.

d. There are five screenings per day.

e. It is in German.

3. Mark the statements *T* (true) or *F* (false). Correct the false statements.

_____ a. This announcement includes information for the weekend of August 6th and 7th.

_____ b. A fifteen-year-old will not be allowed to see *The Edukators*.

_____ c. You can meet the director of *The Edukators* on Sunday night.

_____ d. Soldiers and senior citizens pay the same admission price.

_____ e. Parking prices are higher at night than during the daytime.

f. It has the longest running time.

LISTENING FOR LANGUAGE

3 Read about two pronunciations of the English sound written with the letters "th."

FOCUS ON SOUND
Voiceless and Voiced "th"

In English there are two ways to pronounce the sound written as "th": voiceless and voiced.

- The phonetic symbol for voiceless "th" is /θ/. This sound is heard, for example, in the words *three, Thursday, nothing* and in ordinal numbers ending in "th"—*fourth, seventh, eleventh*, etc.

- The symbol for the voiced "th" is /ð/. This is the sound you hear in the article *the*, demonstratives (*this, that, these, those*), some pronouns (*they, their*), and some words that describe family relationships (*mother, father, brother*).

To pronounce /θ/ and /ð/ correctly, follow these steps:

1. Part your lips and slip the tip of your tongue between your front teeth. Relax. Don't bite down!

2. Put the palm of your hand in front of your mouth. Exhale with your tongue in the position described above. You should feel a rush of air on your hand, and you should hear a voiceless /θ/. Practice by saying the ordinal numbers *fourth, fifth, sixth*, etc.

3. Now add voicing. Keep your lips, tongue, and one hand in the position described above. Put your other hand on your throat so that you can feel your vocal cords vibrating. Now exhale and try to say the word *the*. Make sure you feel the vibration in your throat. Practice with the words listed in this Focus on Sound.

🎧 ④ Listen to words from the recording. Check (✓) the Voiceless or Voiced column to indicate the pronunciation you heard.

	Voiceless /θ/	Voiced /ð/
1. Thursday		
2. there		
3. theater		
4. through		
5. either		
6. thank you		
7. *Stealth*		
8. others		
9. further		
10. with[1]		
11. three		
12. without		

⑤ Work with a partner. Take turns saying the words from Exercise 4 and monitoring your partner's pronunciation.

⑥ Turn to page 272 of the Audioscript. Find the words in Exercise 4 and underline the phrases in which they appear. Practice saying complete phrases with proper stress, linking, blending, and pronunciation of "th."

C. Real Talk: Use What You've Learned

VOCABULARY REVIEW

① The new vocabulary from Part Two is listed below. Review the list with a partner.

bargain matinee	**rated (G, PG-13, R)**	**showtime**
late show	**running time**	**subtitles**
Q and A	**screen (*verb*)**	

---

[1]"With" and "without" can be pronounced with either /θ/ or /ð/, so listen carefully to the speaker's pronunciation.

204 | **Chapter 8**   Part Two

2 Work with a partner. Use the information from Exercise 2 on pages 202–203 and the vocabulary on page 204 to form complete sentences.

Example: *Batman Begins* <u>screens</u> on Wednesday evening at 6:40 P.M.

MOVIE THEATER PHONE RECORDING

1 Work with a partner. Look at the information on page 218. Student A, write a script for telephone recording 1. Student B, write a script for telephone recording 2. Then take turns reading your scripts. Use the chart below to take notes on the information in your partner's "recording."

Name of theater	Running time
Location	Rating
Theater number	Student price
Film	Parking information
Showtimes	

Part Three: On the Air

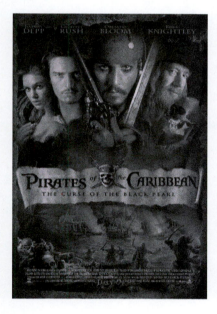

PLOT SUMMARY

The movie *Pirates of the Caribbean: The Curse of the Black Pearl* (2003) is a lighthearted action-adventure story set in the Caribbean in the seventeenth century, a time when Europeans were colonizing the area and pirates were a constant threat. In the film, the governor's daughter, Elizabeth (Keira Knightley), is kidnapped by the evil pirate Captain Barbossa (Jeffrey Rush) and his crew, who need Elizabeth's blood in order to undo an ancient curse which has left them stuck in a state between life and death. Will Turner (Orlando Bloom), her childhood friend, becomes allied with "gentleman" pirate Jack Sparrow (Johnny Depp) in an effort to save her and recover a treasure that Sparrow seeks.

A. Prelistening

DISCUSSION

You will hear part of a radio review of the movie *Pirates of the Caribbean: The Curse of the Black Pearl.* Before you listen, discuss the questions with a partner or in a small group. (*Note:* If you have seen the movie, please answer the third item only. Do not reveal details about the movie.)

- Have you seen or heard of the Disneyland ride called Pirates of the Caribbean, which the movie is based on? Share what you know, or go to the Disneyland website to get information.

- Read the summary of the movie's plot. Based only on this information, do you think you would like to see this movie?

- Which verb tense is used consistently to tell the plot of the film?

- Watch the film trailer on the Internet. What is your first impression? Does it confirm your desire to see or not see the movie?

VOCABULARY PREVIEW

The words and expressions below are from the movie review. Check the ones you already know. Check off the others as you work through the activities in Part Three.

_____ corrupt   _____ scrubbed

_____ eccentric, eccentricity   _____ second-rate

_____ grating   _____ sterile

_____ grit   _____ unbearably

_____ (have) the time of (one's) life   _____ unendurable

_____ mishandled

B. Listening

M A I N   I D E A S

Some Movie-Related Terminology

Press screening: A special showing of a new movie which only members of the media are allowed to attend.

Opening day audience: People who see a film on the first day that it is shown in theaters.

Comic entrance: The first appearance of a character in a movie, filmed in a humorous way.

Flashback: A scene in a film that interrupts the chronological sequence by showing an earlier event or action.

Shot: A picture filmed by a movie camera.

Camera setups: The precise places where a movie director places the cameras before filming a scene.

Romantic leads: Main characters in a film who are romantically involved or will be by the end of the movie.

1 Listen to the review by film critic Henry Sheehan and answer the following questions. Then work with a partner and compare answers.

1. How did the audience and the critic's son respond to the film?

   _____

2. What did the critic think of it? _____

   _____

3. The critic supports his point of view with three criticisms of the film. What are they?

   a. _____

   b. _____

   c. _____

DETAILS AND INFERENCES

1. The critic says his son "had the time of his life." This means his son

    a. was bored.

    b. was not busy, so he had time to see the film with his father.

    c. enjoyed himself very much.

    d. thought it was the best movie he had ever seen.

2. The critic says the film "delivers on" audience expectations. This means the audience was

    a. surprised.

    b. disappointed.

    c. satisfied.

    d. unimpressed.

3. The critic says, "People have become used to taking second-rate as the best they can get." This is an implied criticism of

    a. people's taste.

    b. people's education level.

    c. the film *Pirates of the Caribbean*.

    d. the quality of movies in general.

4. The movie starts with a

    a. flashback.

    b. comic entrance.

    c. bad camera setup.

    d. commercial.

5. How long is the film? _____

6. When the critic calls Johnny Depp's performance "corrupt," he means it was

    a. artificial but amusing.

    b. eccentric but sterile.

    c. boring but authentic.

    d. emotional but second-rate.

7. The critic implies that eccentricity in an actor's performance is good when _____ (Check all that apply.)

_____ a. it is an organic part of the character.

_____ b. it grows.

_____ c. it affects the viewer emotionally.

_____ d. it is external.

_____ e. it is amusing.

8. The critic says watching this movie was "not an unendurable experience." This means the experience was

a. excellent.

b. good.

c. fair.

d. poor.

LISTENING FOR LANGUAGE

③ Read about ways to critique art.

CONVERSATION TOOLS

Criticizing a Work of Art

The word *criticism* has a negative connotation in ordinary conversation, but in the arts it refers to both positive and negative analysis or evaluation of a work such as a film, painting, book, etc. In English, speakers can convey either positive or negative criticism in numerous ways.

Techniques	Examples from the Radio Review
• choice of adjectives and adverbs with positive or negative connotations	This is a *second-rate* film.
• functional categories such as like/dislike, approval/disapproval, etc.	(The audience liked the film.) *I'm kind of sorry about that.*
• sayings and idiomatic expressions that imply a positive or negative opinion	At the screening, Sheehan's son *had the time of his life.*
• comparison	Depp's performance is *not like* one of the great eccentric performances he gives in Tim Burton's movies.
• positive or negative tone of voice— e.g., sarcastic, skeptical, enthusiastic, delighted, etc.²	The critic sounds sorry throughout the review.

²See Chapter 4, Part Two, page 96 for information on using the voice to express strong emotion.

4 Listen to the radio review again. The critic uses many adjectives and adverbs to express his negative opinion of different aspects of the film. Match the items on the left with the descriptions on the right.

_____ 1. Johnny Depp's comic entrance   a. very, very bad

_____ 2. camera setups   b. grating

_____ 3. the two romantic leads   c. emotionally sterile

_____ 4. Keira Knightley's performance   d. miserable performances

_____ 5. Orlando Bloom's performance   e. unbearably bad

_____ 6. Geoffrey Rush's performance   f. mishandled

_____ 7. Johnny Depp's performance   g. badly edited

_____ 8. the film overall   h. corrupt, artificial, amusing

5 Work with a partner. Form complete, true sentences using the language in Exercise 4. If you have seen the movie, state whether you agree or disagree with the critic's opinion.

Example:

The critic thinks the two romantic leads gave miserable performances. I disagree. I thought their performances were funny.

C. Real Talk: Use What You've Learned

VOCABULARY REVIEW

1 The new vocabulary from Part Three is listed below. Review the list with a partner.

corrupt	(have) the time of (one's) life	sterile
eccentric, eccentricity	mishandled	unbearable
grating	scrubbed	unendurable
grit	second-rate	

2 Work with a partner. For each adjective in the list, provide an adjective with the opposite meaning. If you need help, consult a dictionary or thesaurus.

Example:

second-rate ≠ excellent

3 Think of a movie you disliked. Then tell your partner about it, using as many of the Part Three vocabulary items (and their opposites) as possible.

DISCUSSION

Work in small groups and discuss the following questions.

1. What is the purpose of criticism in the arts? Do you think critics have important jobs?

2. In general, do you pay attention to movie reviews? Do they ever persuade you to see or not see a movie? Give an example.

3. Why does it happen sometimes that audiences love a movie that critics hate, or vice versa?

4. If you have seen the movie *Pirates of the Caribbean: The Curse of the Black Pearl*, say whether you agree or disagree with the critic's review. If you have not seen it, say whether or not you would like to see it, based on input from Part Three, the critic, and your classmates.

PRESENTATION: FILM REVIEW

1 Prepare a three- to four-minute oral review of a movie you have seen. Include:

- a short summary of the plot and characters (This should be no more than one minute. See the example on page 205. Use your own words; do not copy from the DVD jacket or from the Internet.)

- what you liked about the movie

- what you disliked

- your recommendation

2 Present your review to your classmates.

Part Four: **In Class**

A movie sound stage

A. Prelistening

ACTIVITY

You will hear a lecture about postproduction movie sound. The speaker is Barry Snyder, a sound executive in Los Angeles, California. Get ready to listen by watching a short (one-two-minute) segment from any movie or movie trailer. Follow these instructions:

1. Watch the segment or clip once without sound. Pay attention to the visual elements and the story. Afterwards, work with a partner and describe what you saw and what was happening.

2. Turn away from the television or computer screen. Play the segment again with sound but no image. Make a list of every sound you hear. Then compare lists with a partner.

3. Now watch the clip again and listen at the same time. Notice how the sound and image are coordinated.

4. Finally, with your classmates, discuss these questions:
   - How did the sound work with the moving image you saw?
   - Which sounds do you suppose were recorded during filming? Which sounds were added later?
   - Look at the photo above. Where was this photo taken, and what do you think is happening?

VOCABULARY PREVIEW

The words and expressions are from the lecture. Check (✓) the ones you already know. Check (✓) the others as you work through the activities in Part Four.

_____ ambient	_____ elements	_____ (movie) set
_____ coherent	_____ inconsistent	_____ shoot (a film)
_____ component	_____ in synch	_____ soundtrack
_____ edit, editor	_____ repetitive	_____ swear word

B. Listening and Note-Taking

LECTURE LANGUAGE: DEFINING TECHNICAL TERMS

1 **Read about defining technical terms.**

Every profession has its own technical vocabulary. When a professional speaks to a group of nonprofessionals, the speaker will usually take care to define technical terms the audience does not know. Definitions are usually marked by specific signaling phrases.

Definitions in a lecture can be very formal and very clearly marked. A speaker might say, "What do I mean by X?" or "The definition of X is . . ."

Other ways of signaling a definition are shorter and more subtle. Definitions may even be implied; that is, there may be no words to signal that the speaker is providing a definition. The listener must use the context to recognize the definition.

The following are examples of some less obvious ways of signaling definition. You will hear these signals in the lecture.

- The music for a movie or television show **is called** the score.
- Dubbing **is** the process of re-recording or replacing dialogue for a motion picture.
- . . . ambient sound, **which is** the natural sound in the environment where you're recording.
- The actors watch the film of their performance and they **dub, they re record** their lines.
- . . . a microphone on a long pole, **what we call** a boom mike.
- Music written for a movie **is (also) known as** the film score.

🎧 ② Listen to sections of the talk containing technical terms. Write the definitions.

1. production sound: _____

_____

2. ADR: _____

_____

looping: _____

3. group ADR, group looping: _____

_____

4. sound effects: _____

5. foley artist _____

6. in synch: _____

7. source music: _____

_____

8. mixing stage: _____

_____

LECTURE ORGANIZATION: LOGICAL DIVISION

③ Read about the logical division method of organizing information.

Logical division is perhaps the most common way of organizing information. Also called *listing* or *enumerating*, it simply means breaking a topic down into smaller parts that the speaker will describe, define, or explain one by one. The parts are not always predictable. For that reason, it is important to listen to the speaker's introduction in order to anticipate the form your notes will take.

The following tips will help you take notes on lectures organized by logical division:

- Listen for synonyms for the word *part*, such as *section, division, component, element, aspect.*

- Listen for transition words that can be used for listing, such as *first, second, also, next, finally,* etc.

🎧 **④** **Listen to the lecture introduction and answer the questions. Then work with a partner and compare notes.**

1. What is the topic of the lecture? _____

2. What three elements will the speaker discuss?

   a. _____

   b. _____

   c. _____

3. What note-taking form will probably work best for this lecture—a list, an outline, or some kind of graphic representation? _____

TAKING NOTES

🎧 **⑤** **Listen to the lecture and take notes on your own paper. Use what you have learned about lecture form, language, and organization. Then rewrite your notes neatly.**

REVIEWING THE LECTURE

⑥ **Work with a partner or in a small group. Use your lecture notes to discuss the questions.**

1. What are the three components of post production sound?
2. What is the meaning of the following terms?
   • production sound
   • ADR (looping)
   • group ADR
3. Why is it necessary to replace production sound with ADR?
4. Why is group ADR necessary?
5. What are sound effects? Give examples.
6. How are sound effects added to the soundtrack?
7. What is a foley stage? What do foley actors do?
8. What does a film composer do?
9. What is source music, and how is it different from a film score?
10. What happens on a mixing stage?

C. Real Talk: Use What You've Learned

VOCABULARY REVIEW

1. The key vocabulary from Part Four is listed below. Review the list with a partner.

ambient	elements	(movie) set
coherent	inconsistent	shoot (a film)
component	in synch	soundtrack
edit, editor	repetitive	swear word

2. Work with a partner. Read the statements. Mark them *T* (true) or *F* (false). Correct the false statements.

_____ 1. Repetitive sounds that are added in post-production are called sound effects.

_____ 2. A movie set must be silent except for the dialogue that the actors are saying.

_____ 3. Source music is an essential element of every movie.

_____ 4. An airplane flying overhead could be an example of an ambient sound.

_____ 5. Foley sound must be in synch with the actors' movements.

_____ 6. A scene may need to be looped if an actor accidentally says a swear word.

_____ 7. The final soundtrack for a movie is produced on a scoring stage.

_____ 8. A film editor takes scenes that were shot at different times and edits them into a coherent soundtrack.

_____ 9. Sound editing is necessary because production sound is inconsistent.

_____ 10. Music, sound effects, and ADR are the basic components of postproduction sound.

PROJECT: ANALYZE A SOUNDTRACK

1 Work in small groups. Each group should view a movie clip or trailer and analyze it in terms of the elements of sound you learned about in the lecture. Follow the steps below.

- Find examples of sound effects, Foley, source music, and the film score.
- Notice places where the dialogue was probably looped and explain why it was probably replaced.
- Comment on the overall quality of the soundtrack and how well it works with the film. Use the vocabulary from Part Four.

2 Present your clip and your group's analysis to the class or another group.

TOEFL® Practice: Synthesizing Listening, Reading, and Speaking

1 Read the passage, which includes descriptions of Foley and sound effects.

> Let's say in a scene the actor grabs his gun, walks to his motorcycle, starts it up and drives away.
>
> A Foley artist would recreate the sounds of the leather jacket and jeans as the actor walks, footsteps (heavy cowboy boots!), the gun pickup and handling, handlebar grab and bike moves, and maybe some key sounds as he puts them in the lock.
>
> The sound effects editor would create the roar of the motorcycle engine starting and driving away, a tire squeal and background ambiances (birds, wind, etc.).
>
> Source: Philip Rodrigues Singer, M.P.S.E., "The Art of Foley," http://www.marblehead.net/foley/index.html
> Used by permission of Philip Rodrigues Singer, M.P.S.E.

2 Review your lecture notes. Then use the information from both the lecture and the reading above to prepare a one-minute oral presentation on the following topic:

- Define *sound effects* and *Foley*. Use examples to explain how these processes are different and how they work together to produce a realistic film soundtrack.

STUDENT A: TELEPHONE RECORDING 1

Name and location of theater: Metroplex 4, 8700 La Palma Blvd.

Theater number: 1

Film: The Da Vinci Code

Show times: 11:00 A.M., 1:45, 4.30, 7:20, 10:10

Running time: 148 minutes

Rating: PG13

Student price: $7.50

Parking information: Behind the theater on Orange St.

Parking cost: $5 Friday through Sunday night; $3 all other times.

STUDENT B: TELEPHONE RECORDING 2

Name and location of theater: Downtown Cineplex, 1842 Western Ave.

Theater number: 3

Film: Friends With Money

Show times: 11:40 A.M., 1:55, 4:45, 7:50, 10:15

Running time: 88 minutes

Rating: R

Student price: $8.50

Parking information: Free parking with theater validation

APPENDIX 1 MASTER VOCABULARY LIST

Items with an asterisk are from the Academic Word List.[1]

CHAPTER 1: TURNING POINTS

(be) on the wrong track
*adjust, *adjustment
adolescence
*anticipate
anxiety
*benefits
bizarre
change directions
changes (one's) mind
come about
come into *contact
    (with)
compromise (n.)
debt
downside
*emerging
entry-level jobs
euphoric
*factor
get your act together
give notice (at work)
go in a different
    direction
in retrospect
judgmental
land on one's feet
make (reach) a decision
make up (one's) mind
*minimize
out of the blue
overreact
put (something) in a
    different *perspective
regret
regroup
*rigid
severe
skills set
stage
start out

stunned
support system
supportive
switch gears
symptoms
turning point
twenty-somethings

CHAPTER 2: LEARNING A NEW LANGUAGE

'zine
*accommodate,
    *accommodation
blog
brainstorm
carjacking
*comprehensive
*comprehensively
easier said than done
elective
endangered species
fit in with (one's) peers
flash cards
fridge
have an ear for
idiomatic
*immigrant
in the habit of
*intensive (program)
metrosexual
motel
*motivation
on the fence
*option
personal trainer
pet peeve
pick up (a language)
rehearse
session
smog
tailored to
under siege
*violation
Y2K
Yuppy

CHAPTER 3: IN THE MONEY

*accumulate
ATM card
*automatic *transfer
balance
bankruptcy
brand-new
checking account
coupons
cut corners
cut down (on)
debit card
do without
double
extras
garage sale
go broke (informal)
go into debt
*grant(s)
*impact
in debt
interest (n.)
interest rate
itemize
*labor market
*linked account
live within (one's)
    means
make ends meet
*minimum balance
money market
    (account)
opening balance
"plastic" (informal)
revolving balance
savings account
segment
service charge
stick to a budget
student loan(s)

CHAPTER 4: MEMORIES

absentmindedness
bring back (a memory)
describe
elaborate
*enhance
evocative (of something)
extend
*facilitate
*filing system
make it up to (you)
*method
mind's eye
*modify
(to have something) on
    one's mind
*phase
picture (v.)
*procedure
recall
recode
remind (someone) of
    (something)
scatterbrain (informal)
*sequence
slip (one's) mind
stages
system
take (someone) back
*target word
(It's not) the end of the
    world (informal)
*transform
*transport (someone)
    back
*trigger (a memory or
    association)
*visualize

(continued)

[1]The Academic Word List was developed by Averil Coxhead at Victoria University of Wellington, New Zealand. The list contains 570 word families which were selected for their frequency and usefulness in academic discourse. For more information, see http://www.vuw.ac.nz.lals/research/awl/awlinfo.html.

CHAPTER 5: BODY TRENDS

account for
all in all
*analyze (*data)
body building
boost one's self esteem
bulked up
bump (n.)
*conduct (a poll,
    *survey, or study)
demographic
    information
disorder(s)
*distorted
dot comers
elective surgery
fired up
fit in
for a change
for one thing . . . for
    another (thing) . . .
get ahead
get tired of (something
    or someone)
give (someone) a hard
    time
in short
not in great shape
on (one's) own
on the whole
regret
run (something) by
    (someone)
self esteem
slim
steroid abuse
The (hand)writing is on
    the wall.
think (something)
    through
washed out
with respect to

CHAPTER 6: DISCOVERIES

ancestor(s)
appraise
as sharp as a tack
claim (n.)
*coincidence
come out of the
    woodwork
*commodities

conducive
*detective
*distinctive
drop in the bucket
fake
*finance
*funding
genealogy
give / take *credit (to
    someone)
Google (someone) (v.)
    (informal)
gut feeling
habitable
(someone's) head is
    spinning
high school reunion
initials
*initiate
*investment *grade
kidnap
legacy resist
microbe
mineral
mission
obsession
run of the mill
sapphire
set foot
*site
take into account

CHAPTER 7: LAW AND ORDER

aboriginal
accelerate
*approach
(be) arrested
assault (n., v.)
capital
case
(be) charged with (a
    crime)
competitor
*comprise
crosswalk
curb
Death Row
defense (attorney)
deliberation (room)
*detective
disorganization
empowerment

end up
*erode
*erosion
*evidence
feel sorry for (someone)
foreman
*generate
guilty
hit and run accident
homogeneous
infuriate
*investigate /
    *investigation
judge
jury, jury duty
keep (someone) away
    from (somewhere)
make (of a car)
manifestation
menacing
*migration
*norms
ordinance
*perspective
property
prosecutor
resist arrest
social *construct
sociologist
speed (v.)
suspect
sweep under the rug
threaten
testify
trial
*violation
witness

CHAPTER 8: LIGHTS, CAMERA, ACTION!

(have) the time of one's
    life
(movie) set
a short (n.)
a thriller
ambient
at the end of the day
bargain matinee
be in the right place at
    the right time
broad (humor)
cast
*coherent

*component
corrupt
eccentric, eccentricity
*edit/*editor
*element
fall apart
flop (n., v.)
genres
grating
grit
gritty
*guaranteed
iffy (informal)
in synch
*inconsistent
intern
juggle
late show
mishandled
miss out on
miss the boat (informal)
multitasking
put all (one's) eggs in
    one basket
Q and A
rated (G, PG-13, R)
repetitive
running time
screen (v.)
scrubbed
second rate
shoot (a film)
showtime
soundtrack
sterile
subtitles
swear word
take a chance (on)
take a shot (at)
*topical
unbearable
unendurable

APPENDIX 2 COMMON ABBREVIATIONS AND SYMBOLS USED IN NOTE-TAKING

Abbreviations		Symbols	
a.m.	morning	&	and
ch.	chapter	± or ~	approximately
cm	centimeter	@	at
e.g.	example	A → B	A causes or leads to B
ex.	example	↓	decreasing, going down
K	thousand	$	dollars
lb	pound	=	equal to, the same as (Use for all forms of be.)
m	meter		
mo.	month	♀	female
Mr.	title used for all men	↑	increasing, growing
Ms.	title used for all women	>	larger than, more than
Mrs.	title used for married women	−	less than, take away, minus
no.	number	♂	male
p. or pp.	page / pages	+	more, and
etc.	etcetera, and so on	≠	not the same as, different
ft.	feet	#	number
i.e.	that is, in other words	%	percent
kg	kilogram	"	same as above (repeated or used again)
km	kilometer		
pd.	paid	<	smaller than, less than
p.m.	afternoon, evening	?	unclear
re	regarding or concerning		
vs.	versus, against		
wk.	week or work		
w/	with		
w/o	without		
yr.	year		

APPENDIX 3 SUMMARY OF STRESS GUIDELINES

Key
capital letters = stressed syllable or word
lower case = unstressed or weakly stressed syllable or word
italics = reduced form

Guideline	Example
"Content" words—nouns, verbs, adjectives, adverbs—are normally stressed. "Function" words—articles, prepositions, pronouns—are normally unstressed. Many unstressed words are normally reduced.	CAROL SWITCHED *'er* MAJOR from BIOLOGY *ta* HISTORY.
Negative words are normally stressed.	Carol CAN'T SPEAK French. She DOESN'T LIKE fish.
A speaker may choose to stress any syllable or word in a sentence in order to 1. emphasize it or 2. show contrast with what a previous speaker has said.	1. Carol switched her major *ta* HISTORY, not SOCIOLOGY. 2. **A:** When's your birthday? September 8th? **B:** NO, it's on September NINTH.
Words or phrases that are normally reduced are not reduced if a speaker chooses to stress them.	Carol switched her major TO history, not FROM history.
Longer sentences are normally divided into short phrases called "thought groups." Every thought group has at least one stressed word. If there is more than one, the *last* content word normally has the strongest stress.	My best friend CAROL / DECIDED *ta* SWITCH *'er* MAJOR / from BIOLOGY *ta* HISTORY / because she wanted *ta* be a MINISTER.
Adverbs ending in *–ly* are usually stressed at the end of a thought group or sentence.	Carol switched her major very SUDDENLY.
Adverbs that tell *where* (e.g., here, there) or *when* (e.g., today, this morning) are normally unstressed at the end of a thought group or sentence.	CAROL has a MEETING with *'er* ADVISOR today.

Guideline	Example
In noun compounds (noun + noun combinations), the first word of the phrase is normally stressed.	TURNING point, CREDIT card, BODY building
In adjective + noun phrases, both words are normally stressed.	MAIN POINT, CREDIT RATING, TALL BUILDING
In inseparable phrasal verbs (verb + preposition combinations), the preposition is normally stressed. In three-word phrasal verbs, the first preposition is stressed.	sit DOWN cut BACK on
Separable phrasal verbs can have 1. an unstressed pronoun or 2. a stressed noun between the verb and preposition. They can also have a stressed noun at the end.	1. turn it ON 2. turn THE LIGHT on, turn on THE LIGHT
Adding a suffix can change the stress. You should consult a dictionary if you're not sure where to place the stress in words of two or more syllables.	1. No change in stress: Home—HOMEless; HAPpy—HAPpiness 2. Stress moves to the last syllable: JaPAN—JapanESE QUEStion—questionNAIRE 3. Stress moves to the syllable before the last: eCONomy—ecoNOMic INstant—instantAneous

APPENDIX 4 Sample Outlines for In-Class Lectures

Chapter 1, Part Four, Exercise 6, page 26

<table>
<tr><td></td><td>Psych 10</td><td>March 14</td></tr>
<tr><td></td><td colspan="2" style="text-align:center">**CULTURE SHOCK**</td></tr>
<tr><td>introduction/
review</td><td colspan="2">I. Intro / Review
   Cult. adjust. process:
     At first: euphoric period
     Stay longer: feel angry, upset, overreact = new stage
     = culture shock</td></tr>
<tr><td></td><td colspan="2">II. Culture shock
   A. Def:
     1. Anxiety when rules we know don't work in new cult.
     2. Psych def: "Cognitive dissonance" = discomfort
       when new exper. don't match what we expect.</td></tr>
<tr><td></td><td colspan="2">   B. Symptoms
     1. Physical: headaches, overeating, sleep disord.
     2. Bizarre behav. or fears, cleanliness, shaking hands
       Ex: friend's son thought new country smelled funny
     3. Emotional = personality changes, e.g., anger,
       homesick, no confidence, lonely, depressed</td></tr>
</table>

C. How to ↓ symptoms

    1. Understand cult. shock is normal

    2. Temporary; 3–6 mos.

    3. Be open-minded, flexible, curious, sense of humor

    4. Be self aware

how to prepare
for life in new
culture
(3 suggestions)

D. How to prepare for life in new cult.

    1. Read, talk to people, watch movies

    2. Learn lang.

    3. Dev. support system ahead of time = get names

      of people, orgs. that can help

CHAPTER 2, PART FOUR, EXERCISE 7, PAGE 54

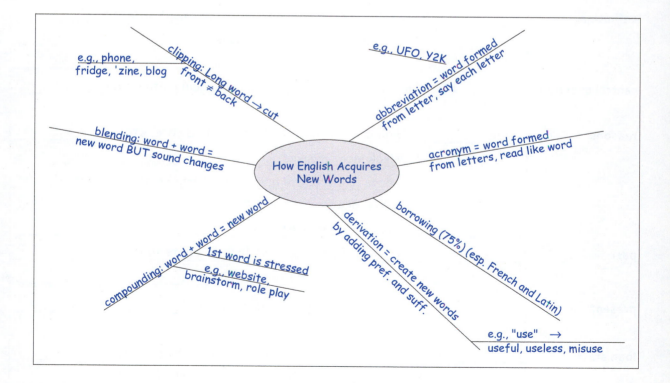

		I. Intro
description	◯	Topic: Credit card debt @ college grads, 25-34
		Recent college grads:
		1st or 2nd job
		maybe newly married
		starting to have kids
		have more debt than any gen. in U.S. history

facts

year
year

II. Facts
- 1992-2001:
  av. cred. card debt ↑ 55%, = $4008 per household
  bankruptcy rate ↑ 19%
- 2001:
  70% had credit cards
  71% had revolv. balance (= make monthly payment)

definition ◯
- Revolv. balance = make monthly payment, interest
  each month → debt increases

central question

III. Central question: Why is this gen. going into debt?

reasons
1. High cost of housing, transp., child care, etc.
2. Weak labor market
   Large % of college grads have temp or pt-time jobs.
   2003: unemp. rate of 10%
3. ↑ student loan debt

past
Past: Sts. used scholarships & grants to pay for
   coll. (don't need to pay back)

present
Present: This gen. pays w/ loans.

loan stats ◯

yr.	% borrowed	av. debt at grad.
1992	42%	$9000
2002	66%	$18,900

result		Diff. financial situation
example		Ex: Typical coll. grad "Caroline"
		Earns $36,000 / yr.
		Takes home $2,058
		Debt: $182 / mo. for loans, $125 for cred. cards
		Doesn't spend on lux.
	○	If unexpected expense? > Use cred. card = more debt
4th reason (2 parts)		4. Easy to get credit + poor money manage. skills

Chapter 4, Part Four, Exercise 6, Pages 108–109

		I. Intro
		A. Previous lect.: Memory works by transforming info
topic		B. This lec.: Memory techniques = mnemonics
		C. Def: Systematic strats. to help us remember
examples	○	e.g. numbers, lists, names, etc.
mnemonic technique		II. Keyword method
		A. History: Dev'd 30 yrs. ago by R. C. Atkinson
		B. Purpose: learn vocab in foreign lang.
		C. Ex: *kaposzta* (Hungarian = cabbage)
		III. Steps
1st step 3 characteristics	○	A. Choose key word
		1. Charac. of good key word
		a. word you know well
		b. sounds like target word
		c. easy to visualize, e.g. concrete noun or verb
		2. Ex: kaposzta →cop

(continued)

2nd step		B. Create mental image
		1. contains key word + target meaning, i.e. cop + cabbage
		2. interacting
		3. best if moving, colorful, exaggerated, silly
		4. Ex: cop w/ cabbage head
3rd step		C. Focus on image to fix in memory
how to study		IV. How to study for test
		A. Ex: kaposzta → cop (key word) → cabbage
		B. "Cop" is bridge from kaposzta to cabbage
	◯	
conclusion		V. Conclusion
		A. Research shows sts. who use keyword method remember
		vocab > sts. who don't
		B. Mnemon. not "magic." Still have to study.

CHAPTER 5, PART FOUR, EXERCISE 5, PAGES 134–135

		I. Intro
		A. Previous topic: Body image disorders in women
topic	◯	B. This lec. topic: Body image disord. in men
		1. 1-2% of Western men have it
		2. Expressed as:
		a. obsession w/ bodybuilding
		b. abuse of steroids
		3. Contrast: East Asian cultures: (a) + (b) rare
new study		II. New study
where research		A. At McLean Hosp., Boston
question		B. Question: Why cult. diff. exists;
subjects		C. Subjects = College men in U.S., France, Austria

method		III. Method
		A. showed pics. of men w/ diff. levels of muscle
	○	B. Asked subs to choose 4 images =
		1. their body
		2. average body (their culture)
		3. ideal body
		4. body women prefer
		C. Also asked women to choose ideal body
		D. Repeated proced. w/ subs from Taiwan
		E. Analyzed data for sim. and diff.
results		IV. Results: 2 sig. diffs.
		A. Ideal body image
		1. West. men said ideal body = 13 kg > their weight
		2. Taiwan. men: only 2 kg >
interpretation		West. men dissatisfied w/ body, Taiw. men satisfied
	○	B. Body women preferred
		1. West. men said: 30 lb (14 kg) more musc. than theirs
		BUT women picked aver. body, no musc.
		2. Taiw. men said: aver. body, like theirs
		Taiw. women picked same
conclusion		C. Findings suggest: West. men have distorted view of ideal body.
		Taiwanese men don't.
discussion		V. Why? 3 hypotheses
1st hypothesis		A. Def. of masc.
		1. West. cult. use muscles to measure masc.
		2. Chinese use intellect, character.
2nd hypothesis		B. Media influence
		1. More images of undressed, musc. men in West than
		2. Taiwan → affect West. idea of ideal body
3rd hypothesis		C. Trad. male roles changing
	○	1. West: More women work → men use muscles for self esteem
		2. Taiwan: More men still in trad. role of breadwinner →
		more secure

topic

4 facts

| | I. Topic: Discoveries of Christopher Columbus |

I. Topic: Discoveries of Christopher Columbus

    Italian explorer and trader

    born 1451

    1492: sailed west to try to reach Asia

    landed in Carib, believed = India

II. Americans give C. credit for:

2 discoveries

    disc. America

    proving earth is round

III. Both beliefs = false

    A. C. did not disc. America

1st assertion

proof

        1. Proof

          • 20,000 yrs ago Asia + No. Amer. connected by land

          • 1st inhab. arrived here from Asia at that time

          • DNA evidence → these people = ancestors of all

            Amer. tribes

        2. C. not even 1st European to reach Amer.

          • 1st = Scandinavian explorer, Leif Ericsson,

            landed in no. east Canada 1000AD

        3. C. kept records, showed he never set foot in no.Amer.

          • 4 voyages: 1492, 1493, 1498, and 1502

          • Closest to Amer. = Bahamas

    B. C. did not prove earth = round

2nd assertion

proof

        1. Greeks knew 2000 yrs. ago

        2. 1492 Euros knew

        3. No doubt C. knew

3 positive accomplishments		IV. What did C. accomplish?
		A. Estab. cult. & econ. link between Euro & Amer.
	◯	B. Initiate trade
		C. Bring Christianity to Amer.
result		D. These accomps → Amer. consider C. great hero
3 negative accomplishments		V. C.'s arrival disastrous for native Amer.
		A. Started slavery as way to repay Spanish king/queen
		for financing voyage
		B. Captured natives & forced them to work in mines
		& plantations; killed those who resisted
	◯	After 4 yrs., 1/3 of native pop. killed or exported
		C. Brought disease, esp. smallpox → killed 1000s
conclusion		VI. Many people today say this is C.'s true legacy.

CHAPTER 7, PART FOUR, EXERCISE 6, PAGES 189–190

topic		**TWO CAUSES OF CRIME**
1st theory		I. Structural-functionist perspective
causes of crime	◯	A. ↑ crime result of
		• social disorg.
		• loss of shared values & norms
		• erosion of social control
origin of theory		B. Based on ideas of Thomas Merton, sociologist
		C. If theory is correct → crime will occur when
		there's rapid social change, e.g.,
examples of social change		• immigration
		• industrialization
		• increased poverty

(continued)

example–country	D. Canada
where is crime? reason	• murders < in east than in west
	• east: more settled, people share sim. cult. →
	less crime
	• west: still migration, so less organized, less
	shared values → more crime
	• same in U.S.
other countries	E. Other countries
examples	• homogeneous, e.g. Japan, Korea → less crime
	• soc. changing rapidly, e.g. So. Africa → more crime
1st theory – conclusion	F. Struc-func = Good theory for understanding
	causes of crime.
2nd theory	II. Conflict theory
origin	A. Based on ideas of Karl Marx
cause of crime	B. Conflict between social classes ↑ crime, i.e., crime →
	inequality
	C. Laws created by people w/ power → protect their interests
examples	• e.g., property rights—help rich, not poor
	• wealthy people influence legal system, get best
	legal advice
	D. Law treats diff. classes differently
examples	• Canada: 12% of prison pop. = aboriginals, but
	abor = 4% of pop.
	• U.S. 41% of prisoners on Death Row = black;
	blacks = 12% of pop.
2nd theory– conclusion	E. Conflict theory can help to explain crime.

topic	Post-production sound = sound for film, TV, commercials, and other media.
	3 elements of post-prod. sound:
	• dialogue and looping or ADR
	• sound effects and foley
	• music composition and music editorial
1st element production sound	I. Dialogue & ADR
	A. Production sound
definition	1. On set, microphones capture sound = "production" sound e.g. actors speaking, ambient sounds
	2. Problem: prod. sound inconsistent
	3. Post prod. takes prod sound and edits, smoothes it out
ADR	B. ADR
	1. Sometimes things in prod. soundtrack can't be saved, e.g. there are loud sounds, swear word, don't like how actor said a line
definition	2. In those cases actors need to go into studio & replace dialogue = ADR = automated dialogue replacement = looping
definition	3. Group ADR = group looping: group of actors re-record. perf
	4. Reason: on set background actors must be silent; need to go back and fill in later

(continued)

2nd element		II. Sound effects & Foley
		A. Sound effects = any sound ↑ dialogue
	○	1. e.g., gunshot, car, dog barking
		2. physically cut / edit them into scenes
		B. Foley = unique way of recording sound
		1. watch picture & foley artists perform sounds
		2. act out characters' movements
		3. e.g., clothes, footsteps, water (repetitive, hard
		to edit one sound at a time)
		4. foley stage = audio environment w/ special
		floor, props
		5. process named after man named Foley
3rd element		III. Music
	○	A. Music composition
		1. composer watches video, dialogue, etc.
		2. composes music
		3. conducts orchestra & records in synch
		w/ picture
		4. can use synthesizers, electronic keyboards,
		or both
		B. Source music
		1. def: something in scene, not background
		2. e.g., music in bar, song on radio
final step		IV. Final step: Go to re-recording or "mixing" stage & mix
	○	dialogue, music, sound effects into final soundtrack
conclusion		V. Sound in film or TV show is almost 100% replaced.

AUDIOSCRIPT

CHAPTER 1: TURNING POINTS

Part One: In Person

Page 2, B. Listening

Exercise 1

Scott: So, uh, what's your major, Carol?

Carol: Well, it's religious studies right now, but I started out as pre-med.

S: Pre-med! Wow, that's quite a switch. Why did you change your mind?

C: Well, in the beginning, because I was always good at math and science and coming from an Asian family, there was always an expectation that I'd go to med school.

S: Umm…

C: And so when I started college, I, I took an amazingly heavy load of, of, of science courses to prepare for med school, but after a while, I just knew that I was on the wrong track.

S: What do you mean?

C: Well, in retrospect, I've always known since age ten that I wanted to be a minister… in essence it was my calling. But when I started college, um, because of the pressure from my family, I never really considered it. But by my third year, by my junior year, I knew that if I didn't change, change directions, I would regret it for the rest of my life.

S: Umm, what did your family say when you told them?

C: Well at first, they weren't… they, they were surprised… they were disappointed… They really wanted me to go to med school. But after a while, I just, they, I kept explaining that this is what I really want to do. And now they're pretty supportive.

S: Good.

C: So tell me, Scott, are there any major turning points in your life?

S: Well, yeah, as a matter of fact, you know um, I started out as a math major, but I just realized I didn't want to spend the rest of my life dealing with formulas and abstract theories and numbers, so… I really wanted to do something where I was helping people. And,

uh I was interested in health sciences. So I started taking pre-med classes, and decided that I would continue…

C: Oh, so, so you're in med school right now?

S: Well, no, actually I'm just finishing nursing school this year.

C: Nursing school! My mom's a nurse! And when I visit her there, they're all women. But, I mean, how did that come about for you?

S: Well, you know, actually, I've just always known that I wanted family and kids. So, I wanted to spend more time with them. And, uh, it's hard to do if you're a doctor …

C: Yeah.

S: So nursing school was a compromise, but I was happy about it because I can have my career in medicine but also have more of my own free time.

C: Oh, well, do you ever think, you know, if you look back in five years, that, you know, you, you, you'll realize that you made a mistake?

S: Um, I doubt it, but, you know, if I change my mind I can go back to school or switch gears, or go into a different direction altogether.

Page 2, Exercise 2. Repeat the recording from Exercise 1.

Page 4, Exercise 4

Group 1

changed, considered, happened, planned, realized

Group 2

passed, stopped, switched

Group 3

decided, interested, needed, started, wanted

Part Two: On the Phone

Page 9, B. Listening

Exercise 1

Shannon: Hello?

Tara: Hi. It's me. Where are you?

S: I'm on my way to work. But traffic's pretty slow. Where've you been all week?

T: Oh, you know. I've been busy with work and the kids and everything...

S: Yeah, I know. So what's... so what's up?

T: Well, I've got news.

S: Good news or bad news?

T: Well, sort of both.

S: Oh?

T: Yeah. Well, remember the business trip I took last month to Atlanta?

S: Well sure, your kids had a ball with us while you and David were gone...

T: Right, yeah. OK. So when I was there they had me sit in on one of their business meetings with all the regional VPs...

S: Yeah...

T: ...and um, and they were talking about creating another VP position...

S: Yeah...

T: and so yesterday, I was just in my office and I got this call out of the blue from the president and he offered me the job.

S: Oh my gosh! Tara! That's fabulous! Were— Were you surprised?

T: Oh, I was totally surprised. I was shocked. I, I didn't know what to say. It was just, the last thing I ever expected.

S: That's so awesome. I mean you've worked so hard for all these years and you're so talented...

T: Yeah well wait, but there's, you know there's more.

S: More?

T: Yeah, there's a real downside to this.

S: Uh oh.

T: OK. Well, I don't even know how to tell you this but the thing is, we have to move to Atlanta.

S: Atlanta.

T: Yeah.

S: Wow. Wow. That puts things in a different perspective.

T: Yeah, I know.

S: Well, you're not going to take it, are you?

T: Well, you know David and I've been talking about it, you know ever since I got the call, and, um, I don't know how to tell you this but I, I think I am going to have to take it.

S: You... You're kidding. Move across country? Leave all your friends and family? For a job?

T: Well it's not just "a" job, Shannon. It's my dream job. You said so yourself.

S: But, but Atlanta? It's so different, it's so far, I mean the food, the climate... Do they even speak English there?

T: Very funny. Well, you know, I think the fact that it's so different, even though it's hard for me to leave, I think that's actually one of the attractions for me 'cause, you know I've lived here my whole life, I haven't seen anything else. And I'd like to just you know try it for a couple of years, 'cause we can always move back.

S: I suppose. Wow. Well it sounds like your mind is really made up.

T: Nyeah, it, I guess, yeah.

S: So when is this big move?

T: Well, they want me to start in a month. So, I have to give notice at work, and, um, David and the kids can't pick up and move that quickly so they'll stay behind and, um, probably come out in the summer.

S: Wow. I need some time to digest this. I'm just stunned... Look, traffic's picking up, I'd better go. Can you, can you meet me for lunch?

T: Oh yeah, that would be great.

S: OK. I'll swing by your office around noon.

T: OK, thanks. See you then.

S: All right. See you.

Page 10, Exercise 2. Repeat the recording from Exercise 1.

Page 12, Exercise 4. Repeat the recording from Exercise 1.

Page 12, Exercise 6

1. I've been busy with work and the kids and everything...

2. ...I got this call out of the blue from the president and he offered me the job.

3. ...you've worked so hard for all these years and you're so talented...

4. ...the thing is, we have to move to Atlanta.

5. Well, you're not going to take it, are you?

Page 12, Exercise 7

1. Well, you know David and I have been talking about it...

2. Well, it's not just a job, Shannon. It's my dream job.

3. I think I am going to have to take it.

4. It's so different, it's so far, I mean the food, the climate...

5. I'd like to just, you know, try it for a couple of years because we can always move back.

Part Three: On the Air

Page 16, B. Listening

Exercise 1

Feldy: This is Talk of the City. I'm Kitty Feldy. Why won't they leave? It's a question many parents are asking these days as more and more often, adult children are moving back home. In fact, there may be more than four million people between ages 25 and 34 who still live at home with Mom and Dad.

Linda Pearlman Gordon and Susan Morris Schaeffer are the authors of Mom, Can I Move Back in with You? A Survival Guide for Parents of Twenty-Somethings. Ladies, thanks for joining us.

Gordon &
Shaeffer: Hi Kitty.

F: Why do kids... I mean economics would seem to be the biggest factor. Is that the biggest factor of why kids move back in with their parents?

G/S: It's the biggest factor, but there's also a sociological factor that is important. Adolescence is, is really longer nowadays, and it's taking longer for the um, emerging adult to really feel adult.

F: That seems like an excuse for bad parenting to me.

G/S: No, it's actually not an excuse for bad parenting. What's happened is our society is changing, and while we do parent differently than the generation of parents before us, it's not bad parenting.

F: Now I remember my mother saying when I hit the big age of 23, that it was time, and I had to have an apartment in the next six weeks or I was going to find my stuff out on the front sidewalk. Was that just a more severe parenting style?

G/S: It was a different time. I mean you mentioned at the beginning, which is a very good point, that economically you're looking at a group over the last three years who have the highest unemployment, they have entry level jobs with few benefits, they're 45 percent of the uninsured population, and they're coming out of college with at least 20,000 dollars' worth of debt. So we think that it's really fiscally responsible for some of the kids to move back in for a period of time in order for them to regroup and be able to build a resume and build a skill set so that they can land on their feet again.

F: So what's the recommended age for you to have parents give that speech of, uh, get your act together or move out?

G/S: It's really... what we're finding and from the parents that we spoke to, what we're noticing is that whether the children are living at home or not, that this speech that you refer to and helping your child to become more adult is something that you have to do with every one of your twenty-somethings. And there isn't a magic moment. There's no magical moment when your child becomes adult.

Page 17, Exercise 2. Repeat the recording from Exercise 1.

Page 18, Exercise 4

1. There may be more than four million people between ages 25 and 34 who still live at home with Mom and Dad.

2. That seems like an excuse for bad parenting to me.

3. No, it's actually not an excuse for bad parenting.

4. And they're coming out of college with at least 20,000 dollars' worth of debt.

5. ...and helping your child to become more adult is something you have to do with every one of your twenty-somethings.

Part Four: In Class

Exercise 1

All right, are we ready to go here? OK. We've been talking about the process of cultural adjustment, and we've seen that when people first come into contact with a new culture, there is this euphoric period of a month or so where everything is new and exciting and interesting.

But if someone stays in the new culture for longer than just a short visit, sooner or later the realities of living in the new culture start to sink in, and quite unexpectedly people may find themselves feeling angry or upset, or they might overreact to situations that they really didn't have any trouble handling when they were "back home." So this shift in attitude and behavior is a pretty clear signal that a person is in a new stage of the cultural adjustment process, that's the stage we call culture shock. And that's what I'm going to talk about right now.

So to start off, what is culture shock? It's that feeling of anxiety that overtakes you when you realize that the rules that you thought you knew about how to get things done don't seem to work in the new culture. In psychological terms this is known as cognitive dissonance; cognitive dissonance, which is defined as the sense of discomfort that we feel when our new experiences don't match what we already know or expect.

So... this dissonance or discomfort can be expressed in all kinds of strange and unexpected symptoms. Some people develop physical symptoms such as headaches, or over- uh huh, overeating, sleep disorders. Other people develop kind of bizarre behaviors or fears, like maybe they worry a lot about cleanliness, or they're afraid of shaking hands with people in the new culture. I have a friend who took his family to live overseas for a year and his son kept complaining that the air smelled funny. That's a little weird.

So... OK, then there are the emotional symptoms of culture shock... personality changes... irritation, anger, homesickness, loss of confidence, loneliness, depression... you know, you wake up in the morning and feel like another person is suddenly living inside your body. This is culture shock.

But as terrible as all of that sounds, there are things that people can do to avoid... well not, not avoid but you can minimize the symptoms. So, uh, first of all it's important to recognize that culture shock is normal; OK, everyone can relax, and nearly everyone living in a new culture goes through culture shock to a greater or a lesser degree. And, uh, it's also helpful to know that it's temporary. Culture shock typically lasts three to six months and then most people start to adjust and feel better.

Now a third thing that can help is for people to understand that... psychological factors that make some people suffer from culture shock more than others. For example, research has demonstrated that people who are open-minded, flexible, curious about new things, uh, people who have a good sense of humor, are less affected by culture shock than people who are more kind of rigid and judgmental. Uh, research also shows that people who are more self-aware, who understand themselves in situations, they understand their own strengths and weaknesses, and they're obviously going to be able to anticipate the effects of culture shock and prepare for them better.

But even if you're not the most flexible person in the world, there are a few things that you can do to prepare yourself for the experience of living in a new culture. First of all, try to learn as much as you can about the new culture before you get on the plane. Read, talk to people, watch movies, and of course try to learn a little bit of the language before you go so you're not totally helpless when you arrive. And experts also suggest trying to develop a support system ahead of time... so, in other words getting the names of people and organizations that you can turn to if you need help and then contact them to introduce yourself as soon as you arrive in the new culture.

So to, to sum things up, as I said before, everyone experiences culture shock, some people worse than others, but there are some steps you can take to minimize the cognitive dissonance when you arrive in the new culture and reduce the shock of culture shock.

Page 23, B. Listening and Note-Taking

Exercise 2

1. So this shift in attitude and behavior is a pretty clear signal that a person is in a new stage of the cultural adjustment process, that's the stage we call culture shock. And that's what I'm going to talk about right now.

2. So to start off, what is culture shock?

3. So... this dissonance or discomfort can be expressed in all kinds of strange and unexpected symptoms.

4. Now a third thing that can help is for people to understand that... psychological factors that make some people suffer from culture shock more than others.

5. So to, to sum things up, as I said before, everyone experiences culture shock...

Page 25. Exercise 6. Repeat the recording from Exercise 1.

CHAPTER 2: LEARNING A NEW LANGUAGE

Part One: In Person

Page 32, B. Listening

Exercise 1

Judy: I think one of the key things for me was motivation. I really wanted to learn the language well. And I had to learn the language well because I was a, an immigrant, and uh I needed to learn the language because I couldn't go back to the country I had come from. So I wanted to fit in with my peers, and um really be part of this new society.

Andrew: Uh yeah, I was basically in situations where I had to learn to speak Japanese.

J: Oh! So you, too.

A: Yeah, um, I worked in Japan, and I never really studied Japanese, I never took classes, I don't know the grammar, I can't really read and write. Um, but I basically found myself in situations where I had to speak it, and if you have to speak it, you pick it up usually.

J: Yeah, but, I mean, "pick it up" is, you know that's easier said than done. Did you, how did you learn all that new vocabulary and...

A: Well... [J: ... sentence structure...] well, probably the, actually probably the biggest factor was that, um but I had a girlfriend from Japan, and...

J: Oh that helps.

A: Yeah, pretty well, it helps in some ways. Um... And so, um, I didn't do any formal training or any formal studies, but it was a matter of every day hearing her speak and I'd pick up several new words every day. I wouldn't take notes, I wouldn't have a study session, it would just be an organic process...

J: Hmm, yeah...

A: ...during the course of our communication.

J: Oh, that's nice. Well I did take classes at the beginning.

A: Um-hmm. Where'd you take classes?

J: In high school, actually.

A: Oh wow.

J: 'Cause I was 17.

A: Um hmm.

J: And so I took English as a second language classes, and um I was motivated and I was a pretty good student. I made flash cards to remember vocabulary. I um, copied my friends' pronunciation, I mean the native speakers, um, that I was in contact with... I really wanted to sound like them.

A: I think... I really thought about this and I think probably the biggest thing that helped me, that people never really talk about or they don't really talk about in textbooks is the fact that I started thinking in Japanese. So you know I'd have a very limited knowledge of Japanese, and I did this too when I was studying French in high school. I did it naturally. I didn't plan to, but I would naturally go about my day, and I'd start talking to myself in Japanese. Like, I'll say these words in English but it'd be like "OK let's see, it's 2:30, I've got to, OK, I've got to be at the store at 3:30, and then, wait a second, OK, do I turn left here?" I would be saying that to myself internally in Japanese, and that's what made it so smooth because I was just in the habit of using it all the time.

J: ...Yeah, um, that's, that's a little bit similar to something I did. I would rehearse...

A: A-ha.

J: ...ahead of time if I knew the situation I was going to be in. I would prepare and rehearse, sometimes aloud, to hear myself what it was going to sound like. And, um, so when I was in the actual situation I had the vocabulary, I had the delivery, and I had the confidence.

A: That's interesting. Yeah. Um, I didn't do something so formal, but again, with the thinking patterns in another language, I mean I have a habit of just kind of you know singing songs or humming songs to myself during the day. And even though my ability at first was not very high, let's say, in Japanese, um, I would just naturally start singing the same song and to the best of my ability translate the words to Japanese, or to French before that or to whatever language. And it would be a terrible translation, but, at first, but uh the point is that, um, you know in all these facets, in all these aspects of daily activity, um, you'd be using the foreign language, um, and just applying it daily in so many ways. In other words, what I'm trying to get at, is that I think a lot of people just apply it in one particular case. They have to speak, they have to listen, that's it. But you can really use it much more comprehensively throughout the day.

Page 32, Exercise 2

Repeat the recording from Exercise 1.

Page 33, Exercise 4

Example: I think one of the key things for me was motivation... I really wanted to learn the language well.

Judy: And I had to learn the language well because I was a, an immigrant, and uh I needed to learn the language because I couldn't go back to the country I had come from.

Andrew: But, uh, I basically found myself in situations where I had to speak it, and if you have to speak it, you pick it up usually. And so, um, I

didn't do any formal training or any formal studies, but it was a matter of every day hearing her speak and I'd pick up several new words every day. I wouldn't take notes, I wouldn't have a study session, it would just be an organic process.

J: Yeah, I would rehearse... [A: A-ha.] ahead of time if I knew the situation I was going to be in. And, um, so when I was in the actual situation I had the vocabulary, I had the delivery, and I had the confidence.

Page 34, Exercise 6

1. ...I mean I have a habit of just kind of you know singing songs or humming songs to myself during the day. And even though my ability at first was not very high, let's say, in Japanese, I would just naturally start singing the same song and to the best of my ability translate the words to Japanese or to French before that or to whatever language. And it would be a terrible translation, but, at first, but uh the point is that, um, you know, in all these facets, in all these aspects of daily activity, um, you'd be using the foreign language, um, and just applying it daily in so many ways.

2. In other words, what I'm trying to get at, is that I think a lot of people just apply it in one particular case. They have to speak, they have to listen, that's it. But you can really use it much more comprehensively throughout the day.

Page 34, Exercise 7. Repeat the recording from Exercise 1.

Part Two: On the Phone
Page 38, B. Listening

Exercise 1

Call 1

Worker: Good morning, English Language Center.

Caller: Uh, hi. I'm calling to get some information about your school.

W: OK, great, I can help you with that.

C: OK, well, I have a nephew, who's from Hungary, and he's coming here for, um, about six to eight weeks.

W: Um-hmm.

C: And he's coming here on February 5th. And he has some business to take care of, but he would also like to do some work on his English while he's here. So I just want to find out, um, if you can accommodate him with that schedule and, you know, what the program is and what it costs and stuff like that.

W: Well, we basically have three different programs. We have an intensive English program, which is our most comprehensive. That covers 30 lessons per week. OK?

C: Thirty lessons meaning... 30 hours?

W: Yes, 30 hours, that's it exactly. That covers a grammar class, and a conversation and listening skills class, and a reading and writing class in the afternoon...

C: Oh, OK.

W: ...all the skills that he needs basically.

C: A-ha.

W: And the cost for that is 1150 dollars for a four-week session.

C: Um, that sounds pretty reasonable, for 30 hours a week.

W: We think so. It's a good value. I should also tell you that we keep a maximum number of students of 12 in all of our classes, and presently our average is between 8 and 9, so the students get a lot of individual attention.

C: Oh, that sounds great.

W: Then, the next program is a semi-intensive program which is 24 lessons per week. Instead of Monday through Friday, it's only Tuesday through Thursday for the afternoon classes.

C: Oh that's good 'cause like I said, he has business here.

W: Yeah well, that's great, and this one is 995 for the four-week session.

C: Oh, OK, I see.

W: The third option is the half-day program, and that's 20 lessons per week. This one, there's no classes at all in the afternoon. It's 895 dollars for the four-week session, students are in class from 9 in the morning 'til 12:45 and then they're free in the afternoon.

C: Ah, I see, that sounds really flexible. Now, um, he needs English mainly for his work. He's a businessman. Does that... do you have like special classes for business?

W: Of, of course. That's, we have what we call elective courses that are tailored to people that have specialized needs such as business people. Specifically for business people because we get a lot of requests for that.

C: Elective classes... um, do you mean they get to choose what they want?

W: They get to choose, that's right, but not in the half-day program because the electives are only offered in the afternoons.

C: Oh, OK, I see. That's interesting. Um, now I assume you have a website, and that has more information about the exact, specific classes?

W: Yes, we do, it's a very comprehensive website. I know I've given you a lot of information. If you weren't able to, to write it all down, it's on the website and there are also application forms that you can download... as well.

C: All right, I will definitely check that out, and I'll get in touch with my nephew, and, um, it's going to depend pretty much on his schedule, I think, and then I'll get back to you.

W: Well that, well that's great. I encourage you to take a look at the website, and if you have any further questions just give us a call back. My name is Tom.

C: Thank you so much, Tom. My name is Rosemary.

W: Great. Thanks, Rosemary. Talk to you soon.

C: OK, bye.

W: Bye-bye.

Call 2

W: American Language Institute, this is Carl.

C: Hi. I'm calling to get some information about your programs.

W: OK... uh, oh, can I put you on hold for just a second?

C: Yeah, OK.

W: OK, thanks. So, uh, how can I help you?

C: Uh, like I said, I was wondering if you could give me some in... information about your programs.

W: Day or night?

C: Day.

W: OK, basically we have two daytime programs, they're both intensive programs.

C: Intensive meaning...

W: They're full-day programs but there are some differences I can outline for you, and then I can direct you to our website for more information if you'd like.

C: That sounds fine.

W: OK, so first we have our Intensive English for Academic Purposes program, which is a ten-week course, and that's 23 hours per week, 9 to 3 Monday through Thursday and 9 to 12 on Friday, and the cost of that is 2750 for ten weeks.

C: Just a moment, you said sessions run ten weeks?

W: Correct. Our winter session starts on January 3rd.

C: And a person would have to sign up for the entire ten weeks?

W: Normally yes, though sometimes we do have students starting late or leaving early.

C: And is the fee adjusted for that?

W: No, I'm afraid not.

C: Hmm. I don't think that program will work... Uh, this is for my nephew who's arriving on February 5th...

W: And how long will he be here?

C: I'm not sure... maybe eight or ten weeks.

W: Well then let me tell you about our other program... it's called Intensive English for Everyday Communication, and these are four-week sessions, uh, 20 hours per week... and the curriculum focuses on communication, listening and speaking as opposed to reading and writing. Students can choose an emphasis like business English or tourist English...

C: Um, and did you say this program was 20 hours a week?

W: Yes, 20 hours, it's Monday through Thursday from 9 to 3 with no classes on Friday.

C: Oh, that's good, because actually my nephew is coming here mainly for business.

W: OK, so he would have Fridays free.

C: And how large are the classes?

W: In the Everyday Communication program?

C: Uh-huh.

W: We have a maximum of 18, but that's usually just in the summer. Right now there're about 14 students per class.

C: OK, that's pretty clear. Um, how much does this program cost?

W: It's 1400 dollars for four weeks.

C: Hmm, I see. OK. Hmm. Like I said, he's arriving February 5th, so when...

W: Let me check the dates for you... Yeah, we have a session starting January 31st and the next one after that starts on February 28th.

C: Oh, so he would miss the first week.

W: Yes, but I'm sure we could make an accommodation for him.

C: OK, well, I think what I need to do is pass along the information to him and take a look at your website. Um, this is kind of a lot of information for me to take in, you know?

W: Yeah, of course...

C: And so I'll talk to him and see what he wants to do.

W: All right, that's fine. Please give us a call back if you have anymore questions.

C: Um, I will. Thank you for the information.

W: You're welcome. Bye now.

C: Bye-bye.

Page 38, Exercise 2. Repeat the recording from Exercise 1.

Page 39, Exercise 5

1. OK, so first we have our Intensive English for Academic Purposes program, which is a ten-week course, and that's 23 hours per week, 9 to 3 Monday through Thursday and 9 to 12 on Friday, and the cost of that is 2750 for ten weeks.

2. We have an intensive English program, which is our most comprehensive.

3. That covers a grammar class, and a conversation and listening skills class, and a reading and writing class in the afternoon.

4. And the cost for that is 1150 dollars for a four-week session.

5. The third option is the half-day program, and that's 20 lessons per week. This one, there's no classes at all in the afternoon. It's 895 dollars for the four-week session, students are in class from 9 in the morning 'til 12:45 and then they're free in the afternoon.

6. **Caller:** Um, and did you say this program was 20 hours a week?

Worker: Yes, 20 hours, it's Monday through Thursday from 9 to 3 with no classes on Friday.

Page 40, Exercise 7. Repeat the recording from Exercise 1.

Part Three: On the Air

Page 43, B. Listening

Exercise 1

Korva Coleman: And next on the line from Las Osos, California is James White. Hi James.

James: Hello.

K: Welcome.

J: Thank you.

K: What is your language pet peeve, James?

J: Well I described it as the, the death of the adverb, and I may have overstated, but maybe it's only an endangered species, but for example you go past a bakery and you see a sign for "fresh-baked bread." And I often wonder what happened to "freshly-baked" bread. Another example might be, uh, Apple's ads, telling people to "Think smart."

K: Someone has taken all the -lys.

J: Exactly.

K: Richard.

RL: Yeah, the Apple ad I think is "Think different" and it has received a lot of criticism.

J: Right.

RL: OK, this is a little bit on the fence here. Understand first of all that all adverbs don't have to have -ly. And in certain idiomatic situations, even with a choice you often go with what looks like an adjective, it's still an adverb. Korva, I think we say "go slow" rather than "go slowly." I think that's the idiom. Let's go to the "fresh baked." I think it's idiomatic. You go to the florist; do you get fresh-cut flowers or freshly cut flowers?

K: Uh, I get fresh cut.

RL: I see it as fresh cut. And fresh-baked I think is idiomatic. Now I agree that the adverb is under siege. I think it is in danger in things like "He speaks real good" which is a double violation, it should be "really" and it should be "well." I think good for well, "He bats good," "He speaks good," and the "real good," I think that is the near-death of those adverbs and that concerns me. But despite the so-called grammar, you have to have an ear for natural American speech, and often we get the "go slow" and the "fresh-cut flowers."

K: Thank you James.

J: Thank you.

Page 44, Exercise 2. Repeat the recording from Exercise 1.

Page 45, Exercise 5

Example: For example, you go past a bakery and you see a sign for "fresh-baked bread."

1. And I often wonder what happened to freshly baked bread.

2. Yeah, the Apple ad I think is "Think different."

3. This is a little bit on the fence here.

4. Korva, I think we say "go slow" rather than "go slowly."

5. You go to the florist; do you get fresh-cut flowers or freshly-cut flowers?

6. I agree that the adverb is under siege.

Part Four: In Class

Page 52, B. Listening and Note-Taking

Exercise 3

1. Now in English the main mechanism we have for creating new words is a process called derivation.

2. So to explain these terms we have to look at some other processes that English has for coining words.

3. So another way that new words are formed in English is by blending.

4. So to recap, I've listed seven processes by which English acquires new words.

Page 53, Exercise 4

I mean how do we explain words like *blog* or *Y2K* or *SARS* or *website* or *carjacking*, uh *personal trainer* or like *metrosexual*? These words are all pretty common now but they didn't even exist 10 or 15 years ago. So to explain these terms we have to look at some other processes that English has for coining words. One of these is compounding.

When my daughter was little she used to say "stummy," which was obviously a blend of *stomach* and *tummy*. And it's a great example of a blend because it shows how blends often occur organically, by accident, and then some of them become actual real new words and while others don't become words.

Page 54, Exercise 7

OK, so, uh, we've been talking about the origins of English words, where our vocabulary comes from. And we've talked about the way that languages borrow words from each other. In English, for example, 75 percent of our words are imported from other languages, mostly French and Latin.

Um, so a language can acquire new words by borrowing them, but all languages also have ways of coining or creating new words. And so what I want to do today in this talk is to introduce you to some of the linguistic gimmicks, the techniques, that English uses to coin new words.

Now in English the main mechanism we have for creating new words is a process called derivation, which means we create—or we derive—new words from existing ones by adding prefixes or suffixes to them. Uh, so for example, we can take the word, the root "use," u-s-e, and by adding prefixes and suffixes we get *useful, useless, misuse, unusable, abuse,* and so on. So that's an example of derivation.

But derivation isn't the only mechanism for creating new words in English, of course. I mean how do we explain words like *blog* or *Y2K* or

SARS or *website* or *carjacking*, uh *personal trainer* or like *metrosexual*? These words are all pretty common now but they didn't even exist 10 or 15 years ago. So to explain these terms we have to look at some other processes that English has for coining words.

One of these is compounding. OK, so compounds are two words, like two nouns or an adjective and a noun, that we put together to form a new word, such as *website, brainstorm,* or *role play*. Now you notice how each part of the compound retains its original pronunciation, but when we put the words together they form a new meaning. And the word on the right is the one that gives the compound its core meaning, so for example a *race car* is a kind of car, right, but a *car race* is a kind of race. OK? And another feature of compounds which you probably noticed already is that the first word is stressed: *brainstorm, website, carjacking,* and so on.

OK, so another way that new words are formed in English is by blending. Blending is a little similar to compounding because a blend consists of two words that are combined to form a new meaning, just like a compound. But what's different about a blend is that one or both words undergo a sound change. So let me give you a couple of examples so you'll see what I mean. So *smog* is a blend of the words *smoke* and *fog*. You'll notice how the /k/ in *smoke* and the /f/ in *fog* drop out and the remaining sounds are combined into one word. Another example is *motel*. *Motel* is a combination of *motor* and *hotel*. And here's a really cute one. When my daughter was little she used to say "stummy," which was obviously a blend of *stomach* and *tummy*. And it's a great example of, of, of a blend because it shows how blends often occur organically, by accident, and then some of them become actual real new words while others don't become words.

OK, another process for forming new words is called clipping. This is when we take a long word and clip or cut out the front or the back, so for instance *telephone* becomes *phone*, and *refrigerator* becomes *fridge*, uh, or how about the word *'zine*, which is a really popular word nowadays—it's a clipping of *magazine*. And some words come about as a result of both compounding and clipping. A great example of that is *blog*, which started out as a compound of *web* plus *log* and then got shortened or clipped to just *blog*. A lot of the slang you hear is created by compounding and clipping just because these processes are so easy from a linguistic standpoint.

All right. So finally, two other sources of new words that I want to mention are abbreviations and acronyms. An abbreviation is a word that is formed from the names of the letters in a phrase, like *UFO*, *unidentified flying object*. Another example is *Y2K*, which as you probably know stands for *year 2000*. But now an acronym is a little different. In an acronym we form a word by combining the letters of a phrase into a word which we read phonetically. We don't say the names of the letters, in other words, so for example *SARS* is an acronym, it stands for *sudden acquired respiratory syndrome*, which is just too much of a mouthful to say, so we use the acronym instead. Another good example is the word *yuppie*, a *young urban professional*.

OK, so to recap, I've listed seven processes by which English acquires new words: borrowing, deriving, compounding, blending, um clipping, abbreviating, and acronyms. And of course there's more to say about each of these, this is just a quick survey, but what I hope I've done is to enable you to see how inventive and flexible the English language is, and I hope I've stimulated your curiosity to find out more about the origins of your favorite English words.

CHAPTER 3: IN THE MONEY

Part One: In Person

Page 60, B. Listening

Exercise 1

Interviewer: So I understand that you lost your husband at a pretty early age, didn't you.

Mrs. Grant: Yes.

I: And your kids were how old at the time?

MG: My son was 14 and my daughter was 17.

I: Wow. Were you working at the time, or were you a housewife?

MG: I was working. I had a secretarial job in a children's agency, in the adoption department.

I: But that wasn't a high-paying job, was it?

MG: No, it wasn't, especially in the beginning because at the time of my husband's death I'd been working just part-time. Eventually I was promoted and became the executive secretary to the director, but that was years later.

I: Um. So how did you manage?

MG: That's a good question. It was very difficult to manage on my salary and pay a mortgage, maintain the house, the cars, the schools for the kids. We did not have money for extras, you can believe me.

I: Well you must have had some sort of strategy for making ends meet...

MG: I lived within my means. My kids didn't expect extra things. For example, one of my daughter's friends had a cashmere sweater, but my daughter knew, from the outset, that she wasn't ever going to get a cashmere sweater. I did sewing for her, I bought clothes on sale, and both kids had part-time jobs. We never ate in restaurants either.

I: When you say you lived within your means, um, what do you mean by that?

MG: Well, I just never spent more than I had coming in. I had a budget and I stuck to it.

I: A budget?

MG: I'd sit down and itemize what I spent every month. This is what I spent for rent every month, this was for utilities, car expenses, car payments, education, clothing, medical insurance. And then I'd compare that with what I had coming in, and if the expenses were greater than the income, well then if it meant cutting down on things I wanted to do, then that's what I had to do.

I: Did you have to... did you ever have to borrow money?

MG: Oh no. No, I was brought up that you never do that. You know, we never had money growing up, so I was used to cutting corners and doing without, if necessary. That's how it's always been for me.

I: Do you have some kind of financial advice that you would give to young people today who are, uh, just starting out now?

MG: For me, the most important thing is that you put money away into a retirement plan. And when I hear about people with their credit cards, how they go overboard, 20,000 dollars, 25,000 dollars in debt, well I don't spend what I can't pay for. I've never had to pay interest on a credit card.

I: That's great. Do you have any other tips or suggestions?

MG: Well there's lots of little things people can do to save money. My kids and I used to go to garage sales... We'd find all kinds of treasures, designer clothes, practically brand-new.

I: Those are such great ideas, is there anything else you could tell us?

MG: Well, don't pay for your lunch. Bring it from home. Take the bus or walk whenever you can. Let's see... don't go grocery shopping when you're hungry... and I'm sure I have saved hundreds if not thousands of dollars by using coupons. And one more thing, always ask for a discount wherever you go. You'd be surprised how much you can save.

I: That's great.

Page 60, Exercise 2. Repeat the recording from Exercise 1.

Page 61, Exercise 4

1.   **Man:** Guess what! I got a raise at work!

    Woman: Great! The extra money will help us make ends meet so we don't have to borrow anymore money from my parents.

2.   **Son:** Hey Dad. Can I borrow 100 dollars for some concert tickets?

    Father: No you can't, Son. It's time you learn how to live within your means.

3. **Woman 1:** Do you find it difficult to stick to a budget?

    Woman 2: Not really. It's easy as long as I pay for everything with cash and don't use credit cards.

4.   **Man 1:** What's the first step in making a budget?

    Man 2: Itemize your expenses. Make a list of every single thing you buy for one month.

5. **Woman:** Look at this water bill! It's the biggest we've ever had!

    Man: I guess it's time to cut down on our water use.

6. **Woman:** How are we going to pay for a new car?

    Man: Don't worry, we'll find a way. We'll just have to cut corners for a while.

7. **Woman 1:** How are you managing since George lost his job?

    Woman 2: Well, we're living off of my salary and we're doing without extras like vacations.

Page 63, Exercise 7

1. Have you ever borrowed money?
2. When did Mrs. Grant's husband die?
3. Your kids were how old at the time?
4. That job didn't pay very much, did it?
5. It was hard for you to live on such a small salary, wasn't it?
6. Did you have a job at that time, or were you a housewife?
7. A budget?

Part Two: On the Phone

Page 66, B. Listening

Exercise 1

Banker: New accounts, this is Carmen Delgado. How may I help you?

 Caller: Hi, I was interested in getting information on the different types of account options you offer.

B: Savings or checking?

C: Uh, both, I guess.

B: OK, I can help you with that. Um, can I get some information from you first?

C: Sure.

B: Are you over 18 years of age?

C: Yes.

B: And are you working full-time?

C: Em, no, I'm a student, actually.

B: All right then. Would you like me to start with the savings options?

C: OK.

B: OK, our basic ... oh, how much money did you want to put in?

C: About 5,400 dollars.

B: Well then there's a couple of options. So our basic savings account, um, requires a 300-dollar minimum balance. Otherwise there's a three-dollar fee each month. If you keep it at least 300 dollars there'll be no monthly service charge. The opening balance is 100 dollars. It comes with a debit card, which is just like an ATM card...

C: Just to be clear, to avoid the service charge there needs to be 300 dollars in the account at all times?

B: That's right, or also the fee is waived if you have a linked account, which is a checking account, that, that's where they automatically take a minimum of 25 dollars a month and transfer it from checking into the savings.

C: Oh, OK, can you tell me more about that?

B: OK, sure. Well, we offer a free checking account which is just... there's... it's 12 dollars for the checks but the account is free. It's only one dollar to open it up. And there's no monthly service charge. You can set it up so you have your income directly deposited into the account, um, but I guess you don't need that if you're a student. But you would need to link the checking account to your savings in order to avoid that monthly fee.

C: What do you mean by "linking"?

B: Oh, it means that you set up an automatic transfer each month from checking to savings, and it can be as little as 25 dollars a month.

C: OK, I understand. Now you said... by the way, what's the interest rate on that savings account?

B: On the savings account you're at point four percent.

C: Wow, that's really dismal...

B: Yes, it is. But with 5400 dollars you could also qualify for our basic money market account. This one has a thousand-dollar opening balance. It's a ten-dollar monthly service charge, and the minimum balance to waive that is 2,500 dollars.

C: How much was that to open again?

B: A thousand to open.

C: And 2,500 to avoid the service charge.

B: Yes.

C: And what's the interest rate?

B: Right now you're looking at point five percent.

C: That's not much better.

B: No, but if you're looking to grow your money then a savings account probably isn't the best place these days.

C: OK. What are the requirements for opening an account?

B: OK, so to open an account you'll need two forms of ID, your social security number and one other like a driver's license.

C: Oh, I guess I should've mentioned that I'm a nonresident... I'm actually a visiting scholar so I don't have a social security number.

B: Oh well, that's all right. You can use your passport and one other form of ID such as a credit card or your school ID card.

C: Well that's fine then. And what are your branch hours?

B: Monday through Friday from 8:30 a.m. to 6 p.m., Saturday 9 to 12, closed on Sundays and holidays.

C: Thanks.

B: You're welcome. Have a nice day.

Page 67, Exercise 2. Repeat the recording from Exercise 1.

Page 69, Exercise 4

1. B: So, our basic savings account, um, requires a 300-dollar minimum balance. Otherwise there's a three-dollar fee each month. If you keep it at at least 300 dollars, there'll be no monthly service charge. The opening balance is 100 dollars. It comes with a debit card, which is just like an ATM card...

2. C: Just to be clear, to avoid the service charge

there needs to be 300 dollars in the account at all times?

B: That's right, or also the fee is waived if you have a linked account, which is a checking account, that, that's where they automatically take a minimum of 25 dollars a month and transfer it from checking into the savings.

3. **C:** What do you mean by "linking"?

B: Oh, it means that you set up an automatic transfer each month from checking to savings, and it can be as little as 25 dollars a month.

4. **C:** By the way, what's the interest rate on that savings account?

B: On the savings account you're at point four percent.

5. **B:** But with 5400 dollars you could also qualify for our basic money market account. This one has a thousand-dollar opening balance.

6. **B:** Oh well, that's all right. You can use your passport and one other form of ID such as a credit card or your school ID card.

Page 70, Exercise 6. Repeat the recording from Exercise 4.

Part Three: On the Air

Page 73, B. Listening

Exercise 1

Chadwick: Michelle, was Shakespeare right? Should we just not loan money?

Singletary: Well, we shouldn't, but then again we should. I mean the fact of the matter is, people are going to be in need, and if you're kind and if you do your money right, you can have money that you can lend to people. So I say if you have it and you can let it go, give it.

C: What do you mean, "let it go"? If you have it, you can lend it out, and you wouldn't absolutely have to have it back?

S: That's right. My number one rule in lending to either a relative or friend or coworker is doing lend them money that you need back. Don't give them your rent money; don't give them money that you have to pay for your car note,

absolutely not. If that is the case, then you're not in the position to give them any money.

C: So if you do loan money, what do you do, do you set a deadline and say, "You have to give it back in six months," or a year, or every month you have to give some back?

S: You know, I play the banker. I ask why they need the money, and I have to be sure that it's something that I think is appropriate. So if it's money, you came up short with your rent, or you got laid off or something like that, I think that's appropriate, and I think it's OK to be, to ask that question "What do you need the money for?"

C: It's a hard question, though, with friends and relatives, isn't it?

S: It is, but you know what, some people just don't handle their money right, and I am not going to be the banker to people who mismanage their money.

C: So deadlines and paybacks?

S: Absolutely. I say do a contract. If it's a large amount of money, make it formal: How much they're borrowing, when you expect the money back and talk to them, get a realistic idea of when they're going to have the money. I mean it make is no sense to say give me my money back in a month if they're not going to have it. Some people charge interest; I don't happen to, but some people do. I think it's really important to put it down on paper if it's a large amount of money 'cause you may have to end up in small claims court, and the more documentation you have, the better your case is going to go.

C: Well is that what you would do if the person doesn't pay you back, go to small claims court or do something else or do you just say "Well, that was it, and I learned from this."

S: For me, I probably wouldn't, I'm not a very litigious kind of person. And I have had people who borrowed money and who did not give it back, and I just kissed the money off because my husband and I have actually created a pot of money, so people who need loans, it comes out of this sort of pot of money. And it's our way of giving back to our family. Now in some cases I absolutely want my money back and I hound you down. "Give me my money!" So... but if it's someone who just, you know, they're just not going to have it... My sister asked for some... ooh, I shouldn't say that, should I, anyway...

C: That's all right, never mind your sister. At least I now know who to go to: "The Bank of Michelle."

Page 74, Exercise 2

Segment 1

Chadwick: Michelle, was Shakespeare right? Should we just not loan money?

Singletary: Well, we shouldn't, but then again we should.

Segment 2

Singletary: I mean the fact of the matter is, people are going to be in need, and if you're kind and if you do your money right, you can have money that you can lend to people. So I say if you have it and you can let it go, give it.

Segment 3

Singletary: You know, I play the banker. I ask why they need the money, and I have to be sure that it's something that I think is appropriate. So if it's money, you came up short with your rent, or you got laid off or something like that, I think that's appropriate, and I think it's OK to be, to ask that question "What do you need the money for?"

Segment 4

Singletary: I say do a contract. If it's a large amount of money, make it formal: How much they're borrowing, when you expect the money back and talk to them, get a realistic idea of when they're going to have the money.

Segment 5

Singletary: I think it's really important to put it down on paper if it's a large amount of money 'cause you may have to end up in small claims court, and the more documentation you have, the better your case is going to go.

Segment 6

Singletary: And I have had people who borrowed money and who did not give it back, and I just kissed the money off.

Page 75, Exercise 4

Inseparable	Separable
need back	lend it out
end up	give it back
come out of	get your money back
give back	put it down
catch up on	pay you back
	kiss the money off

Page 76, Exercise 6

1. Ahmet cut back on entertainment in order to save money.
2. You need to cut down on your spending.
3. Students have to cut out unnecessary expenses.
4. It's hard for me to do without a car.
5. While Mr. Smith was unemployed, the family got by on Mrs. Smith's salary.
6. I'll pay you back after the first of the month.
7. The Diaz family recently paid off their house.

Part Four: **In Class**

Page 83, B. Listening and Note-Taking

Exercise 4

1. Between 1992 and 2001, the average credit card debt of this group increased by 55 percent to an average of 4,008 dollars per household.
2. During the same period of time, this group's bankruptcy rate grew by 19 percent.
3. Seven out of ten, that's 70 percent of these young Americans had credit cards in 2001.
4. In the year 2003, for example, this group had an unemployment rate of about 10 percent.
5. In 1992, 42 percent of students borrowed money for college, and they graduated with an average debt of 9,000 dollars.
6. In 2002, ten years later, 66 percent of students were borrowing money and the average student loan debt had doubled, to 18,900 dollars.

Page 84, Exercise 7

OK, so for the next few minutes I want to talk about the problem of credit card debt among one particular segment of the U.S. population. That's the group of college graduates in the 25- to 34-year-old range. Now this is the group of young adults who are just starting out.... They're on their first or second job, maybe they're newly married or they're just starting to have children. And for a variety of reasons, which I'll clarify in a minute, according to statistics this generation has more debt than any other generation in U.S. history.

So here are some facts. Between 1992 and 2001, the average credit card debt of this group increased by 55 percent to an average of 4,008 dollars per household. During the same period of time, this group's bankruptcy rate grew by 19 percent. OK, so... seven out of ten, that's 70 percent of these young Americans had credit cards in 2001, and of those 71 percent had revolving balances. Revolving balances means that they don't pay the full amount of their bill off each month but rather they only make partial payments. Meanwhile, the interest charges keep accumulating from month to month, and it leads to this pit of debt that's just almost impossible to climb out of.

So now the central question I want to address is, why is this generation going into debt and in many cases going broke? What's really causing it?

Well, first and... first and most obvious is the high cost of housing, transportation, childcare, healthcare, all of these have risen dramatically in the last 10 to 15 years. In the second place you have a weak labor market for this segment of the population. What I mean by that is, a large percentage of college graduates have jobs that are either temporary or part-time or both. In the year 2003, for example, this group had an unemployment rate of about ten percent.

The third factor, which may be unique to the United States, is a rising student loan debt... Let me explain, uh, give you some background on that. Traditionally, it used to be that one way of paying for college in the U.S. was through... was through

government scholarships or grants, which don't need to be paid back. But the amount of available grant money has been shrinking, so this generation I've been talking about is the first generation that is paying for college mainly through loans instead of through grants. And to give you an idea of the impact that this has had, in 1992, 42 percent of students borrowed money for college, and they graduated with an average debt of 9,000 dollars. In contrast to that, in 2002, ten years later, 66 percent of students were borrowing money and the average student loan debt had doubled, to 18,900 dollars.

So now if we combine all the factors that I've listed so far, what they add up to is a pretty difficult financial situation, as you can see by looking at the handout of the sample budget that I've provided for you of a typical graduate, college graduate... let's call her Caroline, OK. All right, so Caroline actually has a pretty good job, she's making 36,000 dollars a year. But, as you can see, her monthly pay after taxes is only 2,058 dollars. And every month, besides her ordinary living expenses, look at the amount of debt Caroline is carrying: 182 dollars per month on her student loans and 125 dollars on her credit cards. You can notice that she really doesn't spend any money on luxuries, yet she has almost nothing left at the end of the month. So what happens to Caroline if she loses her job or has an accident or some other unexpected expense comes up? Well really, what choice does she have but to pull out the plastic and once again add to the credit card debt that she's already carrying.

Now as you know, the credit card companies make this a very easy thing to do. It's remarkably easy to get a credit card in this country. Already in high school young people start getting credit card applications in the mail. But, the problem is that typically young adults don't have much experience with money management, and with the illusion of "free" money that comes with owning credit cards they can quickly accumulate a debt that may take years to pay off. So I would say that the easy availability of credit cards together with poor money management skills is the fourth reason for the financial difficulties of young college graduates today.

CHAPTER 4: MEMORIES

Part One: In Person
Page 91, B. Listening

Exercise 1

Segment 1

Lida: Do you ever walk into a room and um... there'll be like a smell, and you'll go, "Oh, I know this smell." And it takes you back to some time when you were a child.

Donna: Yes, smells, uh... Uh, the smell of wood, sawdust...

L: Uh-ha.

D: ...has a very strong uh pull on my memory because my father worked with wood, so our garage always had the smell of fresh-cut wood and sawdust on the floor. And, um, I love the smell of sawdust, [um - hmm..] wood, cut wood... um...

L: You know what reminds me of my father? The smell of pipe tobacco. 'Cause my dad smoked a pipe. And you know, I can, I can... Not that many people smoke anymore, but every once in a while I'll be somewhere, and I smell tobacco and it's as if my dad were in the room. You know, it just transports me back to being a child. And I love that smell. 'Cause it reminds me of my dad.

D: Right.

Segment 2

D: The taste of something also brings back a memory. I was in Trinidad, Tobago, after university, and hanging out on the small island of Tobago, and on Sundays, uh, one of the, uh, beach restaurants would make a big Sunday barbecue. And they went out fishing in the morning, brought back the fish; they'd be on the... the cooks would sit on the sand, uh, clean the fish, soak the fish in fresh lemon and barbecue it... Uh, and you'd get a big glob of wonderful potato salad with this fresh, fresh fish. It was... my mouth is watering as I speak of it. It was the most incredible piece of fish I've ever eaten in my whole life...

Segment 3

Fran: I have a favorite color combination, and it's not a color combination I go out and wear. But for some irrational reason I like these two colors together. And they're purple and green. And you know me, and I don't wear a lot of purple and green combinations, but it triggers some happy association. And I remember as a child playing with blocks that were painted, and that my favorite ones were the purple and green ones together and building all sorts of intricate purple and green combinations. And to this day I still like it...

Segment 4

Matt: So I think a baseball or a softball would be very evocative of childhood and youth. Because um, when I was a kid, the um major league baseball came to, to Los Angeles and it was a big, big deal. And everyone played baseball all the time. And, um, if you closed my eyes and put one in my hand, I could recognize it by the weight, and by the sort of s... roughness, but, smooth, but just a little bit rough texture of the ball, and the seams, the raised seams that held it together. And it has a sort of faint smell of leather, and um, all those things remind me of uh, childhood.

Page 91, Exercise 2. Repeat the recording from Exercise 1.

Page 92, Exercise 4

1. **Man 1:** I have a question.
   Man 2: I have a question, too.
2. **Woman 1:** Joe will e-mail you tomorrow.
   Woman 2: Tell Joe to call me tomorrow.
3. **Woman:** Hannah will bring the coffee to the meeting.
   Man: No, Mark will bring the coffee.
4. **Woman 1:** Lynn has a doctor's appointment tomorrow.
   Woman 2: Cathy has a doctor's appointment today.
5. **Man:** Please put the chair here. And please put the table there.

Page 93, Exercise 5

1. No, Jack's mother planted FLOWERS in the spring.
2. No, Jack's MOTHER planted flowers in the spring.
3. No, Jack's mother planted flowers in the SPRING.
4. No, JACK'S mother planted flowers in the spring.
5. No, Jack's mother PLANTED flowers in the spring.

Part Two: On the Phone

Page 95, B. Listening

Exercise 1

Man: Hello?

Woman: Hi honey.

M: Hi honey.

W: I'm just checking in. I'm on my way to pick up Joseph. We should be home by...

M: Wait wait wait. You're on your way to pick him up? Oh, didn't I tell you? His game got cancelled.

W: What? Howard, you didn't tell me!

M: The school left a message... the game got cancelled. A sprinkler broke and the field got flooded so they couldn't play. I'm sorry, I forgot to call you. I already picked him up.

W: Howard! I can't believe you did this again! This is like the tenth time you've done this...

M: I know, I'm sorry.

W: No, but this really is a problem. Your absent-mindedness... I mean, last week you forgot to give me two important messages, and then those videos... they were five days overdue...

M: Now, hold on. Look who's talking. What about my birthday last month? You forgot it. I didn't make a big deal out of that, did I?

W: Yeah, you've got a point there, but that was just one time, and it was right after my mother had surgery. You, on the other hand...

M: Oh, come on. I've got a thousand things on my mind too, so it's not the end of the world if things slip my mind once in a while...

W: Slip your mind? You've been a total scatterbrain lately...

M: [sigh]

W: We've got to do something about this...

M: Yeah, you're right. It's my fault. Guess I should start writing things down.

W: Yeah, I've been telling you to do that!

M: Yeah, I know. I apologize.

W: All right, all right, let's forget about it for now. We'll talk about this when I get home... but who knows when that's gonna be... I'm stuck in traffic here.

M: I really am sorry... Listen... let me make it up to you... I'll get dinner ready, okay?

W: Okay, that sounds good.

M: Good.

W: Just... just...

M: What?

W: Just... don't forget to turn the oven off when you're done.

Page 96, Exercise 2. Repeat the recording from Exercise 1.

Page 97, Exercise 4. Repeat the recording from Exercise 1.

Part 3: On the Air

Page 101, B. Listening

Exercise 1

Interviewer: Well, give us an idea of some of the tricks, the basic tricks that teachers could lay out for kids. And I was interested in one thing that you wrote, that the best way to remember something, say for a test, is to transform it. In other words, if something you're trying to remember is verbal, make it visual, make a diagram for yourself. Is that what you mean, to to...trans...

Levine: Absolutely. That's one method, is keep recoding information. If it comes in visually, like a diagram, put it into words, describe it. If it comes in verbally, uh, try to make a diagram of it, try to make a chart, try to picture it, try to think of examples of it in your own life. The more you extend information, the more you elaborate it, uh, the more you modify it in one way or another, the more effectively it gets filed in memory. It's also important to teach kids that they need to put information in categories, that you don't put things in memory without attaching them to something. Uh, let me give you an example that shows this. Along about age nine, children develop a filing system in their minds. They actually develop folders that they can put information in. If you ask a seven-year-old to name as many animals as he can in 30 seconds, he'll say, um, robin, shark, cow, dog, spider. If you ask a 13-year-old with a well-organized memory to name as many animals as he can in 30 seconds, he'll say "cow, chicken, turkey, pig, lion, tiger, giraffe, elephant, rhino, spider, ant, bee"— do you see what he's doing?

I: Yeah. They put them in phylum, in classes...

L: Yes, he's going from one folder to another. He can name ten times as many animals as that 7-year-old. And if you see a 13-year-old, and you ask him to name as many animals as he can in 30 seconds, and he sounds like a seven-year-old, you know he's failing tests in school. He has no folders. He's got to be taught how to do that. And so often, what comes intuitively and naturally to certain kinds of minds has to be taught formally to other kinds of minds. Every single one of us has things that we can do so well intuitively and things that we're going to have to be led through formally.

I: There is a little, uh, trick that you wrote about in the book that I didn't... that and I never thought of, that long-term memory filing works best right before you go to sleep.

L: Absolutely.

I: How would you apply that?

L: Well, kids have to know that you study for exams right before you go to sleep, and, and by all means do not study and then take a shower and then go to sleep 'cause then all you remember in the morning is the shampoo. Uh, you have to take the shower first, and then study, and then go to sleep. And what you study right before you go to sleep gets replayed about five times after you fall asleep. It has instant replay built into it. Uh, this is one of the many many, sort of memory tricks of the trade, that I think students ought to know about.

Page 102, Exercise 2. Repeat the recording from Exercise 1.

Page 104, Exercise 4

L: Along about age nine, children develop a filing system in their minds. They actually develop folders that they can put information in. If you ask a seven-year-old to name as many animals as he can in 30 seconds, he'll say, um, robin, shark, cow, dog, spider. If you ask a 13-year-old with a well-organized memory to name as many animals as he can in 30 seconds, he'll say "cow, chicken, turkey, pig, lion, tiger, giraffe, elephant, rhino, spider, ant, bee" — do you see what he's doing?

I: Yeah. They put them in phylum, in classes...

L: Yes, he's going from one folder to another.

Part Four: In Class

Page 107, B. Listening and Note-Taking

Exercise 2

So now, another way of facilitating recall is through the use of memory techniques called mnemonics... I'll spell that for you: m-n-e-m-o-n-i-c-s... OK, uh, as I said before, mnemonics are techniques for improving memory. A little more formally, uh, they're systematic strategies that we can use to help us remember information, especially information that is hard to recall like numbers, lists, names, things like that.

Page 107, Exercise 4

1. Suppose you have a new friend and you learn that your friend's phone number is 934-1971. And suppose that, coincidentally, you were born in 1971.

2. OK, so let's say you are a student in a language class and you're trying to learn a new word.

3. So let's pretend that you're studying English and one of the words on your vocabulary list is the word *expeditious*.

4. OK. So now imagine that it's a week later and you have a vocabulary test the next day.

Page 108, Exercise 6

OK, we've been talking about how memory works, right, and what we can do to improve our memory. So we've seen, for example, we can enhance our ability to recall new information if we transform or extend it in some way. So, for instance, we're more likely to remember verbal information like directions to someone's house for example uh, if we transform it into something visual like a diagram or a map or something.

So now, another way of facilitating recall is through the use of memory techniques called mnemonics... I'll spell that for you: m-n-e-m-o-n-i-c-s... OK, uh, as I said before, mnemonics are techniques for improving memory. A little more formally, uh, they're systematic strategies that we can use to help us remember information, especially information that is hard to recall like you know numbers, lists, names, things like that.

So about 30 years ago, there's a psychologist named R.C. Atkinson, and he developed this mnemonic technique to help students learn vocabulary in a foreign language. And he called it the keyword method, and what I'd like to do now is demonstrate this method for you using an example from a language that none of you know. All right, so then you can use this technique in your own language studies. Uh, anybody know Hungarian? You speak Hungarian? No? OK, good.

Uh, so let's say you're learning Hungarian, right, and you're learning the names of foods, and one of your target words is the Hungarian word for cabbage, which is called *kaposzta*. And how can you remember that?

Well, the first step in the keyword method is to choose your key word. And a good key word has three characteristics: One, it's a word you know very well. You're real familiar with it. Two, it's a word that sounds like the target word—you know, the word you're trying to remember—or at least the first part of the target word. And number three, the last characteristic, the third characteristic of a good key word, is that it should be something that's easy to visualize, easy to picture, so a concrete noun or action verbs, those make you know the best keywords.

All right let's apply those three criteria to our example, *kaposzta*. OK, so what's a familiar word that sounds like *kaposzta* and is easy to visualize?

What comes to mind? Well, how about "cop," you know, a police officer. So that's a good keyword because it sounds like our target word *kaposzta*, it's familiar, it's easy to visualize, easy to picture.

So OK now we've got a keyword, and what's the next step? What we're going to do is, we're going to create a mental image, a picture, that contains both the keyword, in this case cop, and the target meaning, which is cabbage. In other words, in your mind's eye I want you to imagine the cop and the cabbage interacting—you know, doing something. Um, it's best if the image is moving, if it's colorful, exaggerated, silly, it's even better. So the more absurd or ridiculous, the better. Uh, let's imagine a cop wearing a uniform. OK, you got that? And his head is a big, green cabbage, all right? So let's give it eyes, put a nose on it, and a mouth, cop's hat, put a cop's hat on it. OK, what else? Maybe a mustache? A mustache?

So take that silly image and just focus on it for a minute. Hold it in your mind's eye... OK... Really concentrate so it's fixed in your memory.

OK. Now let's suppose it's a week later, all right, and you've got to review because tomorrow you're going to have a test on your new Hungarian vocabulary. Let's see how you can use this keyword method to painlessly study for your test. Make it easy, right?

First you take out your list of words and, you know, there's the word *kaposzta*. Immediately you think of your keyword, cop, which automatically triggers the image you created of the cop, you know with the cabbage head, and voila! There it is! Your definition. See how it works? So, you see the sequence? *Kaposzta* leads to cop; cop leads to cabbage. Now "cop" is the bridge that connects the new word, *kaposzta*, with the definition, cabbage. The association is so powerful you couldn't even forget it if you tried.

So research does prove this. It proves that students who use the keyword technique remember vocabulary better than students who don't. But let me give you a word of caution, in conclusion. I don't want you to think that this mnemonic or any other, you know, techniques are magical. All right, for mnemonics to work you still have to practice and rehearse. You have to study for the test.

Mnemonics don't eliminate the need to study, but you know they can definitely make it easier for you to remember some kinds of information.

CHAPTER 5: BODY TRENDS

Part One: In Person

Page 114, B. Listening

Exercise 1

Jennifer: Mom and Dad, I have a question for you.

Father: OK.

Mother: OK, what is it?

J: OK. Can I get a tattoo?

F: No, absolutely not.

M: Well, wait a minute. Let's hear what she has to say. Tell us what you're thinking, honey. Why do you want a tattoo?

J: Well they're just so cool, I mean Maxine has one of a butterfly and it's so pretty, you know, I just really like the way it looks.

F: And just where is this pretty little butterfly?

J: On her ankle, Daddy, where did you think it was?

F: I don't know, I'm not sure I want to.

M: Well what kind of tattoo did you have in mind, Jennifer?

J: OK, I was thinking of like a rose, you know, a small one, maybe on my shoulder.

F: But why? What's the point?

J: It's just cool, Dad. And all the kids are doing it, and their parents aren't giving them a hard time.

M: Jennifer, you know perfectly well we don't care what all the other kids are doing. You're going to have to come up with a better reason than that. Have you really thought this through? You know once you get a tattoo, that's it, it's permanent.

J: Well so is piercing my ears and you let me do that when I was 12.

M: Well yes, that's true, but it's not the same.

J: Why not?

M: Well because for one thing the holes don't show, and for another, if you change your mind you can just stop wearing earrings and the holes close up. Tattoos don't go away when you get tired of them.

J: But I'm not going to get tired of it!

F: How do you know? You change your clothes three times every day, and you tell me five years from now you're not going to get tired of a rose branded into your skin?

J: Daddy!

M: Well but that's a good point, Jennifer. You really don't know how you're going to feel five years or ten years from now.

J: So if I don't like it I'll have it removed.

M: Honey, removing tattoos is painful, and it leaves scars.

J: I don't care!

M: Well, what about henna? Couldn't you use that? At least it washes off and you can have different designs...

J: Mom, honestly, henna is for kids. Nobody my age does henna. Really, all my friends have tattoos.

F: I find that hard to believe.

M: Arthur please. Jenny, that is just not a good enough reason to do something you may regret six months or a year or five years from now.

J: You are so old-fashioned, you never let me do anything I want to do. I get good grades and I've never been in trouble. You say you trust me so why can't I do something I want for a change?

F: For a change? Seems to me you get to do just about everything you want. Wasn't it just last week that we let you drive to Santa Barbara with Jody and...

M: Arthur, don't start debating with her, OK? Let's stick to the main issue here. Jennifer, honey, I understand how you feel. You want to be cool and you want to fit in. But a tattoo just isn't something we can support, OK? Once you've finished school and you're living on your own, then you can decide for yourself, but right now, our answer is no.

J: All right. How about a diamond stud in my nose? Can I do that instead?

F/M: Jennifer!

Page 114, Exercise 2. Repeat the recording from Exercise 1.

Part Two: On the Phone

Page 119, B. Listening

Exercise 1

B: Hello.

A: Good morning. My name is Jason Rafferty and I work with the Northwest Public Opinion Research Group. And this week we're conducting a nationwide poll of Americans' attitudes about beauty and body image. Would you have approximately five minutes to participate in our survey?

B: Umm, OK, as long as it doesn't take any longer than that 'cause I'm expecting someone any minute here.

A: Very good. Um, here's the first question. Now thinking about physical attractiveness, that is, how beautiful or handsome someone is—how important do you think a person's physical attractiveness is in our society today in terms of his or her happiness, social life, and ability to get ahead? Would you say it is very important, fairly important, not too important, or not at all important?

B: Hmm. In, in today's society I would say that it's very important. I mean, you know, the way you look, it's the first thing that people notice, and maybe that's unfair but it's, it's the truth, especially if you're a woman, right?

A: OK, thank you. Uh, the second question is, if you had to describe yourself to someone who didn't know you, how would you describe your physical appearance? Would you say you are— beautiful or handsome, attractive or above average, average, somewhat below average in attractiveness, or unattractive?

B: Uh, could you, could you run those choices by me again?

A: Sure. Beautiful or handsome, attractive or above average, average, somewhat below average in attractiveness, or unattractive?

B: Hmm. Well, well no one's ever told me to put a bag over my head, so I'll say attractive or above average.

A: OK, thank you. Uh, the third question. All in all, are you satisfied with how attractive you are, or do you wish you could be more attractive?

B: On the whole... I'd say I'm satisfied, though between you and me I sure wouldn't have minded, you know, being a little taller.

A: All right. Uh, next, all in all, would you say you are generally pleased with the way your body looks, or not?

B: I guess pleased.

A: Pleased...

B: Yeah.

A: OK, have you ever had elective cosmetic or plastic surgery to improve the appearance of some part of your body, or not?

B: Well, I'd rather not answer that.

A: No problem, we'll mark that as a "No Opinion." The last question, would you consider elective cosmetic or plastic surgery to improve the appearance of some part of your body, or not?

B: Would I ever consider it? Like in the future, you mean? Well... yeah, I might.

A: All right, thank you. Now to conclude the survey may I verify some demographic information about you?

B: I suppose.

A: All right, are you male or female?

B: Female.

A: Is your age group below 25, between 25 and 34, 35 to 44, 45 to 54, or 55 or older?

B: Between 25 and 34.

A: Thank you. And is your income level below 25,000 dollars a year, in between...

B: I'd rather not say.

A: All right, and are you never married, married, divorced, or widowed?

B: Never married.

A: All right. Thank you for your participation. If you'd like to read about the results of this nationwide survey, feel free to consult our website at www.northwestporg.net in approximately two weeks. Anyway, good-bye and thank you very much for your time.

B: You're welcome. Bye.

Page 120, Exercise 2. Repeat the recording from Exercise 1.

Page 121, Exercise 5

1. Would you say it is important, fairly important, not too important, or not at all important?

2. Would you say you are beautiful or handsome, attractive or above average, average, somewhat below average in attractiveness, or unattractive?

3. Are you satisfied with how attractive you are, or do you often wish you could be more attractive?

4. All in all, would you say you are generally pleased with the way your body looks, or not?

5. Have you ever had elective or cosmetic surgery to improve the appearance of some part of your body, or not?

Part Three: On the Air

Page 125, B. Listening

Exercise 1

Announcer: Looking for a job may not be easy, but some people hope to improve their chances by making themselves look younger. The Stanford Medical Center reports that about half of its cosmetic surgery patients from the last few years have been people who were looking to improve their image so they can improve their lives. And joining us now is one of Stanford's patients, Maria in California. She asked us not to use her last name. Welcome Maria.

Maria: Hello.

A: What kind of work have you done in the past?

M: Mostly sales.

A: You're in the Silicon Valley area, so...

M: Absolutely.

A: It's tech stuff that you're working with.

M: Yeah.

A: You're unemployed right now?

M: Uh, about to be.

A: Your company's not in great shape.

M: The writing's on the wall, so it's a matter of, uh, going out and looking for another one.

A: So what have you decided to do about this?

M: In order to compete with a lot of the dot-comers, um, you've got to look and feel good.

A: This is an industry that has thrived on youth, isn't it, I mean it's a lot of 22-year-old kids starting companies, or at least that's been the image of it anyway.

M: Yes, absolutely, and there are a lot of them here in the Valley.

A: And you're not a 22-year-old kid.

M: No, no, thank God, no.

A: Such a rude question, but how old are you exactly?

M: Uh, I'm in my late thirties.

A: OK. You feel that you need to look younger in order to have a chance in the job interviews that you hope to have soon.

M: Absolutely.

A: What have you done?

M: Uh, well, I went to Stanford, and I had my eyes basically refreshed. I look like I'm awake now. Um, and now it's boosted my self esteem, and so now I'm just sitting here, looking for jobs like crazy, and before I wouldn't do it because I didn't want to see anybody.

A: You had bags under your eyes, is that...

M: Yeah, and also on top. It kind of looked like I was very tired.

A: And you're telling me that when you began thinking again about going out again to look for a job, you felt so bad about yourself you didn't even want to face anybody in a job interview.

M: Right. Because to me it wasn't even worth trying to go out and look for a job because even if they did call me in for an interview, they would take a look, and they'd probably have a 25-year-old, and, who looks fresh, and ready to go, versus me, who looks ready to go to bed.

A: How long had you been at this job?

M: Um, I've been at this job now for three years.

A: Did you have trouble with your age the last time you were looking for a job?

M: Oh no, no, not at all.

A: The change in the eyes, the refreshing the eyes, as you call it, was that the only plastic surgery you had?

M: Uh, no, actually I had a little bit of work on my nose.

A: A little bit of work.

M: A-ha.

A: What sort of work?

M: Uh, taking the bump out and making it look a little bit more cosmetically pleasing.

A: You feel pretty confident that you need to look young in order to get a job. This is a young person's field.

M: Yes, you have to compete, and you have to look good. No one's going to want somebody that looks washed out and tired.

A: Did you ever hear of anybody who actually suffered from age discrimination?

M: You know what, you do see it. People who are older, in their forties and fifties, that try and find a job over here, it's extremely hard. And I've seen it, because the young kids get in and they bump'em out. And it does happen. Even though that's discrimination and they'll tell you that doesn't happen, it does happen. And if I was to be called to go in, I think my chances are a lot better just because I'm fired up and I'm ready to go. I feel like I can do anything, conquer anything, and people see that.

A: Maria, who recently underwent plastic surgery in hopes that a new look will lead to a new job. We heard about her courtesy of the Knight Ritter news service. Maria, thanks very much for taking the time.

M: Great. Thank you so much.

Page 126, Exercise 2. Repeat the recording from Exercise 1.

Page 127, Exercise 4

1. A: You're in the Silicon Valley area, so...

   M: Absolutely.

   A: It's tech stuff that you're working with.

   M: Yeah.

2. A: This is an industry that has thrived on youth, isn't it, I mean it's a lot of 22-year-old kids starting companies, or at least that's been the image of it anyway.

   M: Yes, absolutely, and there are a lot of them here in the Valley.

3. A: You had bags under your eyes, is that...

   M: Yeah, and also on top. It kind of looked like I was very tired.

4. A: You feel pretty confident that you need to

look young in order to get a job. This is a young person's field.

M: Yes, you have to compete, and you have to look good. No one's going to want somebody that looks washed out and tired.

Part Four: In Class

Page 132, B. Listening and Note-Taking

Exercise 2

1. Now, we've talked quite a lot in this course about the subject of body image disorders in women and the rising incidence of conditions like anorexia and bulimia.

2. Researchers at McLean Hospital in Boston were interested in finding out why this cultural difference exists, why body building and steroid use were so much more prevalent in the West than in the East.

3. The subjects in this study were male college students from three Western cultures: the U.S., France, and Austria.

4. Now what the researchers did is that they showed these male students pictures of men with varying levels of muscularity and body fat...

5. Then, in the next phase of the study, the researchers showed the same series of pictures to a group of male university students in Taiwan.

6. In other words, the researchers interpreted this to mean that the Western men saw themselves as skinny and underdeveloped whereas the Taiwanese men were basically satisfied with the way they looked.

7. So in short, the findings suggest that Western men may have an unrealistic or even distorted idea of what they should look like and what women want, but that Taiwanese men don't seem to have this problem.

8. Another explanation could be the influence of the media.

Page 134, Exercise 5

Now we've talked quite a lot in this course about the subject of body image disorders in women and the rising incidence of conditions like anorexia and bulimia. And I think we're so accustomed to thinking of these disorders as women's problems, that you might be surprised to learn that an estimated one to two percent of Western men also suffer from body image problems. These are often expressed in the form of a pathological concern with body building, the abuse of muscle-building drugs like steroids, or both.

Now in contrast, in East Asian cultures, such as China, male body image disorders and steroid abuse are extremely rare. Researchers at McLean Hospital in Boston were interested in finding out why this cultural difference exists, why body building and steroid use were so much more prevalent in the West than in the East, and this led them to conduct a very interesting study, which I'd like to summarize for the next few minutes.

All right. Um, the subjects in this study were male college students from three Western cultures, the U.S., France, and Austria. Now what the researchers did is that they showed these male students pictures of men with varying levels of muscularity and body fat, ranging from very slim at one extreme to really bulked up at the other, and they asked them to choose four images: one, the image that most closely resembled their own bodies. Two, the body of an average man of their age in their culture. Three, the body they would ideally like to have, and four, the body they thought women would prefer the most. In addition, for purposes of comparison, the researchers also asked a group of women to look at the pictures and choose the body they liked best.

Then, in the next phase of the study, the researchers showed the same series of pictures to a group of male university students in Taiwan, and asked the same questions. Afterwards they analyzed the two sets of data looking for similarities and differences. And what they found were two significant differences between the Western and the Eastern group.

First, with respect to the question of what the men considered to be the ideal body image, the Western subjects picked an ideal body that was about 28 pounds, or 13 kilos, more muscular than they perceived themselves to be. But the Taiwanese men picked an ideal body that was only two kilos bigger than their own.

In other words, the researchers interpreted this to mean that the Western men saw themselves as skinny and underdeveloped whereas the Taiwanese men were basically satisfied with the way they looked.

Second, regarding the question of which body type the men thought women preferred, the Western men predictably guessed that women preferred a male body that was about 30 pounds, or 14 kilos, more muscular than theirs. Yet when the researchers asked actual Western women to choose the male body they liked, they didn't choose a bulked up Arnold Schwarzenegger body; they chose an average body, without the extra muscle. Conversely, the Taiwanese men guessed that women would prefer an average body, similar to their own. And in fact, that is what the women chose.

So in short, the findings suggest that Western men may have an unrealistic or even distorted idea of what they should look like and what women want, but that Taiwanese men don't seem to have this problem; and that brings me to the next part of my talk, which is: Why? What accounts for the difference? The researchers proposed three hypotheses.

Now, the first possible explanation may lie in the different ways that Western and Eastern cultures have traditionally defined masculinity. You know Western cultures going all the way back to ancient Greece and Rome have measured it in terms of muscles and physical power. You can go to any art museum and look at the male statues for proof of what I'm talking about. But as the researchers explain, in traditional Chinese culture, masculinity has much more to do with things like intelligence, strength of character, and courage, rather than muscles.

Another explanation could be the influence of the media. Studies show, for instance, that images of undressed, muscular men are far more common in the West, especially in the United States, than in Taiwan. And the greater exposure to these images could be affecting Western notions of what the ideal male body ought to look like. And finally, the third explanation, might be that the traditional role of Western men has changed over the last generation, with more and more women working and supporting themselves, you know, leading some men to focus on their bodies as a way of maintaining their masculine self esteem. But in Taiwanese culture, there has been much less of a change in the traditional family structure, at least so far. So the satisfaction that Taiwanese men appear to feel with their bodies may be related to the security they derive from their traditional role as breadwinner and head of the family.

Now let's examine each of these hypotheses more closely, keeping in mind that further research is needed on all three...

CHAPTER 6: DISCOVERIES

Part One: In Person
Page 140, B. Listening

Exercise 1

A: Well so, um, these rovers, what were they looking for, and what did they actually discover?

B: OK, well, this mission was all about finding water or signs of past water on Mars... And what they found, and this is the big important discovery of these rovers, they both found geological evidence that there was water in the past. Not last year, and not a hundred years ago, but thousands, millions of years ago, there was definitely water on the surface of Mars.

A: How'd they discover that?

B: Because they looked at the rock formations, they, they looked at the minerals that the rocks were made of and they found distinctive signs that there was definitely water on the surface. At Meridiani, they discovered a mineral called hematite which can only be formed in the presence of water, which leads to the possibility that Meridiani may have been the site of a lake millions of years ago.

A: That's amazing. But well, what does that mean... that there was life on Mars at one time?

B: Not exactly. In all the missions that we've flown so far to Mars, what we've discovered is that we can't prove that there wasn't life on Mars. But we can't prove that there was life on Mars, either.

A: OK, but what's your gut feeling?

B: My gut feeling, is that there's no... well, there are no little green men on Mars. Whether there are tiny microbes hidden hundreds of feet deep in what might be ice near the poles, that's a possibility.

A: Well let's suppose that in the future they do find microbes or bacteria or whatever on Mars, why would that be important?

B: Well, these discoveries are important because they're the first small steps in discovering whether another planet is, or could have been in the past, habitable. And so we might find that Mars could be a place that people could live in the future...

A: Come on. You don't really think that people are ever going to live on Mars, do you?

B: Yes, yes I really do think that people are going to live on Mars. I mean, I don't know about big cities, but I think that, at sometime in the next hundred years, there will be astronauts on Mars.

A: So what's the next step?

B: The next step is to find, uh, to maybe go back to the same places or to go some other places where there might have been water, and then to do some more sophisticated chemical analysis of the soil to find out what kind of minerals there are, and are they conducive to, would they have been in the past conducive to, life being there in the past.

A: OK, but I have to ask you this, what's the point? Why spend taxpayer money...

B: Why, what, what's the point, well look. The spirit of exploration has always taken us places where we've never been before. Otherwise, we never would have discovered Antarctica or gone to the moon or any of the other places that people have explored throughout history. And as for the money, I mean, you have to understand that the amount of money that's spent on the space program is just a drop in the bucket of the budget of the United States. And this is a rich country, rich enough to be able to devote a very tiny portion of its budget to be the Columbus of the twenty-first century.

Page 141, Exercise 2. Repeat the recording from Exercise 1.

Page 143, Exercise 4

1. At Meridiani, they discovered a mineral called hematite which can only be formed in the presence of water, which leads to the possibility that Meridiani may have been the site of a lake millions of years ago.

2. Whether there are tiny microbes hidden hundreds of feet deep in what might be ice near the poles, that's a possibility.

3. Well, these discoveries are important because they're the first small steps in discovering whether another planet is, or could have been in the past, habitable. And so we might find that Mars could be a place that people could live in the future...

4. The next step is to find, uh, to maybe go back to the same places or to go some other places where there might have been water, and then to do some more sophisticated chemical analysis of the soil to find out what kind of minerals there are, and are they conducive to, would they have been in the past conducive to, life being there in the past.

5. Otherwise, we never would have discovered Antarctica or gone to the moon or any of the other places that people have explored throughout history.

Part Two: On the Phone

Page 147, B. Listening

Exercise 1

Rose: Hello?

Brent: Is this Rose Green?

R: Um, it used to be.

B: I beg your pardon?

R: My father's name was Green. My married name... Wait a minute, who is this?

B: My name is Brent Knoop. And uh, you don't know me, I'm from Boston, and I'm in town for a few days on business...

R: OK.

B: The reason I'm calling is, uh, well, this may sound strange but I think you and I might be cousins.

R: I, I don't have any cousins in Boston, that I know of anyway...

B: Well that's what I want to find out, if you have a few minutes to talk.

R: Well sure, this is starting to get interesting. Um, so you're from Boston?

B: Yes, but I was born in Amsterdam.

R: Really. My mother was born in Amsterdam.

B: Um-hmm. And what is her name?

R: Well, she died nine years ago, but her maiden name was Blits. B-l-i-t-s.

B: A-ha, there it is, my mother's name was also Blits, same spelling.

R: You're kidding! What was her first name?

B: Clara.

R: Oh my gosh. I remember my mother talking about an aunt named Clara. Wow...

B: What was... what was your mother's first name?

R: Branca, though she had a funny nickname, Beppie.

B: And what was her mother's name?

R: Uh, Rozette.

B: Well then, we're certainly related. My grandmother on my mother's side was named Branca, same as your mother. And this Branca had eight children, including my mother, Clara, and your grandmother, Rozette...

R: Hold on, hold on, my head is spinning. So... your mother Clara and my grandmother Rozette were... sisters.

B: Yes.

R: And that means that you and my mother were...

B: First cousins. And that makes you my first cousin once removed.

R: Wow. I didn't think I had any cousins in this country. How in the world did you find me?

B: Well that's another interesting story. About five years ago I became interested in genealogy. [Oh] It was through my wife really, she's Irish, and she has a huge family. And we started putting together a family tree for her family, and so I got the idea to do the same for mine. [Mmm.] So on my next visit to Amsterdam I sat down with my mother...

R: Is she still alive?

B: Yes, she's 92 years old and sharp as a tack.

R: Ah, that's incredible.

B: Uh-huh, uh-huh. Well, so I was talking with my mother and I started writing down all the names, and very quickly it became sort of a small obsession, you know, trying to find people. My mother knew your maiden name, she was at your mother's wedding in Holland, before your parents left for the States, and I guess they used to correspond...

R: Oh. But that still doesn't explain how you found me.

B: Actually I've been searching for you for several years, but you know, Green is such a common name, and my mother didn't know your married name...

R: It's Nessen, that's what I use...

B: A-ha. Well I tried to Google you about three years ago, and nothing came up. And then a couple of weeks ago I tried again, for some reason, and this time, I got lucky, I found a link to an announcement about a high school reunion...

R: That's right!

B: Mm-hmm. So I followed the link, and there was a photo with the name Rose Green in the caption.

R: You are quite a detective. I used my maiden name at the reunion so people would remember who I was. What an amazing coincidence. I can't believe it.

B: Well now that I've found you, would you like to get together and learn more about your family?

R: By all means, where are you staying?

B: I'm at the Plaza.

R: We're about fifteen minutes away.

Page 148, Exercise 2. Repeat the recording from Exercise 1.

Page 149, Exercise 4

1. This may soun' strange.
2. your mother's firs' name
3. my gra-mother
4. try to fin' people
5. on my nex' visit
6. You foun' me.
7. don' know
8. He lef' for work.

Page 150, Exercise 5

1. Ya kin always fin me at this number. [You can always find me at this number.]
2. My firs'cousins live in lotsa diff-rent cities. [My first cousins live in lots of different cities.]
3. I don feel comftable using 'er firs name. [I don't feel comfortable using her first name.]
4. I'm gonna bring my gra-mother some choc-late. [I'm going to bring my grandmother some chocolate.]
5. Joseph lef'for work sev-ral minutes ago. [Joseph left for work several minutes ago.]
6. On yer nex visit, tell me more about yer famly. [On your next visit, tell me more about your family.]
7. Wus wrong wi that piano? It souns strange. [What's wrong with that piano? It sounds strange.]

Part Three: On the Air

Page 153, B. Listening

Exercise 1

Host 1: Doug, in South Bend, Indiana, Doug, tell us about your great discovery.

Doug: Well, it was some years ago, about 22 or 3 years ago, actually, I got a metal detector for Christmas.

H1: OK.

D: And after waiting all winter long to get to use the thing, we ended up uh, we ended up being in a local...

H1: Are we getting some background ukulele there?

D: No, that's actually my other phone, but I'm gonna ignore it for right now.

Host 2: Wow, that's quite musical.

H1: That's your cell phone, that's your cell phone ring?

D: Yeah, my cell phone.

H1: Hmm. OK.

D: But um, at any rate, um.

H1: Back to the metal detector.

D: And, uh, after finding, you know, a few pennies and a whole bunch of bottle caps and whatever, I hit, uh, a pretty loud signal, which back then was really the only thing you could use to tell anything...

H1: Mm-hmm.

D: ... and...

H1: ... started digging...

D: ...started digging, and found a large man's diamond and sapphire ring.

H1: Wow.

D: And as it, and I really kind of thought it was fake because it was as big as it was. I had it appraised... first of all, he wanted to buy it, which that's usually a good indication that it's worth something.

H1: Right.

D: But I found out that the sapphires, they were, um, just your run-of-the-mill sapphires, but the uh, the diamond was what the gentleman referred to as an investment grade.

H1: Um, I'm sure those were very pleasing words to hear.

D: Yeah, it really was, and all with a, uh, you know, an 80-dollar metal detector that I got for Christmas.

H1: Now this was somebody's ring, right?

D: Yeah, and I put an ad in the paper, and nobody responded...

H2: Are you questioning Doug's integrity?

D: I'm sorry?

H1: No, I'm just trying to find out the story.

D: No, no, no, I mean, it was somebody's ring, it was a man's ring.

H1: And so how much...

D: There were initials inside the ring, but there was no way to...

H1: What were the initials?

D: Oh, I'm sorry I honestly don't remember.

H1: 'Cause I lost a ring in South Bend, Indiana.

D: I figured if I gave too much information I'm sure people'd be coming out of the woodwork to claim it.

H1: Well how much did you sell the ring for?

D: I still have it.

H1: Oh you still have it. What was it appraised at?

D: Huh?

H1: What was it appraised at?

D: Uh, at the time, it was like 15,000 dollars.

Page 154, Exercise 2. Repeat the recording from Exercise 1.

Page 155, Exercise 4

1. **H1:** Are we gettin' some background ukulele there?

    D: No, that's actually my other phone, but I'm gonna ignore it for right now.

2. **D:** And I really kind of thought it was fake because it was as big as it was.

3. **H1:** What were the initials?

    D: Oh, I'm sorry I honestly don't remember.

    H1: 'Cause I lost a ring in South Bend, Indiana.

4. **D:** I figured if I gave too much information I'm sure people'd be coming out of the woodwork to claim it.

Page 156, Exercise 6

D: Well, it was some years ago, about 22 or 3 years ago, actually, I got a metal detector for Christmas.

H1: OK.

D: And after waiting all winter long to get to use the thing, we ended up uh, we ended up being in a local...

H1: Are we getting some background ukulele there?

D: No, that's actually my other phone, but I'm gonna ignore it for right now.

H2: Wow, that's quite musical.

H1: That's your cell phone, that's your cell phone ring?

D: Yeah, my cell phone.

H1: Hmm. OK.

D: But um, at any rate, um.

H1: Back to the metal detector.

D: And, uh, after finding, you know, a few pennies and a whole bunch of bottle caps and whatever, I hit, uh, a pretty loud signal, which back then was really the only thing you could use to tell anything...

H1: Mmm-hmm.

D: ... and...

H1: ... started digging...

D: ... started digging, and found a large man's diamond and sapphire ring.

Part Four: In Class

Page 161, B. Listening and Note-Taking

Exercise 2

1. In the first place, Columbus did not discover America. How do we know this? Well, we know that 20,000 years ago, Asia and north America were connected by a land bridge, and the archaeological evidence is clear that the first humans arrived in north America from Asia around that time.

2. Also, Columbus and his men also kept written records, and on the basis of those, historians know that Columbus never actually set foot in North America. In fact, in four voyages to the New World—in 1492, 1493, 1498, and 1502, the closest he ever came was the Bahamas, in the Caribbean.

3. And as for the second claim, well, Columbus didn't really prove that the world was round, either. The Greeks already knew that 2000 years ago, and written records show that by 1492, educated Europeans knew it too.

Page 161, Exercise 4. Repeat the recording from Exercise 2.

Page 162, Exercise 6

I'd like to spend some time, at this point, talking about the discoveries of Christopher Columbus. As you may know, Columbus was an Italian explorer and trader, born in the year 1451, and according to the first line of a poem that many American children learn in school, in 1492, Columbus sailed the ocean blue, which refers to the fact that in 1492, Columbus received funding from Ferdinand and Isabella, the king and queen of Spain, to try to reach Asia by sailing west across the Atlantic, which had never been done before. After about a month at sea, his ships landed on an island in the Caribbean, and until the day he died, Columbus was convinced that he had landed in India.

Now traditionally, Americans have given Columbus credit for two things, for discovering America and for proving the wo—that the earth is round. If you go out and ask ten Americans who discovered America, I'll bet that nine of ten of them will say, I bet, that it was Christopher Columbus. And yet today, we have unmistakable archaeological and historical evidence that both of these beliefs are false.

In the first place, Columbus did not discover America. How do we know this? Well, we know that 20,000 years ago, Asia and North America were connected by a land bridge, and the archaeological evidence is clear that the first humans arrived in North America from Asia around that time. We also have DNA evidence that shows that these people were the ancestors of all the native tribes in North and South America.

Not only did Columbus not discover America, he wasn't even the first European to reach this continent. That honor belongs to a Scandinavian explorer named Leif Ericsson who landed on the northeastern shore of Canada 500 years earlier than Columbus, around the year 1000.

Columbus and his men also kept written records, and on the basis of those, historians know that Columbus never actually set foot in North America. In fact, in four voyages to the New

World—in 1492, 1493, 1498, and 1502, the closest he ever came was the Bahamas, in the Caribbean.

So, Columbus didn't really discover America, at least not North America. And as for the second claim, well, Columbus didn't really prove that the world was round, either. The Greeks already knew that 2000 years ago, and written records show that by 1492, educated Europeans knew it too. So, in short, there's no doubt that Columbus knew when he sailed west that he wasn't going to fall off the edge of the earth.

OK. So if Columbus didn't discover America, and he didn't prove that the earth was round, what in the world did he accomplish? Well his main contribution, of course, was establishing the cultural and economic links between Europe and America that continue until today. He initiated trade between Europe and America and of course it was Columbus and his followers who brought Christianity to America. And it's because of these accomplishments, I think, that most Americans have always viewed Columbus as one of the great heroes of history.

But the problem with this romantic point of view is that it doesn't take into account the disastrous impact that the arrival of Columbus had on the native people of North and South America. I never learned in school, for instance, that it was Columbus who initiated the trans-Atlantic trade in slaves. And how that came about is actually a sad but interesting story. As I mentioned before, Columbus got money from Ferdinand and Isabella, the king and queen of Spain, to finance his first voyage, but you probably don't know, I certainly didn't, that they agreed to pay for it only if Columbus promised to repay their investment by bringing back gold, spices, and other valuable commodities from Asia. Obviously, Columbus failed to connect with any Asian merchants or traders, and so he came up with the idea of kidnapping native people and selling them as slaves in order to finance his journey. Columbus and his followers also captured natives and forced them to work in the gold mines and the plantations that they established all over the Caribbean, and those who resisted were killed. In fact it's estimated that within four years of

arriving in the Caribbean, Columbus and his men had either killed or exported one third of the native population. And finally, it's now well known that many thousands and possibly millions of native Americans died of European diseases like smallpox, which hadn't existed in the New World before European colonists arrived. So in conclusion, there are many people today who claim that slavery, forced labor, and disease are the true legacy of Christopher Columbus.

CHAPTER 7: LAW AND ORDER

Part One: In Person
Page 168, B. Listening

Exercise 1

Juror: The one time I was chosen for jury duty it was for a criminal case that lasted I think it was about four days, and it was very interesting because it was very emotional, which I was surprised about, I didn't expect it.

Lida: Well what was the case about?

J: The case was about this down-and-out young man who wasn't exactly homeless, but he lived in one of those flea-bag hotels in the downtown area, and the c—and he had attacked some security guards or some bicycle officers or something downtown and thrown bottles at them and resisted arrest. Apparently he was drunk or on drugs or something. And uh, and so he was arrested and charged with assault. The witnesses were injured officers, um, who testified that he attacked them and threw a bottle at them which, uh, one of the bottles hit one of the officers in the arm, and the o—and the officer came to trial with his arm in a sling. And what was interesting was that we knew nothing about this man's background. We didn't know if he had ever been arrested before. We had to go based only on the evidence presented in the courtroom. And the evidence was pretty one-sided. The guy took the witness stand himself and he was a very poor witness, bless his heart; basically he had nothing to say to defend himself. He denied that... what he did, but he couldn't present evidence and neither could his lawyer, for that matter.

L: Well what did this guy look like?

J: He was pretty pathetic, poor fellow. We all kind of felt sorry for him. He looked unhealthy, beat up, inarticulate, clearly very poorly educated. And in a way my heart went out to him, I know that sounds weird, but he was a young guy and already it seemed like he had just given up on life. And his lawyer, what a joke... Oh I have to tell you something that most people don't believe happened, but the judge fell asleep during the case.

L: Really?

J: I am completely serious. The defense attorney was talking, and the delivery was so slow and boring and long-winded that everybody was just nodding off, including the judge. And the other lawyer, the prosecutor, actually had to say "Your honor? Excuse me, your honor?"

L: That is funny.

J: Anyway so each side concluded its case and then it was time for the judge to give us our instructions. And she explained that we had to decide based only on the evidence and on the legal definition of aggravated assault. Whatever our personal feelings were we had to leave those outside the door and go strictly by the law. So then the twelve of us went into the deliberation room with about 154 pages of what they call "the law" and elected a foreman and started going over everything. And even though it seemed like an open and shut case, it took us a long time to decide because we took the judge's instructions very very seriously, and any time we had a question we had to go back and see what "the law" had to say about it.

L: So, uh, who, who were the other people on the jury, besides you?

J: It was a diverse group. There was a teacher, a housewife, an unemployed guy, you know different ages, different ethnic groups. But we all took it very seriously. Everyone contributed.

L: So what did you finally decide?

J: In the end we all agreed that he was guilty but it was a very emotional decision for all of us because we knew we were sending him to jail. And we didn't take that lightly, believe me. It's a huge responsibility.

Page 169, Exercise 2. Repeat the recording from Exercise 1.

Page 170, Exercise 4

1. The case was about this down-and-out young man.

2. ...and so he was arrested and charged with assault.

3. ...one of the bottles hit one of the officers in the arm

4. ...and the officer came to trial with his arm in a sling.

5. He was pretty pathetic, poor fellow.

6. We all kind of felt sorry for him.

7. And in a way my heart went out to him.

8. Oh I have to tell you something that most people don't believe happened...

9. ...any time we had a question we had to go back and see what "the law" had to say about it.

10. ...but it was a very emotional decision for all of us because we knew we were sending him to jail.

Part Two: On the Phone

Page 174, B. Listening

Exercise 1

Witness: Hello.

Detective: Is this Mr. Collins?

W: Uh, yes...

D: This is Detective Walters from the Metropolitan Police. I'm investigating a hit and run accident that occurred at the intersection of Elden and Olympic yesterday afternoon.

W: Umm...

D: I understand you were a witness to this accident?

W: That's right.

D: Would this be a good time for me to ask you some questions about what you observed?

W: Yeah, OK.

D: OK. Well, why don't you just tell me about what you remember.

W: Right. It was about 3:15, and I was sitting in the passenger seat of a car on Elden Street and I was facing, uh we were facing north at a traff—traffic light, um a red light, waiting to turn left. And uh then I saw a white van approaching very fast coming from east to west on Olympic. And just then the light changed, so now it was a red light for the east west traffic and green for us, uh so the cars on Olympic were slowing down, but this van didn't stop. And I looked in the crosswalk and there was a lady. And I said to my friend who was driving, "Oh no, that van's gonna hit that lady." And the next thing I know, the van didn't slow down, and it turned, and it hit the lady and... she went flying. Uh, but it didn't stop, in fact it accelerated as it turned north and just sped on. Uh, and a couple of other cars took off after him. So then I jumped out and ran over to where the woman was lying, and uh, she was lying in the street there, not moving, uh, but it looked like she was breathing. And I just stayed with her 'til the police arrived.

D: OK. So when you say the van turned... it turned right? Onto Elden?

W: Right.

D: Before or after it hit the lady?

W: Uh seemed like... during.

D: All right, and now just to clarify, which crosswalk was the woman crossing in? Was she going east to west or was she going north to south?

W: Uh well I've been thinking it over since yesterday, and, uh, originally I thought she was going east to west, on Elden, but on second thought... Well, if she was doing that and the van hit her, she couldn't have... well she would've ended up on, on the north side of Elden. So that means...

D: Where did she end up instead?

W: On the west side of the intersection, on Olympic. So I think she must have been crossing Olympic when the van hit her.

D: OK. Can you tell me anything more about the driver?

W: I never saw the driver.

D: OK, what about the van—year, make, model, license plate?

W: It was a white van. That's it.

D: Can you think of anything else that would help us catch the driver?

W: Uh, not really. I've gone over it in my mind a hundred times but it was so fast, and then that poor woman...

D: All right Mr. Collins. Thank you for your time.

W: You're welcome.

D: Good-bye.

W: Bye.

Page 175, Exercise 2. Repeat the recording from Exercise 1.

Page 176, Exercise 4

1. the intersection
2. yesterday afternoon
3. I understand
4. show up
5. now and then
6. snow and ice
7. three elephants

Part Three: On the Air

Page 181, B. Listening

Exercise 1

Danny Solomon is a 57-year-old trained chef, but his fellow Atlantans might see him standing outside at McDonald's asking for money. "And then I would say 'Pardon me sir, my name is Danny and I'm homeless and I'm very hungry, I haven't eaten in about two days. I'd appreciate any spare change that you may have, whatever you can spare me. Thank you.

For the last five months he's been staying in Atlanta's Open Door Community, which houses and feeds some homeless people. Solomon says he averages 25 or 30 dollars a day from panhandling and uses it to buy food or cigarettes. "I do know people that... from my experience on the street, that do panhandle for a living. This is how they survive, and it's, to them it's just a hustle. But there are, the majority of people that ask people for money, actually need it."

A proposed city ordinance would make that illegal in much of downtown Atlanta. The idea infuriates Murphy Davis, a Presbyterian minister who works at Open Door. "This is empowerment of police power to sweep the poor under the rug, and I think the important issue here is the criminalization of poverty, which has been a trend in the United States for a long time."

A group called the Martin Luther King Campaign for Economic Justice launched a protest against the ordinance. Vice president Tony Singfield was once homeless himself. "It's a violation of uh freedoms of speech and the right to exist."

An Atlanta city council member who's leading the effort for the ban says it would curb freedom of speech, but, he says, there's a compelling governmental interest. "We're trying to make sure that we don't erode the economic base of the city." Lamar Willis says panhandling is keeping some people away from downtown, threatening the convention and tourism business that generate three billion dollars a year. "When businesses refuse to remain in downtown Atlanta, when conventioneers and tourists refuse to come in to downtown Atlanta, if we can't undergird that then we are going to be in a world of trouble."

A group called Central Atlanta Progress helped shape the legislation. Its president, A.J. Robinson, says visitors and locals frequently complain that panhandling makes them feel unsafe. "Absolutely. And particularly at night. If you're accosted on the street at night by somebody who looks menacing, it creates a lot of fear. It's the number one thing that people complain about our downtown community." He says there's no hard proof panhandling has cost Atlanta a convention, but he says it's a real problem. Competitor cities like Las Vegas and Miami have tough anti-panhandling laws.

Page 181, Exercise 2. Repeat the recording from Exercise 1.

Page 183, Exercise 4

1. courageous
2. questionnaire
3. ridiculous
4. photography
5. educational
6. unhappiness

7. indecision
8. neighborhood
9. destiny
10. Lebanese
11. critique
12. homogeneous
13. reality
14. legislation
15. illegal
16. menacing

Part Four: In Class

Page 187, B. Listening and Note-Taking

Exercise 2

Sociologists can help us to understand the causes of crime because it's difficult to talk about what we should do about crime until we understand what are the causes of crime. Clearly any attempts to reduce crime are going to be based on what is causing crime. So there are three starting points, three major sociological theories that will assist us to understand the causes of crime.

Page 188, Exercise 5

1. The first is the structural-functionist perspective. This proposes that crime, and especially increases in crime, are a result of disorganization...

2. There's still a great deal of migration to the western provinces, so we would expect the west to be less organized [for] their less shared values and ideas, and therefore there will be more crime.

3. This is the conflict theory, based on the original ideas of Karl Marx, in which crime is a manifestation of the conflict between the classes in any society. In other words, crime is caused by inequality.

4. So it could well be that because aboriginal peoples are at the bottom of the class system, they tend to be unfairly treated by the legal system.

Page 189, Exercise 6

The first is the structural-functionist perspective. This proposes that crime, and especially increases in crime, are a result of social disorganization, as a result of a loss of shared values and norms and an erosion of social control. These ideas are based on Robert Merton, who was a very famous sociologist. And if this is what we think are at the root of crimes, then we would expect increases in crime to occur when there's rapid social change, when there's a great deal of immigration or industrialization or increased poverty. In fact in Canada, it's interesting, if we take a look at the number of murders per 100,000 people, it is far lower on the east coast than on the west coast. And we can use this theory to explain this change from east to west, because we can say that the eastern part of Canada—it's been settled for several hundred years, especially the Atlantic provinces; all the people that are residents there tend to share a similar culture. But as you go to the western provinces, they've been settled more recently by groups of people from very many different cultures. There's still a great deal of migration to the western provinces, so we would expect the west to be less organized, for there to be less shared values and ideas, and therefore there will be more crime.

We can use this structural-functional approach and also look at other countries. And we would expect countries which are quite homogeneous, such as Japan and Korea, to have lower crime rates while societies or countries which are changing quite rapidly—think of South Africa—those countries should have higher crime rates. And in fact, we do find some of this, which will lead us to the conclusion that yes, this is a good way to try to understand some of the causes of crime.

But it isn't going to tell us everything about the causes of crime. We have to use a second theory. This is the conflict theory, based on the original ideas of Karl Marx, in which crime is a manifestation of the conflict between the classes in any society. In other words, crime is caused by inequality. And that makes sense; if everybody was equal in Canada, there would be a lot less crime, obviously. As well, this theory draws our attention to the fact that laws are social constructs. They're created, and they can change, as we've already discussed. But they tend to be created primarily the people in position's of power, by the wealthy, powerful people in any society. And therefore those laws are going to protect the interests that group. Think about the kinds of laws we have in Canada. A great many of the laws we have in Canada and the U.S. and other capitalist

countries deal with property rights—what belongs to whom, what happens if property or capital is transferred. And these types of laws tend to work to the advantage of the people who do have a great deal of capital or property and don't work as much to the advantage of those who are poor. Clearly you already know that individuals who are wealthy have the ability to influence the legal system, to purchase the very best legal advice, to influence the way decisions are made. And there [are] examples from everyday occurrences where we know that the law treats people of different classes differently. Just some examples about this: In Canada, 12 percent of people in prisons in Canada are aboriginals. But aboriginals are only three percent of Canada's population. So it could well be that because aboriginal peoples are at the bottom of the class structure, they tend to be unfairly treated by the legal system. In the U.S., 41 percent of those prisoners on Death Row are black, but blacks comprise only 12 percent of the U.S. population. Again, we see great inequalities in the way that different groups in society are treated, and these are the kinds of things we tend to learn when we use the conflict theory to understand crime.

CHAPTER 8: LIGHTS, CAMERA, ACTION!

Part One: In Person

Page 194, B. Listening

Exercise 1

Lida: How do you prepare to be a mov—I mean what did you do to prepare to be a movie producer?

Rachel Miller: The thing about producing is that there's no one way. And then, my path and everyone's is different. I did a short in high school...

L: What do you mean a "short"?

RM: A short film, a 20-minute short film that I found and financed and produced and made happen. Found the cast, found the director.

L: In high school.

RM: In high school.

L: And then I interned, which means working

for someone for free but getting experience, um before I went to college, and then I went to NYU film school, and focused on um, law and business and took a lot of producing classes, but also took a lot of technical classes like editing and sound and directing and writing because the best producers are ones that can do everything.

L: ... and so what are you doing now?

RM: I started my own company. I have about ten projects that I am working on. And it's just, you know, trying to make it happen.

L: So how do films come together; how does a movie make it to the big screen?

RM: A movie is chance, opportunity, luck, hard work, being in the right place at the right time. It's about getting that material to the producer or the director who will take a shot at it. And, who'll stay with the project and fight for the project. And someone to champion you. And it's about... nothing is guaranteed in this business. There's no formula to make a fantastic movie. For example, *The Island*, which cost a hundred million dollars to make, Michael Bay directed it, he did everything from *Bad Boys* to *Armageddon,* and *Pearl Harbor,* the biggest action director of our time, starring Scarlett Johanssen and Ewan McGregor, Dreamworks made it, and it flopped. And it only made ten mil—12 million dollars the opening weekend. So everything is iffy in this business. And for a producer, it's about not putting all your eggs in one basket, about having ten projects, so if one falls apart, one might go and one might be in this stage and one might be in this stage. And then fighting for it until it gets a director, it gets a talent and it gets money, and it gets a studio, gets a distributor, and then it gets made.

L: When you say "fighting for it," how do you do that? You just, you're on the phone all day, or?

RM: On the phone 12 hours a day, on e-mail or just not giving up.

L: Let's go back to what you're working on now. And just more examples of the types of projects that are in the works.

RM: Um, they're all different. One is a family comedy, very broad, very fun and smart. One is a very dark, gritty look about four teenage boys and how they deal with grief. One is a thriller, you know, scary thriller, lots, we burn down a house at the end of it. One is an urban relationship movie. One is a big romantic comedy that's fun. One is a very topical action movie. And I work in all genres but at the end of the day all my projects have great stories and great characters.

L: How do you juggle all those things at the same time?

RM: Welcome to the life of a producer. You have to just be very well organized, and very good at multitasking, and remembering everything on every project. And following up on everything. And just being on top of every single project all the time and working every day.

Page 195, Exercise 2. Repeat the recording from Exercise 1.

Page 196, Exercise 3

A movie is chance, opportunity, luck, hard work, being in the right place at the right time. It's about getting that material to the producer or the director who will take a shot at it. And, who'll stay with the project and fight for the project. And someone to champion you. And it's about... nothing is guaranteed in this business. There's no formula to make a fantastic movie. For example, *The Island*, which cost a hundred million dollars to make starring Scarlett Johanssen and Ewan McGregor, Dreamworks made it, and it flopped. And it only made ten mil—12 million dollars the opening weekend. So everything is iffy in this business. And for a producer, it's about not putting all your eggs in one basket, about having ten projects, so if one falls apart, one might go and one might be in this stage and one might be in this stage.

Part Two: On the Phone

Page 201, B. Listening

Exercise 1

Hello and thank you for calling the New Age theater complex, located on the Promenade in the newly renovated downtown entertainment center.

The following showtime information is effective for Friday, August 5th to Thursday, August 11th only. In theater number one we are proud to present *March of the Penguins*, rated PG, with a running time of one hour and 36 minutes. Showtimes are 12:15, 2:30, 4:40, 7 o'clock, and 10:15. In theater number two, *The Edukators*, rated R, in German with English subtitles, with a running time of two hours and 11 minutes, showing at one o'clock, 4:15, 7:35 and 10:25. On Friday, August 5th and Saturday August 6th, there will be a Q and A after the 7:35 show of *The Edukators* with the film's director.

In theater number three we present *Stealth*, rated PG-13, with a playing time of two hours and 15 minutes. *Stealth* will screen at 11:00, 4:00, 7:00 and 9:50, and on Friday and Saturday nights only there's a special latenight show beginning at 12:30 a.m. with a special admission price either night of seven dollars and fifty cents. And in theater number four, *Batman Begins*, rated PG-13, with a running time of two hours and 35 minutes. *Batman* will play at 12:40 and 6:40 p.m. daily except for Thursday, August 11th, when there will be no screening of *Batman* due to a special engagement.

Admission prices to the New Age theaters are as follows: We have bargain matinees daily for seven fifty, first show of the day ONLY. All other shows are nine dollars. Seniors 62 and older and children under 12 are eight dollars all day. Students and active members of the military with valid ID are eight fifty.

Please note that for movies rated R, no one under the age of 17 will be admitted to the theater without their parents at the same time. Photo ID will be required.

Parking is located behind the theater on Grand Avenue. Parking prices are five dollars on weekends and holidays, three dollars Monday through Thursday.

In consideration of others we ask that there be no talking or noise during the performances. For further information please visit our website or call us direct at 310-555-3904. Thank you for selecting the New Age Theater Complex, and we'll see YOU at the movies!

Page 202, Exercise 2. Repeat the recording from Exercise 1.

Page 204, Exercise 4

1. Thursday
2. there
3. theater
4. through
5. either
6. thank you
7. stealth
8. others
9. further
10. with
11. three
12. without

Part Three: On the Air

Page 207, B. Listening

Exercise 1

Henry Sheehan: Well, I didn't see this movie at the press screening, excuse me. I saw it yesterday, at the El Capitan, with a paying audience. And, I brought my sixteen-year-old son, Brian. And, he had the time of his life. He loved it. And, so did the entire audience. There was, you know, the film was interrupted by cheers, including at moments when the film had tableaus that mimicked the ride at Disneyland, upon which the film is based, Pirates of the Caribbean.
There are several times in the movie where, you know, the setups on the ride are repeated in the movie. And, people would erupt in recognition. And, four times, in the movie, they sing the song that's sung at the ride. So, people, you know, the film is clearly set up to meet the expectations of the people who love the ride. And, people go there for that, and they like it. And, they like lots of stuff in the film.

And, so, you know, in terms of a film that delivers audience expectations, I think it's worth mentioning that this film clearly does that, at least, for an opening day audience. I'm kind of sorry about that. Because, this is a second-rate film. And, I think, just, people have become used to taking second-rate as the best they can get. I just have three quick points to make. The film is very badly directed by Gore Verbinski, who started out making commercials.

And, it's apparent almost right from the first. Where, after an opening flashback Johnny Depp makes, what is supposed to be, a comic entrance. And, it's just really mishandled. I won't get into how it's done. But, it should be done in just a couple of shots. And, Verbinski has to resort to a really badly edited series of bad camera setups. The second thing is, it's really badly acted. The two romantic leads just give miserable performances. What's her name? Keira Nicely is...

Andy Klein: Knightley.

HS: Knightley. It's just unbearably bad. And, Orlando Bloom is very, very bad.

AK: In ways that will endear him to his fan audience.

HS: I don't think, I don't know, I don't get that feeling.

AK: Ahhhh. He does.

HS: Geoffrey Rush doesn't just play the character, he gives a kind of performance, instead of just playing the bad pirate, he gives a kind of performance which he sat down and said, hmm, what's the kind of performance an actor would give if he was playing a pirate, instead of just playing the pirate. It's like he was trying to do a pirate for, like, his four-year-old nephew. Which would probably be great for his four-year-old nephew, but, for someone sitting in a theater for two hours and twenty minutes, gets a little grating. Johnny Depp gives, what I would call, a corrupt performance. It's not like one of his, it's not...

Larry Mantle: I've never heard that described before.

HS: Well, it's not like one of the great eccentric performances he gives in Tim Burton's movies, like Edward Scissorshands, where the eccentricity is a completely organic part of the character, in which the eccentricity grows and affects you, emotionally. It's like the producer said, Johnny, give us some of that good Johnny Depp stuff, and just apply it. And, it's, so, it's all external. It's all artificial. I admit, it's amusing to watch. But, it has nothing to do with the character, Captain Jack Sparrow, he's playing, because there is no Captain Jack Sparrow. And, so, that all leads to, like, my

third, and final, point, which is that the movie is completely sterile, emotionally. And, even in terms of action. I mean, everything looks, like, scrubbed, and fresh, and, you know, that there's no dirt, there's no grit. There's nothing to it. You don't come out feeling anything.

So, you know, to go back, you know, the audience loved it, my son loved it. And, I can see why. And, it's certainly not an unendurable experience, but, it's a second-, or even third-rate film.

Page 208, Exercise 2. Repeat the recording from Exercise 1.

Page 210, Exercise 4. Repeat the recording from Exercise 1.

Part Four: In Class
Page 214, B. Listening and Note–Taking

Exercise 2

1. That sound is called production sound, and production sound is the most common sound that you can get. It's natural sound from the production. It's the actors speaking, it's the ambient sound of what's in the environment that you're in, and you record that sound.

2. We often have to go back into a studio, a recording studio, and the actor watches his performance, or her performance, and they actually replace their lines. They re-read their lines. And then a sound editor, a dialogue editor, or an ADR editor... uh this is called Automated Dialogue Replacement, or ADR. It's also known as looping, and often we'll go back in and we'll re-record certain lines.

3. We'll also bring in a troop of actors that were not actually in the film to do what we call "group ADR" or "group looping," which is to play all the background characters on the street, or in the restaurant, or wherever we are, to re-record their performances because...

4. Sound effects is just what it seems to be. It, it's the addition of sound, uh, anything that's not dialogue.

5. ... that's what it was named after a guy by the name of Foley, and he was the one that invented this process of specially recording

sound effects for film and television shows and commercials and other kinds of media.

6. and conducts the orchestra and they record the music, uh, what we call in synch, which is at the same time of the, of the uh picture

7. Sometimes we have something called source music. Source music is the music that plays like in the background of a bar, or on a radio, and it's a rock 'n' roll song, or it's a different type of piece of music, but it's coming from something in the scene, it's not playing in the background of the scene.

8. Now once the dialogue, and the music, and the sound effects are all recorded, and they're all edited in synch with the picture, then we go into a re-recording stage, a re-recording or mixing stage. And we take—"mixing" we should tell you—we take all the elements and mix them together into the final soundtrack of the film or television show.

Page 215, Exercise 4

I want to speak to you today about post-production sound: sound for feature films, and television shows, and commercials, and all different types of media, uh, and the work that goes into creating soundtracks for these types of media, these types of entertainment material. Uh, it's a very interesting topic and think that people don't realize how significant the post-production audio, the post-production sound process is. Uh, there are a number of distinct elements of post-production sound, and I can kind of list them for you and then I'll describe each one of them. There is dialogue and looping or ADR, Automated Dialogue Replacement; there are sound effects and Foley; and then there is music composition and music editorial. And those three elements—which are really five or six elements—but those three elements all combine to make the final soundtrack of the film.

Page 215, Exercise 5

I want to speak to you today about post-production sound: sound for feature films, and television shows, and commercials, and all different types of media, uh, and the work that goes into creating soundtracks for these types of media, these types of entertainment material. Uh, it's a very interesting topic and think that people don't realize how significant the post-production audio, the post-production sound process is. Uh, there are a number of distinct elements of post-production sound, and I can kind of list them for you and then I'll describe each one of them. There is dialogue and looping or ADR, Automated Dialogue Replacement; there are sound effects and Foley; and then there is music composition and music editorial. And those three elements—which are really five or six elements—but those three elements all combine to make the final soundtrack of the film.

So let's talk about dialogue first and ADR. When you're on the set of a movie or a television show or any kind of entertainment product that you're working on, uh, you always have a microphone and you shoot with either one or two or three cameras, depending on how it is, and there's always microphones that are open that are capturing the sound. That sound is called production sound, and production sound is the most common sound that you can get. It's natural sound from the production. It's the actors speaking, it's the ambient sound of what's in the environment that you're in, and you record that sound. But because you're recording that sound over the course of a day or two days or even hours, that sound is inconsistent. The background changes; actors' volume change, and it is part of what sound editors do, and post-production sound professionals do, is to take that production sound and smooth it out. So that's the first thing that we do. We take the production sound, the production dialogue that's recorded, and we actually edit it and uh, we fill in with backgrounds, and we fill in with different types of ambient sound so that its sounds like one coherent, smooth, piece of dialogue as opposed to lots of little cuts and little edits. I'm sure you've seen television shows and movies where they cut between two actors. Well, this is a way of making the actors seem like they're in the same scene, even though one side of the shot was filmed at a different time than the other side.

Now a lot of times, there are things in the production dialogue track that can't be, uh, that can't be saved. There are issues that occur. Maybe there's a loud sound that happens on top of somebody's line, or maybe there is a performance issue, where we don't like the way an actor particularly said a line; or maybe there's um, a swear word or something that goes into uh, that that we can't have on television or we can't have in a commercial or we can't have in the film. We often have to go back into a studio, a recording studio, and the actor watches his performance, or her performance, and they actually replace their lines. They re-read their lines. And then a sound editor, a dialogue editor, or an ADR editor... uh this is called Automated Dialogue Replacement, or ADR. It's also known as looping, and often we'll go back in and we'll re-record certain lines. We'll also bring in a troop of actors that were not actually in the film to do what we call "group ADR" or "group looping," which is to play all the background characters on the street, or in the restaurant, or wherever we are, to re-record their performances because we require them to be silent when they're on the production stage, and when we come back in we have to fill back in with those ambient voices that we didn't record when we were on the stage. So that's the dialogue and the ADR component of it.

Now there's a whole, an other aspect of this which is the sound effects and Foley, and I'll explain Foley in a second. Sound effects is just what it seems to be. It, it's the addition of sound, uh, anything that's not dialogue. So any kind of effects, let's say it's a gunshot, or a car, or uh, different types of birds, or, you know, wind, or whatever might be playing, that we visually see, or we want to creatively put in a dog bark. We don't actually see the dog but it's in the background somewhere, just giving the ambient feel of the scene that we want to play and heightening the emotion of the scene. So we'll often add in different kinds of sound effects, um, if there, a lot of times when we're on a set we don't shoot a real gun, but we'll have a recorded sound of a gun that we'll add in afterwards 'cause we're shooting a blank gun on the set. So those types of impact sounds, of ambient sounds, we record them out in the environment and then we cut them in, we physically edit the sounds in to the scenes that we're recording.

Now Foley is a much more unique way of recording sound because what we do is we watch the picture, somewhat how we watch the picture and the performances in ADR, we also watch the picture in Foley, and the Foley artists, which are performers basically, perform the sounds. They watch the screen and they actually act out the characters' movements, whether it's cloth movement for their clothes or footsteps, things that are repetitive in nature, that would be very difficult to edit one sound at a time, we actually do in Foley; maybe water splashing sounds, which are really hard to actually edit by picking pieces of recorded water and editing them, we can perform them live to what's going on. Now Foley is actually, uh, was named the Foley stage, which is a, a, an audio stage or recording environment, that is special, it's special flooring, and special props all around, and that's what it was named after a guy by the name of Foley, and he was the one that invented this process of specially recording sound effects for film and television shows and commercials and other kinds of media and entertainment.

And the final component to the post-production process, the post-production sound process, is music: music composition, where a composer will come in, uh, and write the music. He'll watch the video, the edited video, listen to the sound effects, listen to the dialogue, and write and compose the music, and then come in to either a scoring environment, which is a big theater-type environment where the orchestra sits and conducts the orchestra and they record the music, uh, what we call in synch, which is at the same time of the, of the uh picture, uh, or they will record it using synthesizers, using electronic keyboards and, and sometimes a combination of both. Sometimes we have something called source music. And the source music is the music that plays like in the background of a bar, or on a radio, and it's a rock 'n' roll song, or it's a different type of piece of music, but it's coming from something in the scene, it's not playing in the background of the scene.

Now once the dialogue, and the music, and the sound effects are all recorded, and they're all edited in synch with the picture, then we go into a re-recording stage, a re-recording or mixing stage. And we take—"mixing" we should tell you—we take all the elements and mix them together into the final soundtrack of the film or television show. And that's what we, that's the final sound. And we sit there and we try to weigh the importance of the dialogue in that scene, and the effects in that scene, and the music, and see how they play together, how all of those elements work together to create the final soundtrack of the film. And I don't think people really understand the significance of the amount of work that goes into creating that final soundtrack. Um, you should be aware that most of what you hear in a movie or in a television show or in a commercial or even on the Internet with Internet stu- uh, material, Internet entertainment, the soundtracks are almost 100 percent replaced. They're manipulated, there's a lot of dialogue that's replaced, all the sound effects are added and all of the um, all the music is added after the fact. None of it's recorded during the production process, and so all of that work is done in post-production, post-production audio in this particular case, and that creates the final soundtrack of the film.